V. E. SCHWAB
SHADES OF MAGIC
THE STEEL PRINCE

TITAN®
COMICS

SHADES OF MAGIC: THE STEEL PRINCE

EDITOR
AMOONA SAOHIN

MANAGING EDITOR
MARTIN EDEN

SENIOR DESIGNER
ANDREW LEUNG

Managing and Launch Editor / Andrew James
Production Assistant / Rhiannon Roy
Production Controller / Peter James
Senior Production Controller / Jackie Flook
Art Director / Oz Browne
Sales & Circulation Manager / Steve Tothill
Senior Publicist / William O'Mullane
Publicist / Imogen Harris
Senior Brand Manager / Chris Thompson
Ads & Marketing Assistant / Bella Hoy
Commercial Manager / Michelle Fairlamb
Head Of Rights / Jenny Boyce
Publishing Manager / Darryl Tothill
Publishing Director / Chris Teather
Operations Director / Leigh Baulch
Executive Director / Vivian Cheung
Publisher / Nick Landau

Published by Titan Comics, a division of Titan Publishing Group, Ltd.
Titan Comics is a registered trademark of Titan Publishing Group, Ltd.
144 Southwark Street, London SE1 0UP.

STANDARD EDITION ISBN: 9781785865879
B&N EDITION ISBN: 9781787731790
FP EDITION ISBN: 9781787731806

A CIP catalogue for this title is available from the British Library.

First Edition March 2019

10 9 8 7 6 5 4 3 2 1

Printed in Canada

www.titan-comics.com
Follow us on Twitter @ComicsTitan | Visit us at facebook.com/comicstitan

For rights information contact: jenny.boyce@titanemail.com

V. E. SCHWAB
SHADES OF MAGIC
THE STEEL PRINCE

ARTIST
ANDREA OLIMPIERI

COLOURIST
ENRICA EREN ANGIOLINI

COLOUR ASSISTS
VIVIANA SPINELLI

FLATS, CHAPTER 4
CASSANDRA PEIRANO

LETTERS
ROB STEEN

TITAN®
COMICS

V.E. SCHWAB
SHADES OF MAGIC
THE STEEL PRINCE

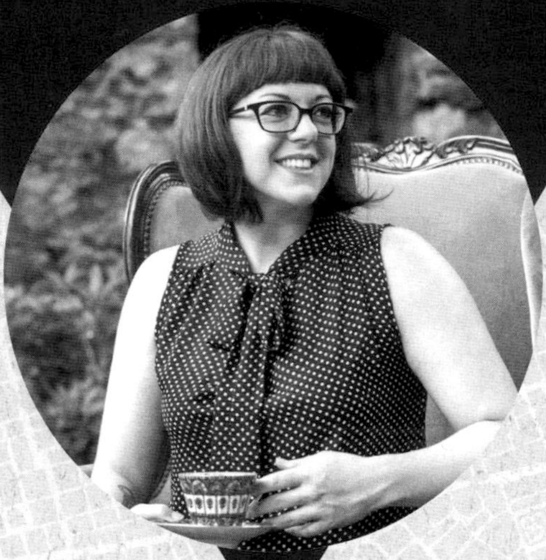

"The Steel Prince," said Sol-in-Ar, and then, reading Maxim's expression: "It surprises you, that the tales of your exploits reach beyond your own borders?" The Faroan's fingers grazed the edge of the map. "The Steel Prince, who tore the heart from the rebel army. The Steel Prince, who survived the night of knives. The Steel Prince, who slayed the pirate queen."

Maxim finished his drink and set the glass aside.

"I suppose we never know the scale of our life's stories. Which parts will survive, and which will die with us."

-A Conjuring of Light

Maxim Maresh became one of the most controversial figures in the *Shades of Magic* series. Father to Rhy, adopted parent to Kell, he was more often painted as an antagonist than a hero. His role was a necessary, but also frustrating, one—there was so much more to Maxim's life than I could fit on the page, and by showing him as he was during the time of someone else's story, I was forced to neglect his own.

When I wrote the above passage, I knew I was cracking open a door, one I so hoped I'd have the chance to walk through. And here we are.

Before he was the King of Arnes, Maxim Maresh was a young, headstrong prince with a penchant for metal magic and a lot to learn about the world beyond Red London. Banished by his own father to Verose, a city on the dangerous Blood Coast, Maxim was plunged into a world of danger and adventure. A place where he would make a few friends and many enemies, and gain a reputation that would follow him onto the pages of *Shades of Magic*.

The title he would earn? The Steel Prince.

This is his story.

CAST OF CHARACTERS

MAXIM MARESH

Crown Prince of Arnes.
Magically gifted with
the ability to bend
steel to his will. He is
known to be a talented
fighter and soldier
who has led troops at
the forefront of the
Arnesian army, but he
desires to do more.

NOKIL MARESH

King of Arnes.
Frustrated with his
son's preoccupation
with the other realms,
he banishes Maxim
to Verose. He hopes
to redirect his son's
attention towards
matters in their own
world and kingdom.

TIEREN SERENSE

Head Priest of the
London Sanctuary and
the adviser to the king.
Wise and powerful
in his own right, he
has watched over and
trained Maxim in
magical combat and
matters of leadership
and statecraft.

ISRA

A royal guard serving
in the Arnesian
army base in Verose.
Toughened by the
harsh streets of the
Blood Coast, she leads
a matchless team with
her loyal companions,
Osili and Toro. There
are dark secrets hidden
in her bloodline that
this story may uncover.

ARISA

A notorious magician
nicknamed the Pirate
Queen, known to be
the most dangerous
woman on water,
wielder of banned
magics and someone
who answers to no
authority but her own.
Feared by outlaws and
soldiers alike, her visits
to Verose are deadly.

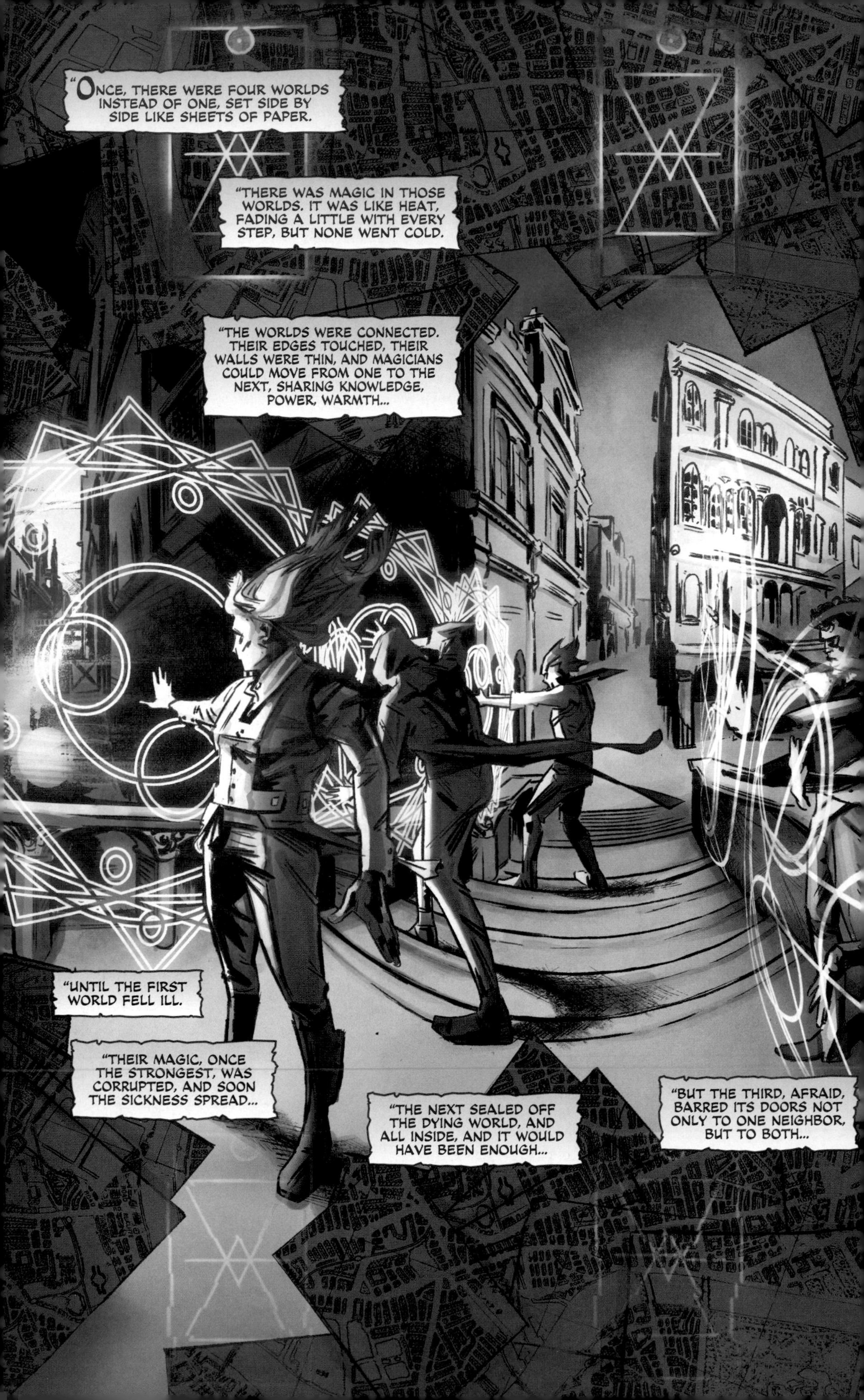
"ONCE, THERE WERE FOUR WORLDS INSTEAD OF ONE, SET SIDE BY SIDE LIKE SHEETS OF PAPER.
"THERE WAS MAGIC IN THOSE WORLDS. IT WAS LIKE HEAT, FADING A LITTLE WITH EVERY STEP, BUT NONE WENT COLD.
"THE WORLDS WERE CONNECTED. THEIR EDGES TOUCHED, THEIR WALLS WERE THIN, AND MAGICIANS COULD MOVE FROM ONE TO THE NEXT, SHARING KNOWLEDGE, POWER, WARMTH...
"UNTIL THE FIRST WORLD FELL ILL.
"THEIR MAGIC, ONCE THE STRONGEST, WAS CORRUPTED, AND SOON THE SICKNESS SPREAD...
"THE NEXT SEALED OFF THE DYING WORLD, AND ALL INSIDE, AND IT WOULD HAVE BEEN ENOUGH...
"BUT THE THIRD, AFRAID, BARRED ITS DOORS NOT ONLY TO ONE NEIGHBOR, BUT TO BOTH...

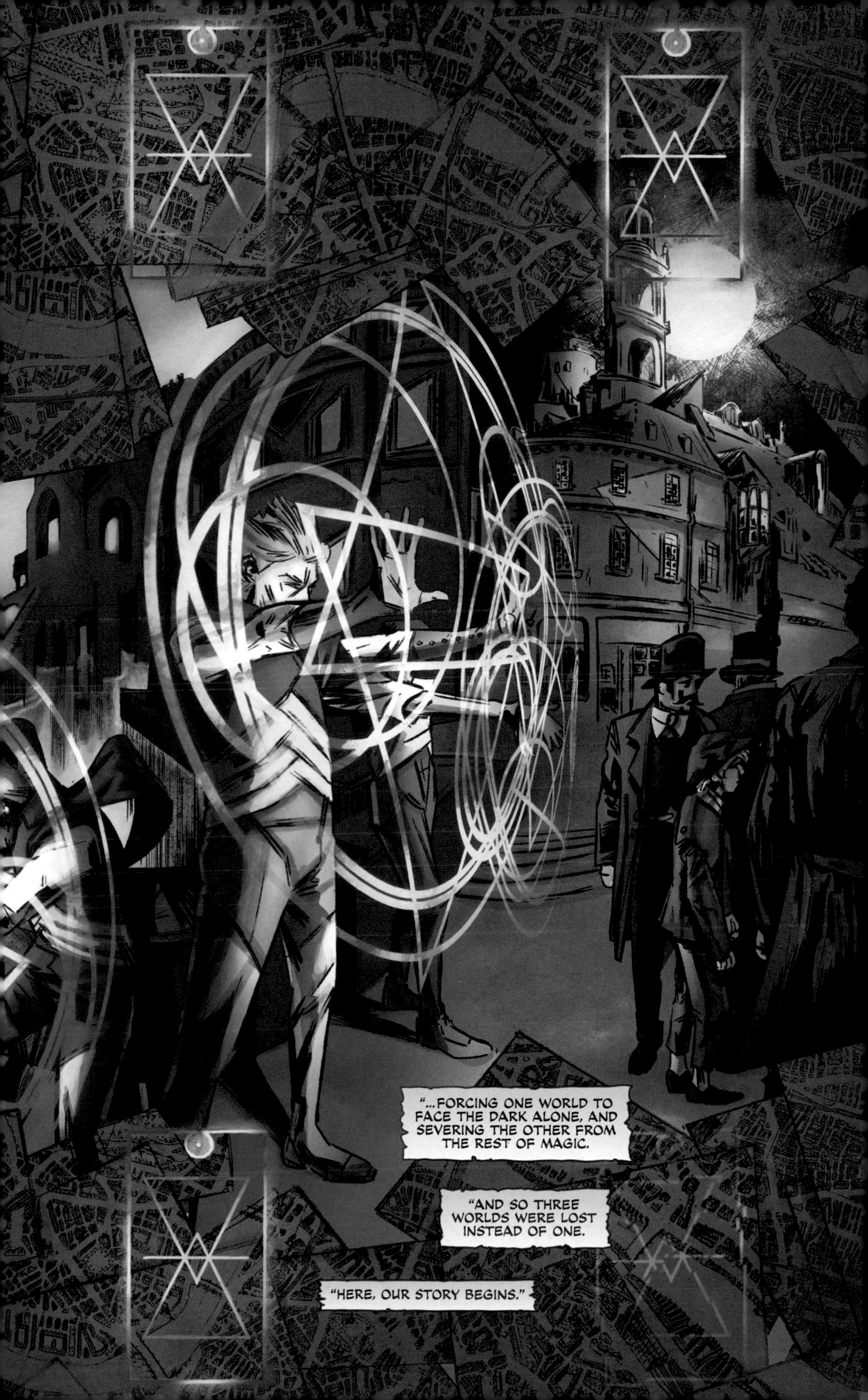
"...FORCING ONE WORLD TO FACE THE DARK ALONE, AND SEVERING THE OTHER FROM THE REST OF MAGIC.
"AND SO THREE WORLDS WERE LOST INSTEAD OF ONE.
"HERE, OUR STORY BEGINS."

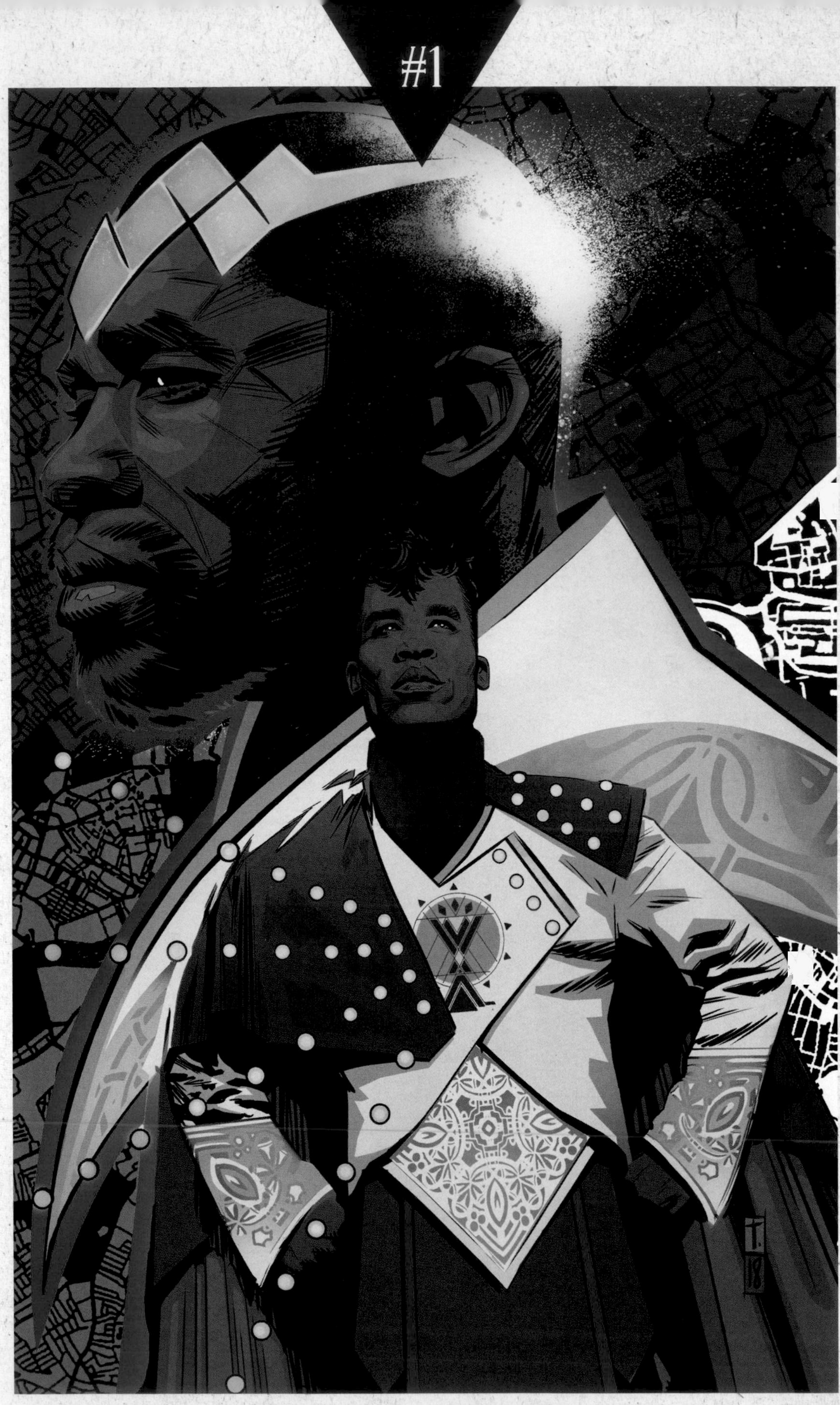
#1

COVER B - TOMM COKER & AMOONA SAOHIN

#1

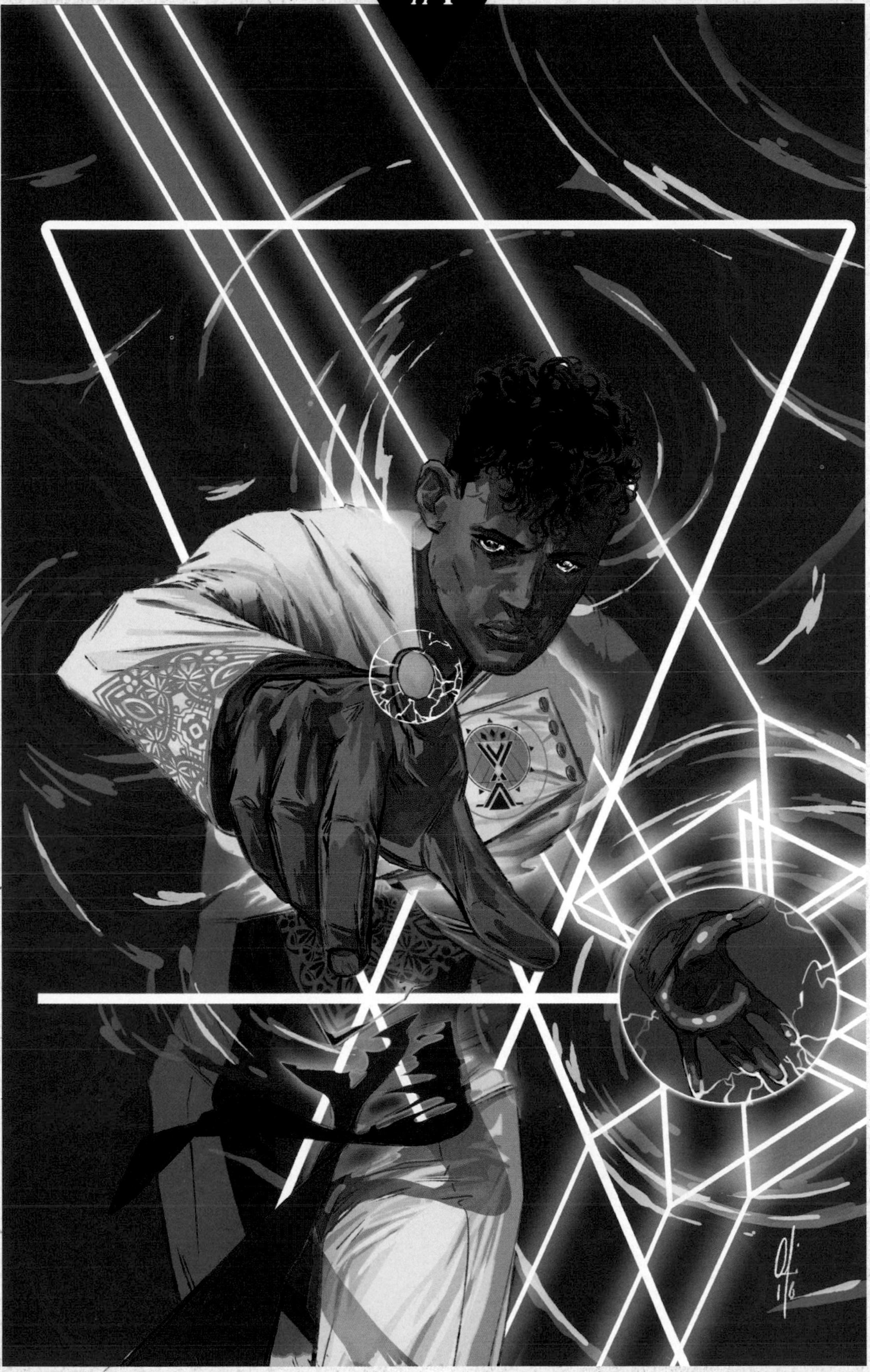

COVER C - ANDREA OLIMPIERI

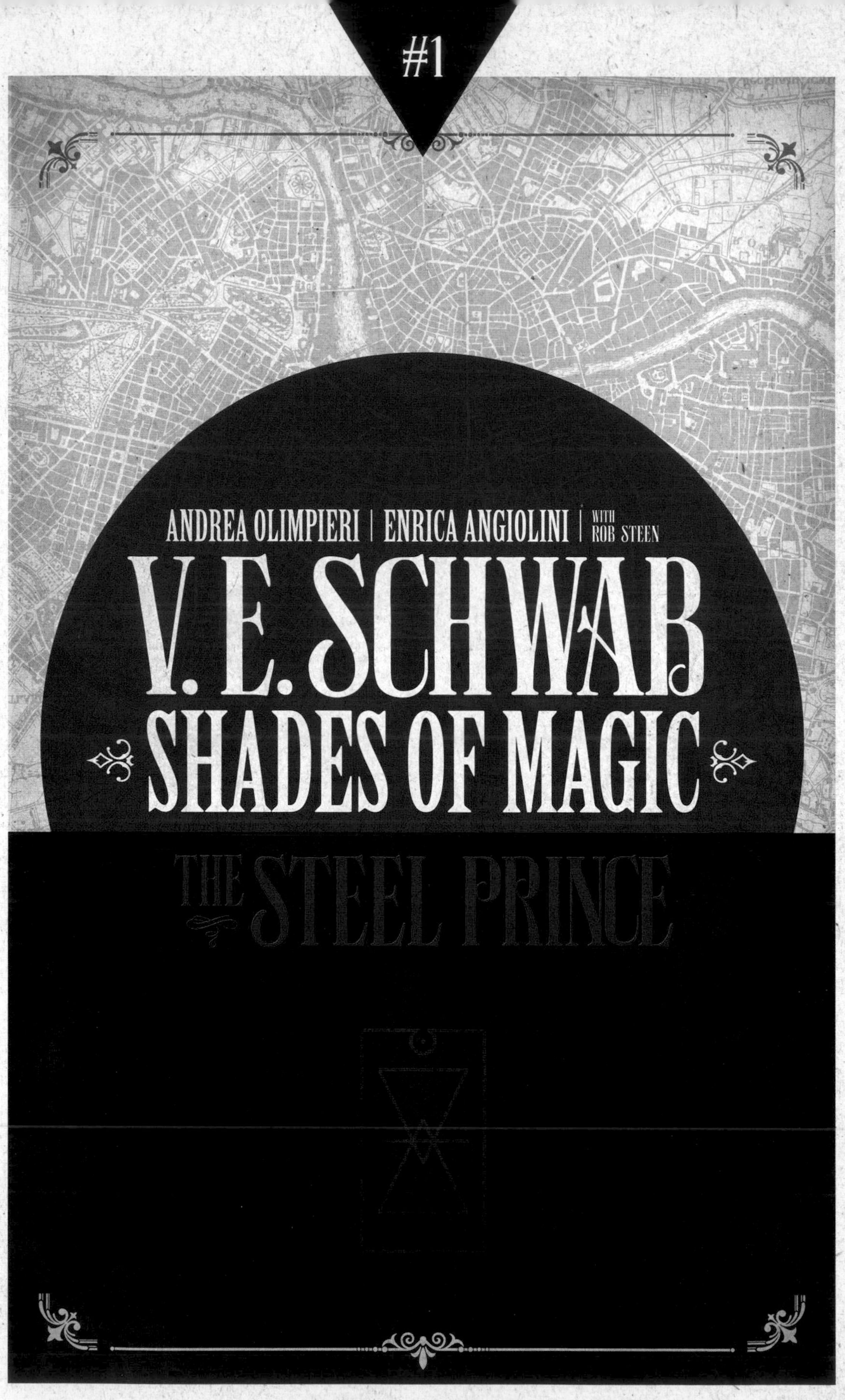
#1
ANDREA OLIMPIERI | ENRICA ANGIOLINI | WITH ROB STEEN
V. E. SCHWAB
SHADES OF MAGIC
THE STEEL PRINCE

COVER D - ANDREW LEUNG

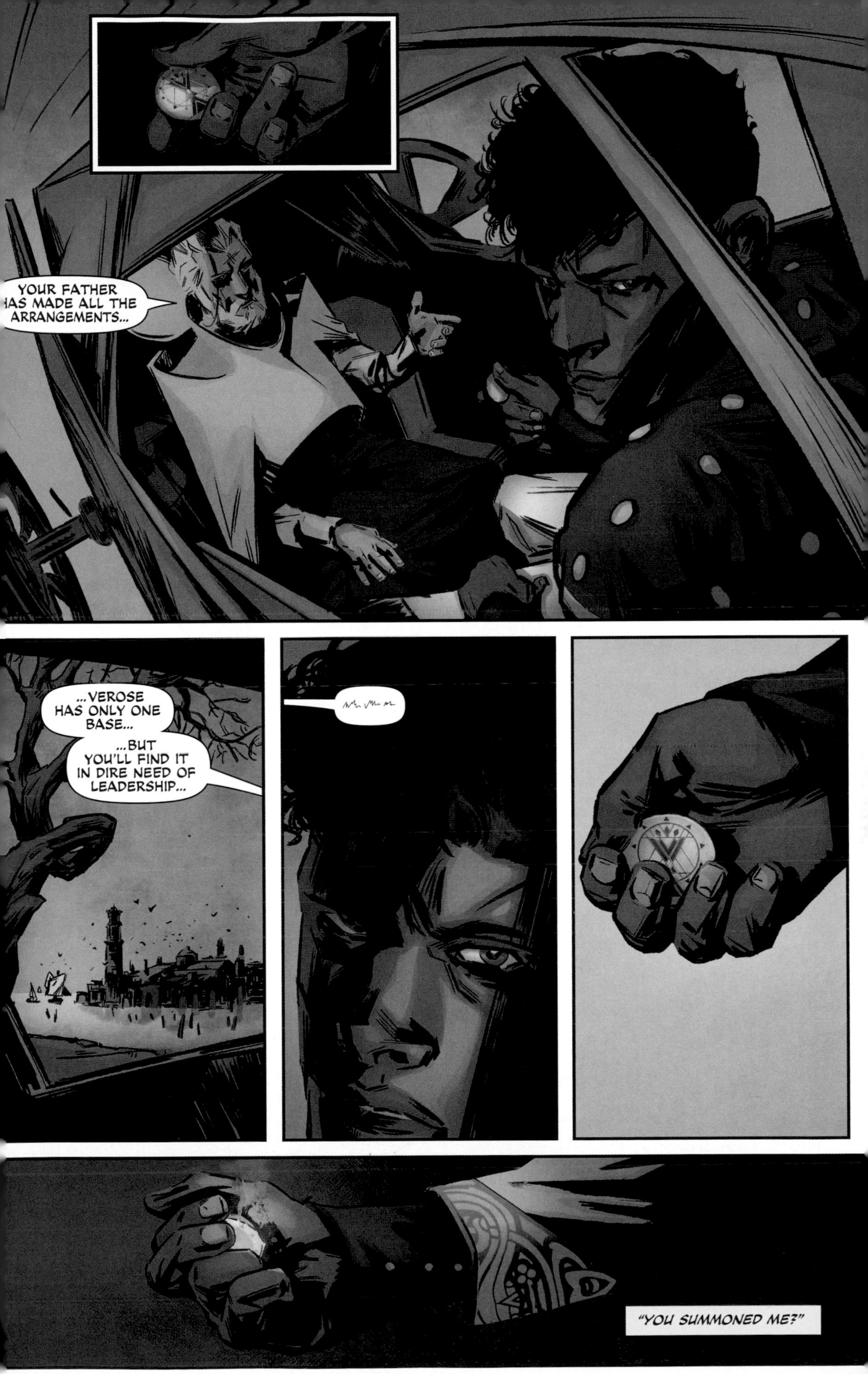
YOUR FATHER HAS MADE ALL THE ARRANGEMENTS...
...VEROSE HAS ONLY ONE BASE...
...BUT YOU'LL FIND IT IN DIRE NEED OF LEADERSHIP...
"YOU SUMMONED ME?"

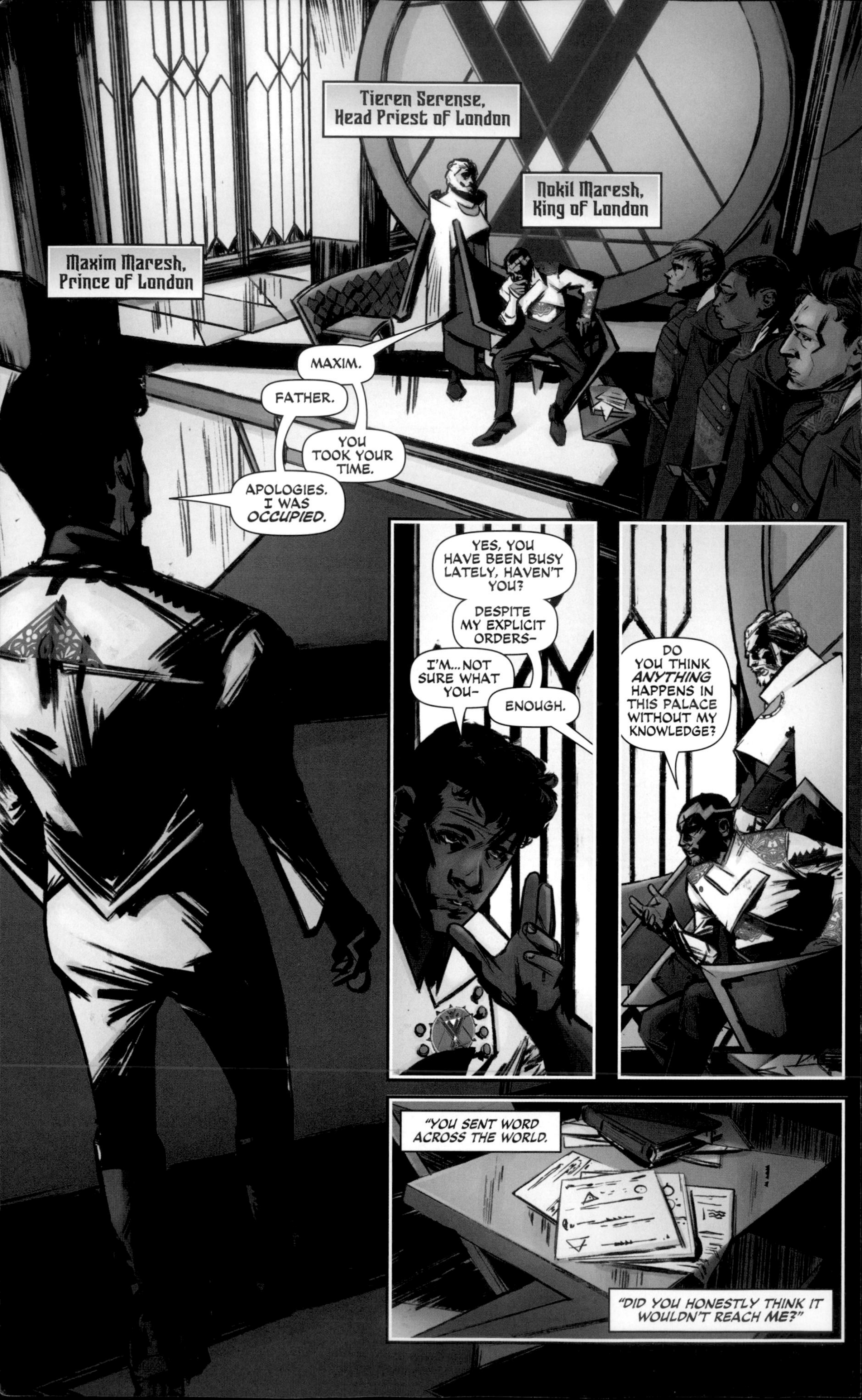
Tieren Serense, Head Priest of London
Nokil Maresh, King of London
Maxim Maresh, Prince of London
MAXIM.
FATHER.
YOU TOOK YOUR TIME.
APOLOGIES. I WAS *OCCUPIED*.
YES, YOU HAVE BEEN BUSY LATELY, HAVEN'T YOU?
DESPITE MY EXPLICIT ORDERS–
I'M...NOT SURE WHAT YOU–
ENOUGH.
DO YOU THINK *ANYTHING* HAPPENS IN THIS PALACE WITHOUT MY KNOWLEDGE?
"YOU SENT WORD ACROSS THE WORLD.
"DID YOU HONESTLY THINK IT WOULDN'T REACH ME?"

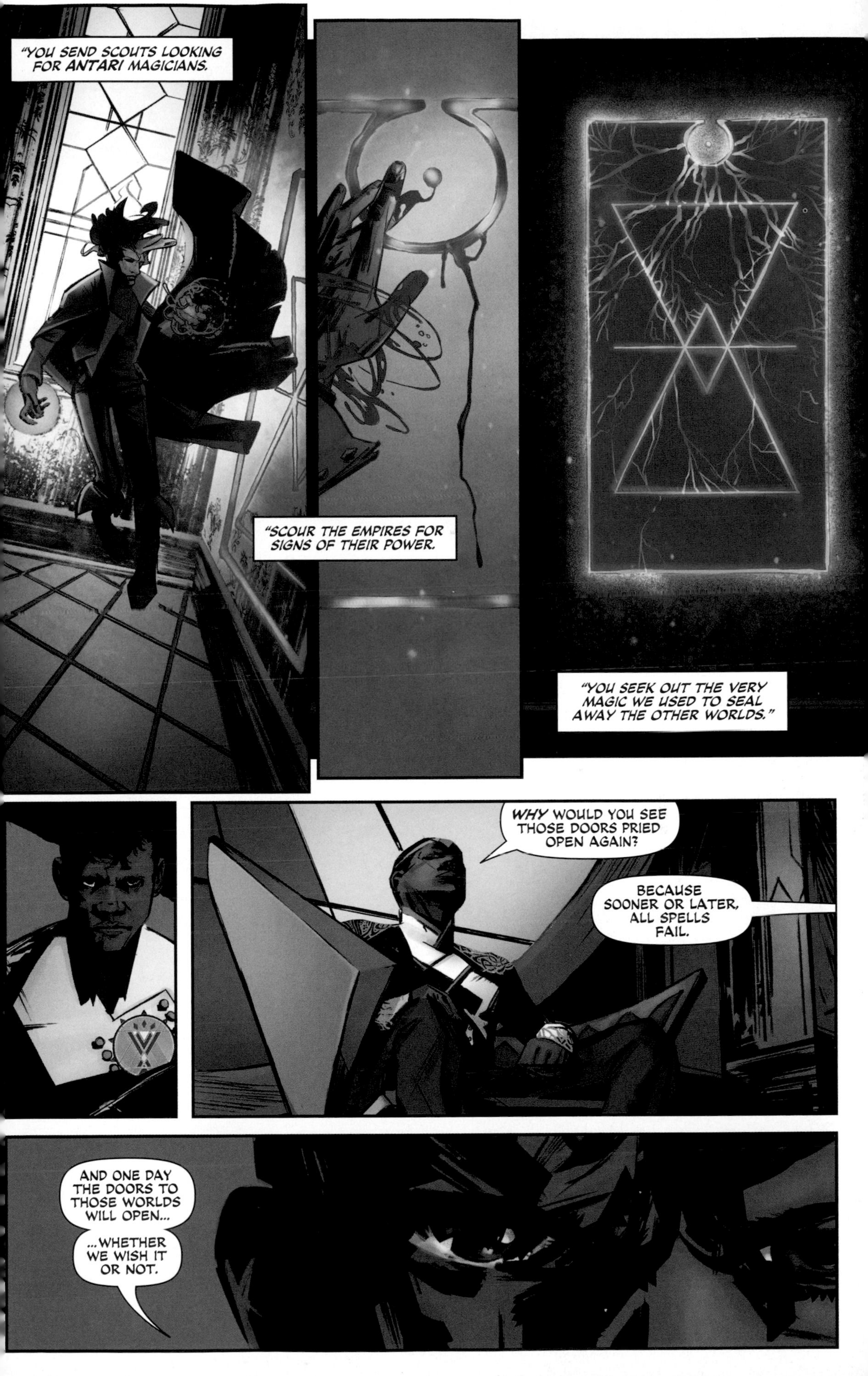
"YOU SEND SCOUTS LOOKING FOR ANTARI MAGICIANS.
"SCOUR THE EMPIRES FOR SIGNS OF THEIR POWER.
"YOU SEEK OUT THE VERY MAGIC WE USED TO SEAL AWAY THE OTHER WORLDS."
WHY WOULD YOU SEE THOSE DOORS PRIED OPEN AGAIN?
BECAUSE SOONER OR LATER, ALL SPELLS FAIL.
AND ONE DAY THE DOORS TO THOSE WORLDS WILL OPEN...
...WHETHER WE WISH IT OR NOT.

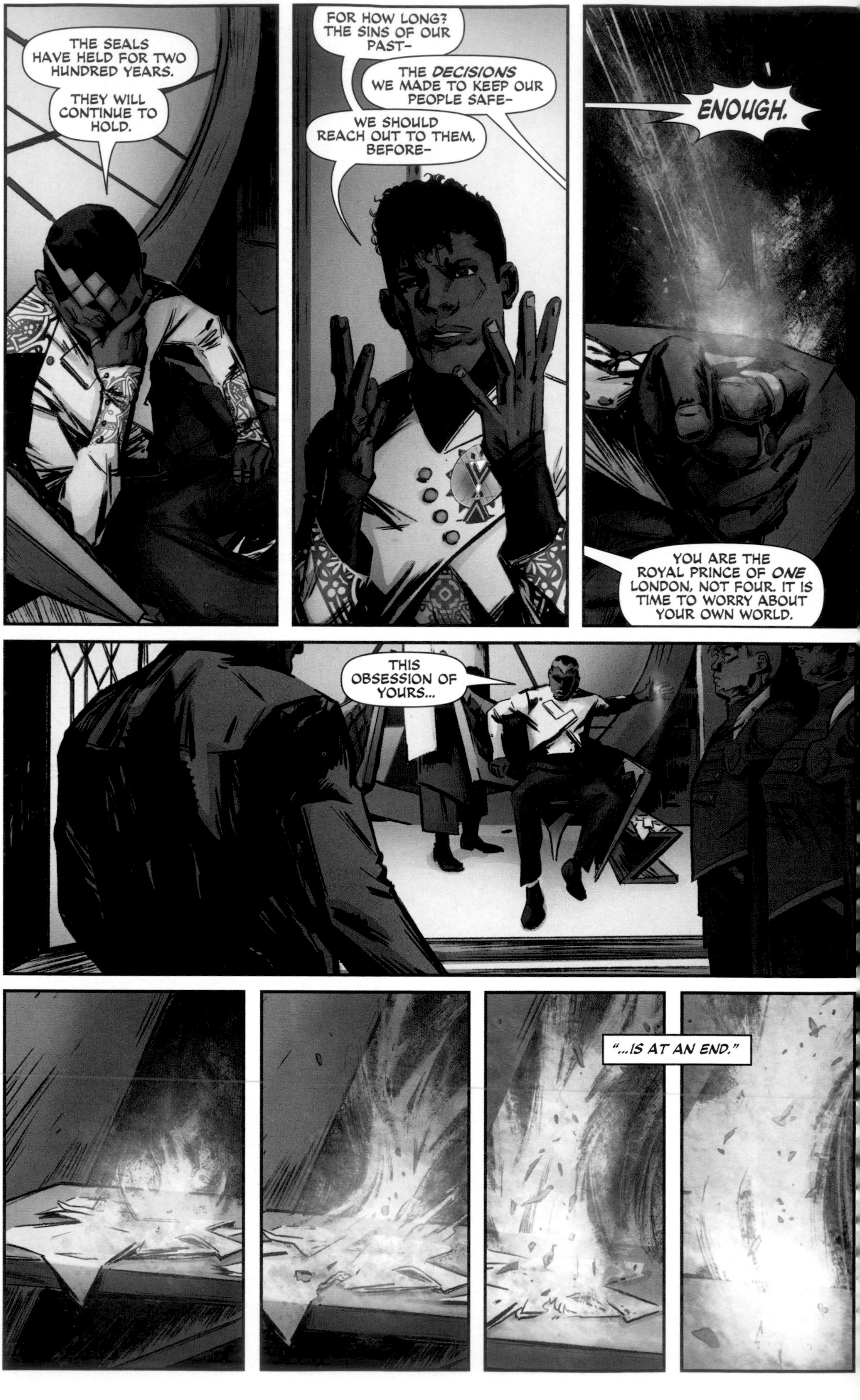
THE SEALS HAVE HELD FOR TWO HUNDRED YEARS.
THEY WILL CONTINUE TO HOLD.
FOR HOW LONG? THE SINS OF OUR PAST-
THE *DECISIONS* WE MADE TO KEEP OUR PEOPLE SAFE-
WE SHOULD REACH OUT TO THEM, BEFORE-
ENOUGH.
YOU ARE THE ROYAL PRINCE OF *ONE* LONDON, NOT FOUR. IT IS TIME TO WORRY ABOUT YOUR OWN WORLD.
THIS OBSESSION OF YOURS...
"...IS AT AN END."

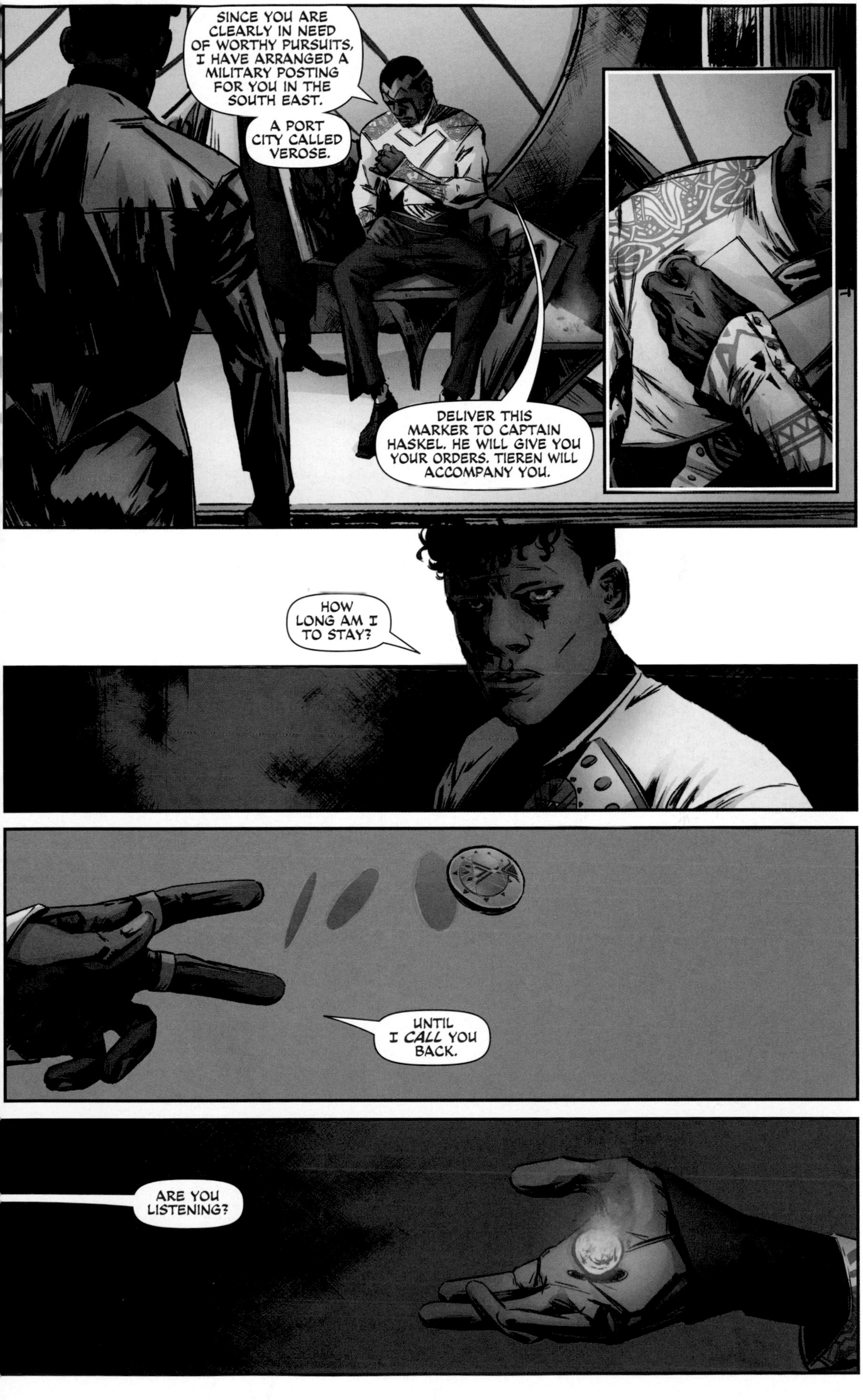
SINCE YOU ARE CLEARLY IN NEED OF WORTHY PURSUITS, I HAVE ARRANGED A MILITARY POSTING FOR YOU IN THE SOUTH EAST.
A PORT CITY CALLED VEROSE.
DELIVER THIS MARKER TO CAPTAIN HASKEL. HE WILL GIVE YOU YOUR ORDERS. TIEREN WILL ACCOMPANY YOU.
HOW LONG AM I TO STAY?
UNTIL I *CALL* YOU BACK.
ARE YOU LISTENING?

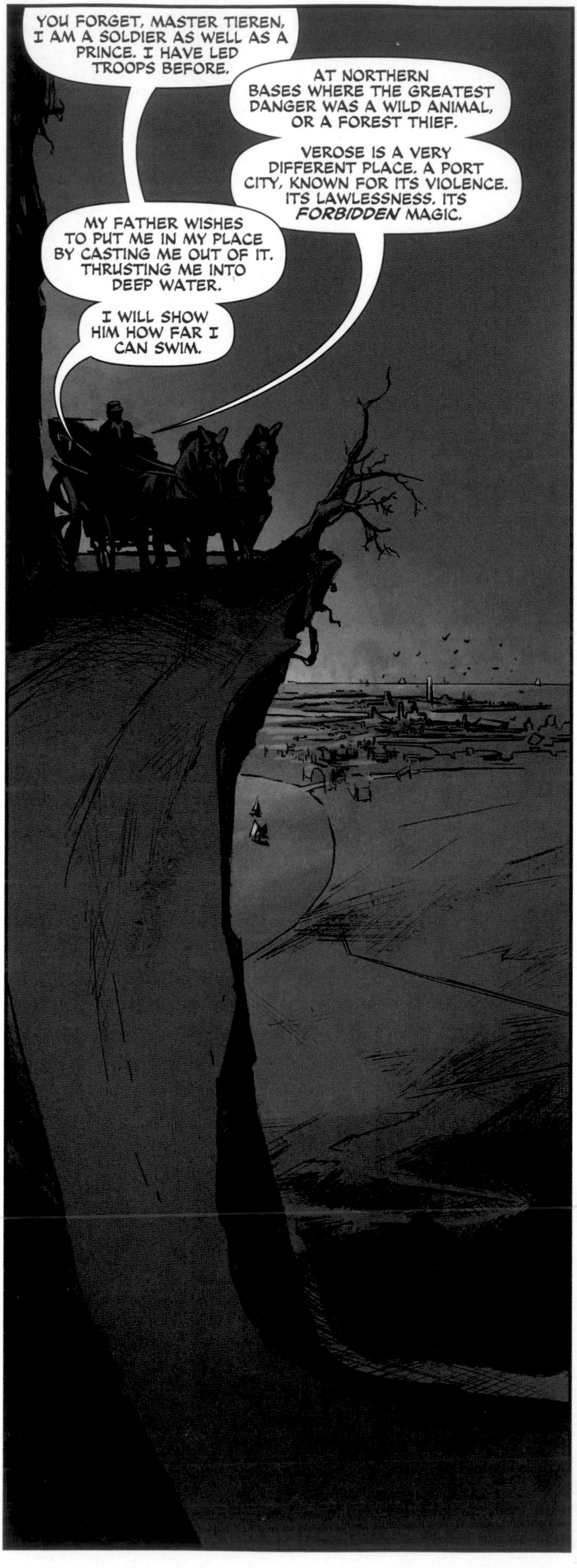
YOU FORGET, MASTER TIEREN, I AM A SOLDIER AS WELL AS A PRINCE. I HAVE LED TROOPS BEFORE.
AT NORTHERN BASES WHERE THE GREATEST DANGER WAS A WILD ANIMAL, OR A FOREST THIEF.
VEROSE IS A VERY DIFFERENT PLACE. A PORT CITY, KNOWN FOR ITS VIOLENCE. ITS LAWLESSNESS. ITS *FORBIDDEN* MAGIC.
MY FATHER WISHES TO PUT ME IN MY PLACE BY CASTING ME OUT OF IT. THRUSTING ME INTO DEEP WATER.
I WILL SHOW HIM HOW FAR I CAN SWIM.
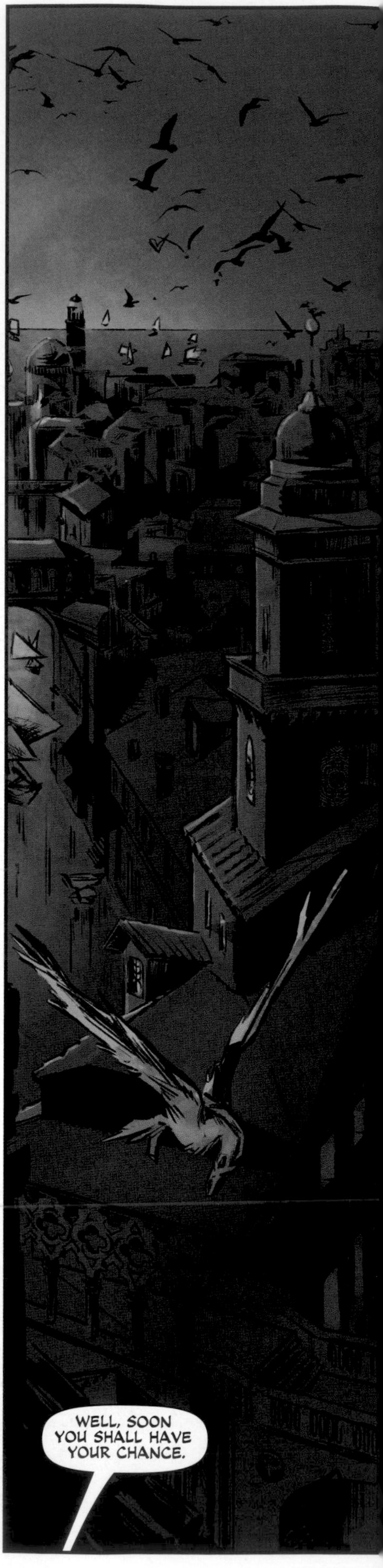
WELL, SOON YOU SHALL HAVE YOUR CHANCE.

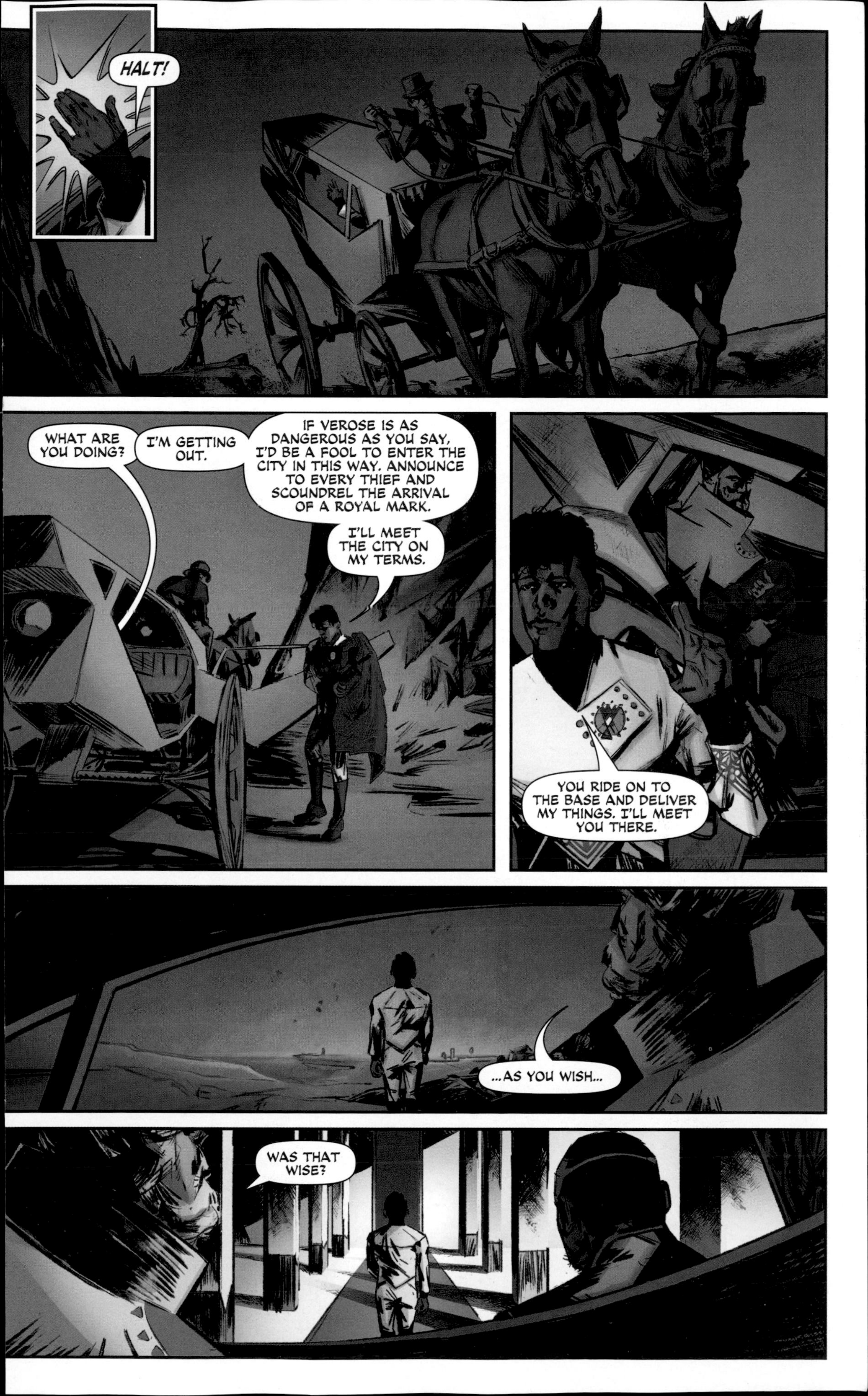
HALT!
WHAT ARE YOU DOING?
I'M GETTING OUT.
IF VEROSE IS AS DANGEROUS AS YOU SAY, I'D BE A FOOL TO ENTER THE CITY IN THIS WAY. ANNOUNCE TO EVERY THIEF AND SCOUNDREL THE ARRIVAL OF A ROYAL MARK.
I'LL MEET THE CITY ON MY TERMS.
YOU RIDE ON TO THE BASE AND DELIVER MY THINGS. I'LL MEET YOU THERE.
...AS YOU WISH...
WAS THAT WISE?

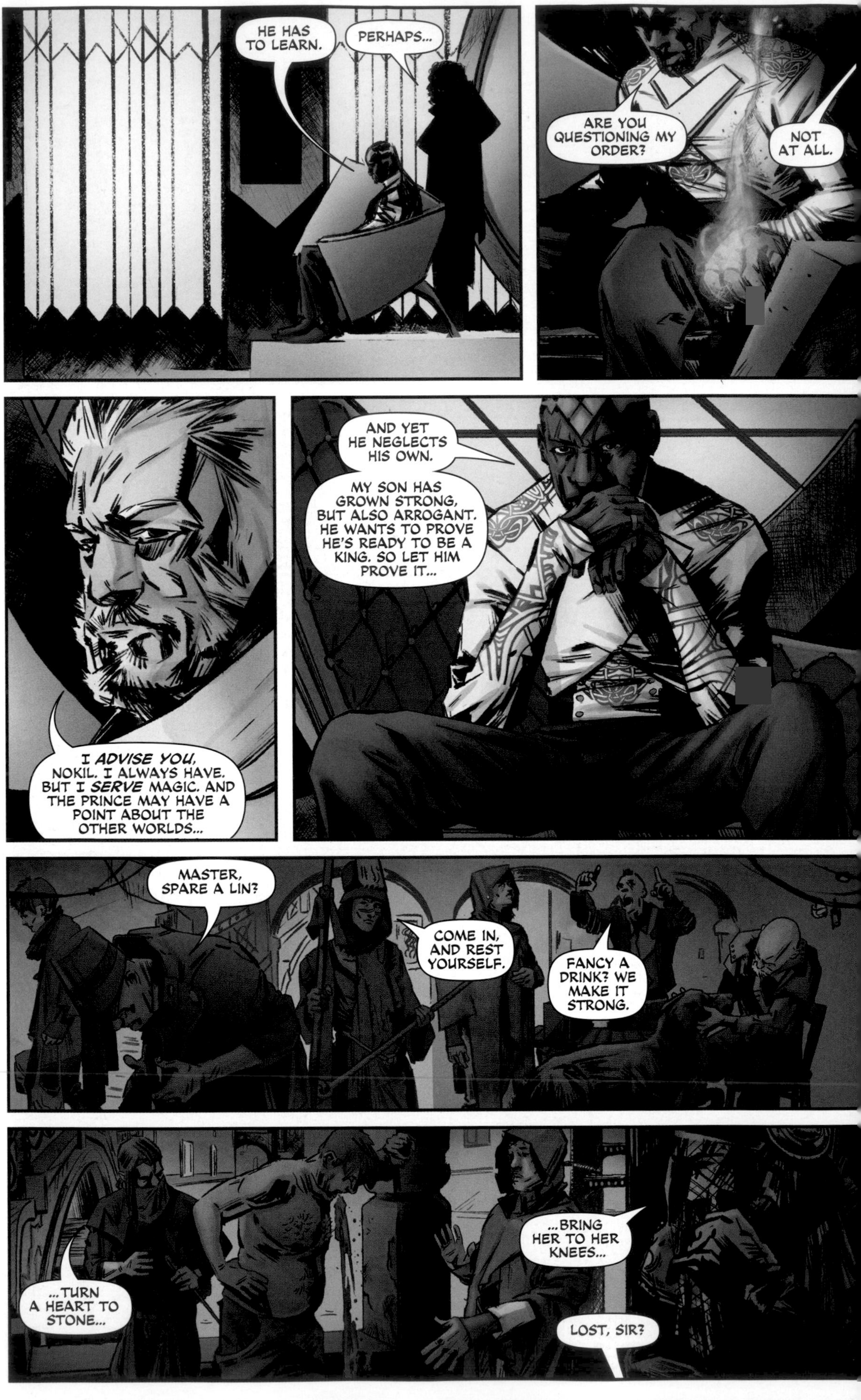
HE HAS TO LEARN.
PERHAPS...
ARE YOU QUESTIONING MY ORDER?
NOT AT ALL.
I ADVISE YOU, NOKIL. I ALWAYS HAVE. BUT I SERVE MAGIC. AND THE PRINCE MAY HAVE A POINT ABOUT THE OTHER WORLDS...
AND YET HE NEGLECTS HIS OWN.
MY SON HAS GROWN STRONG, BUT ALSO ARROGANT. HE WANTS TO PROVE HE'S READY TO BE A KING. SO LET HIM PROVE IT...
MASTER, SPARE A LIN?
COME IN, AND REST YOURSELF.
FANCY A DRINK? WE MAKE IT STRONG.
...TURN A HEART TO STONE...
...BRING HER TO HER KNEES...
LOST, SIR?

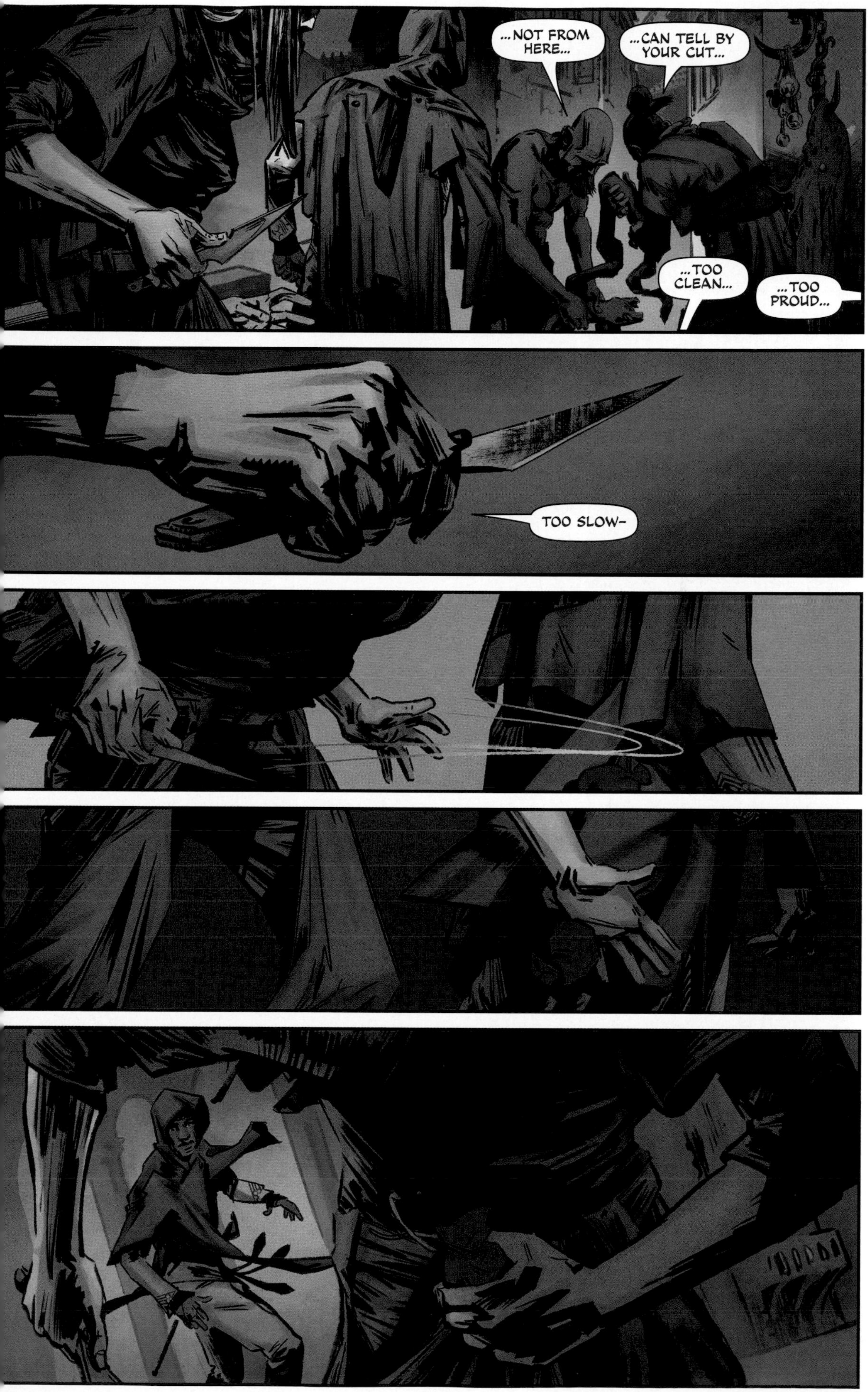
...NOT FROM HERE...
...CAN TELL BY YOUR CUT...
...TOO CLEAN...
...TOO PROUD...
TOO SLOW-

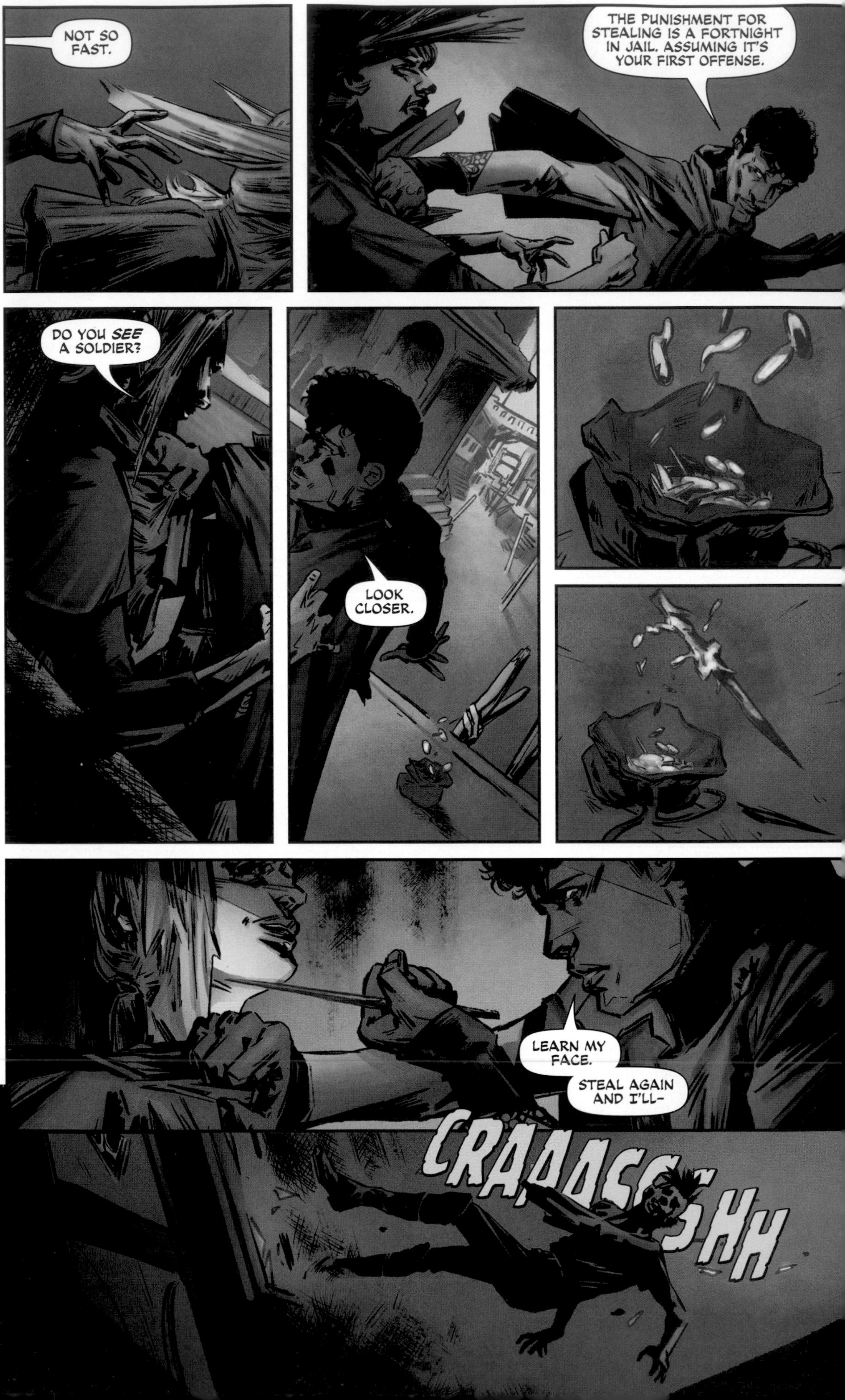
NOT SO FAST.
THE PUNISHMENT FOR STEALING IS A FORTNIGHT IN JAIL. ASSUMING IT'S YOUR FIRST OFFENSE.
DO YOU *SEE* A SOLDIER?
LOOK CLOSER.
LEARN MY FACE.
STEAL AGAIN AND I'LL-
CRAAASSSHH

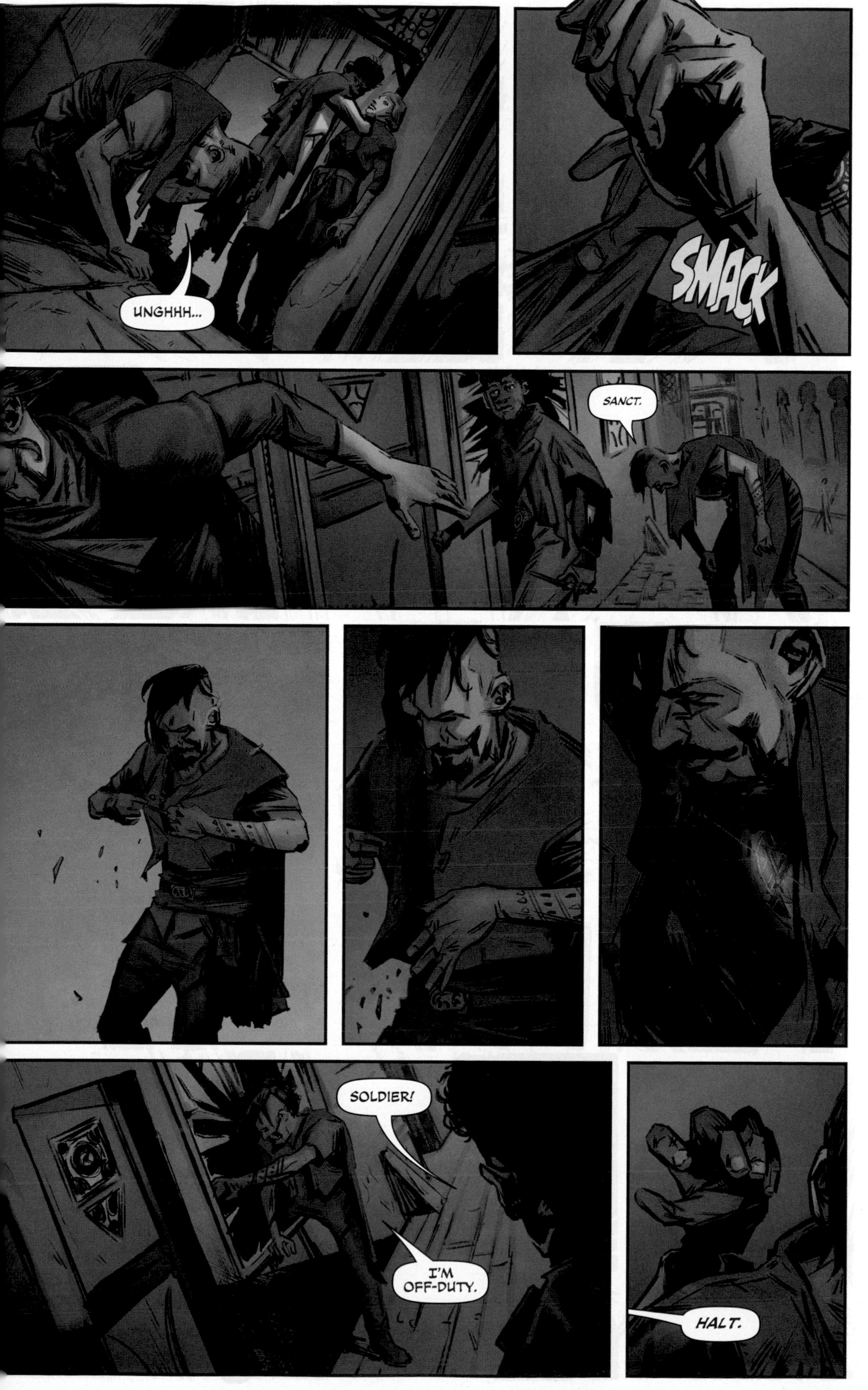
UNGHHH...
SMACK
SANCT.
SOLDIER!
I'M OFF-DUTY.
HALT.

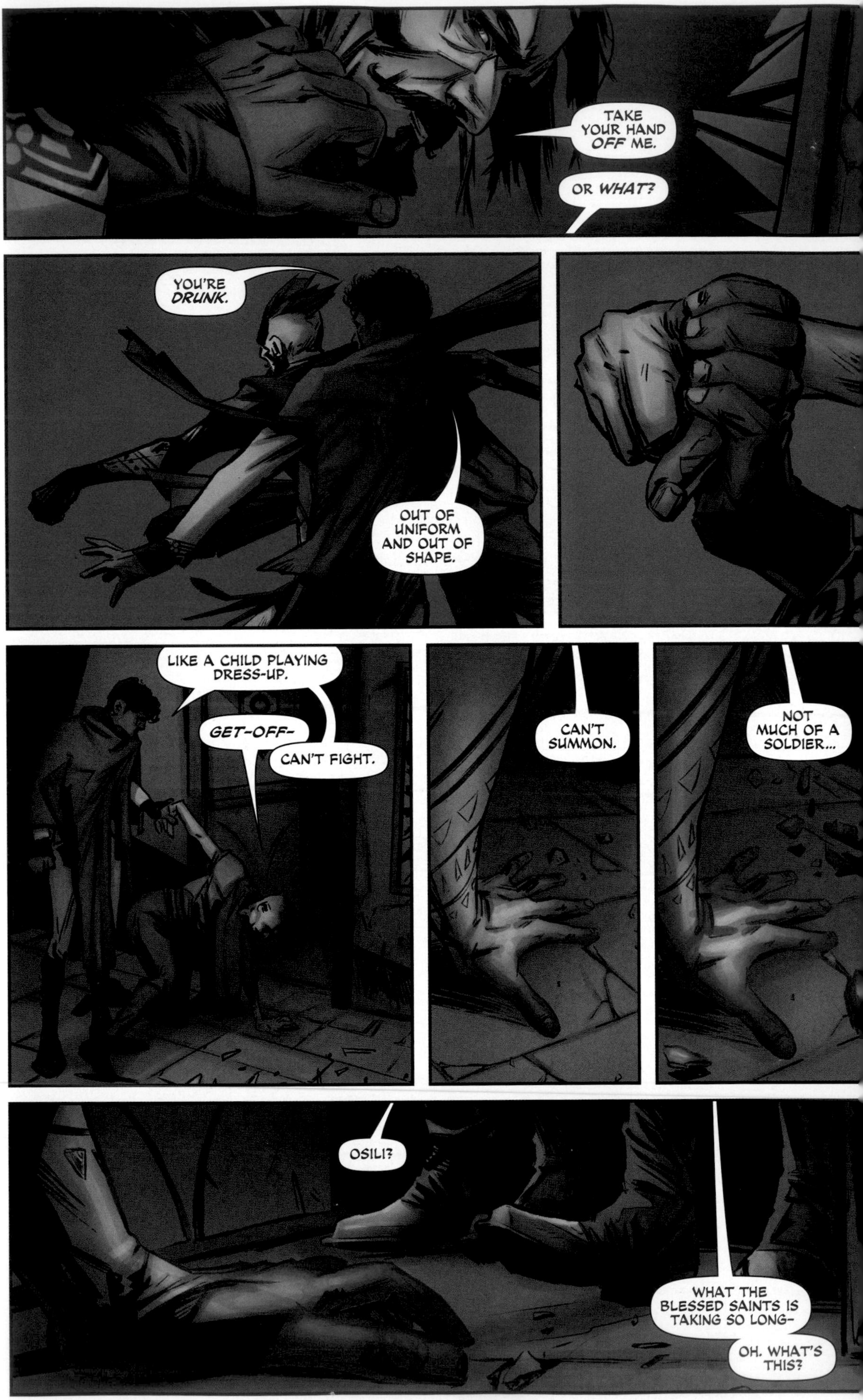
TAKE YOUR HAND OFF ME.
OR WHAT?
YOU'RE DRUNK.
OUT OF UNIFORM AND OUT OF SHAPE.
LIKE A CHILD PLAYING DRESS-UP.
GET-OFF-
CAN'T FIGHT.
CAN'T SUMMON.
NOT MUCH OF A SOLDIER...
OSILI?
WHAT THE BLESSED SAINTS IS TAKING SO LONG-
OH. WHAT'S THIS?

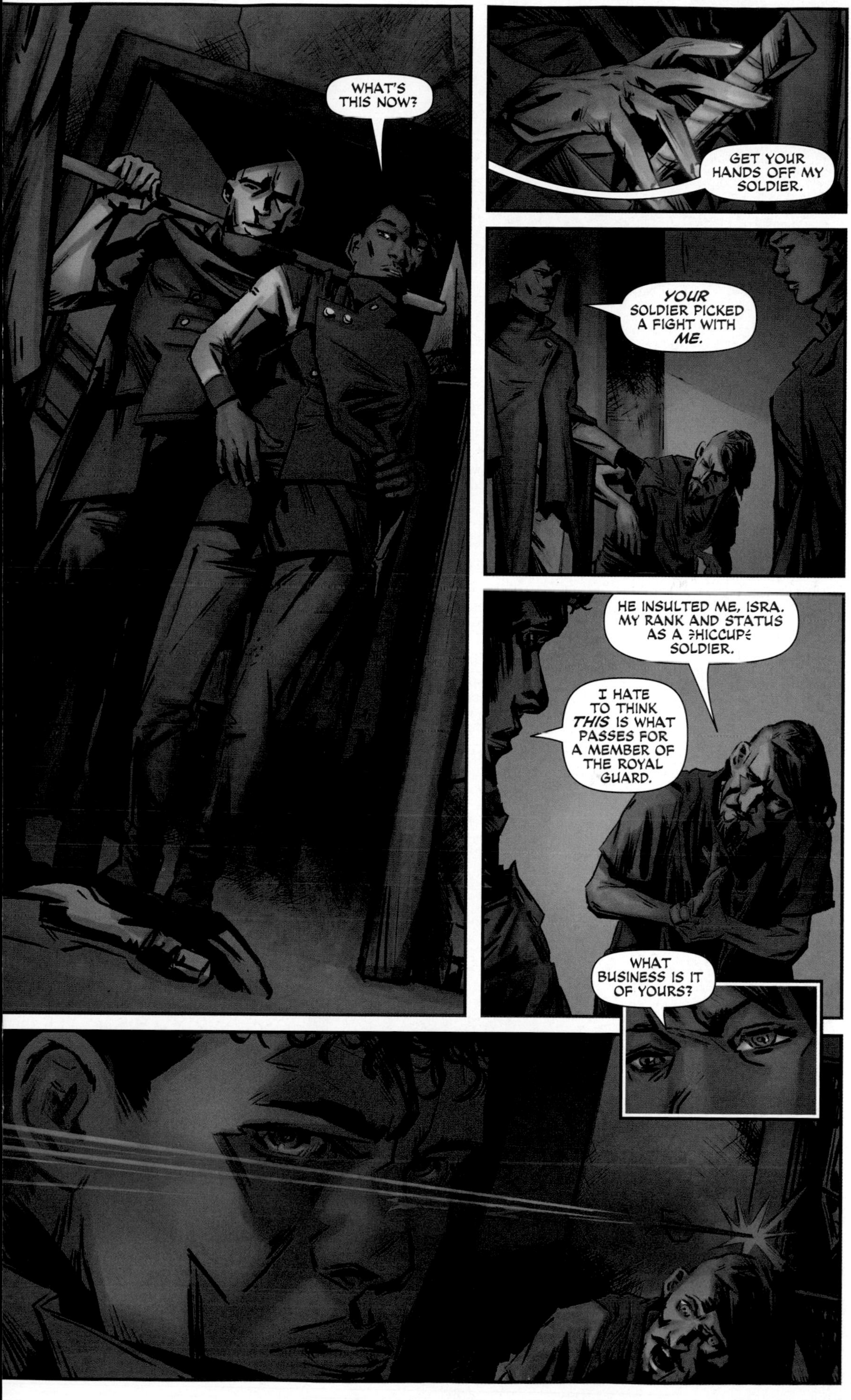
WHAT'S THIS NOW?
GET YOUR HANDS OFF MY SOLDIER.
YOUR SOLDIER PICKED A FIGHT WITH ME.
HE INSULTED ME, ISRA. MY RANK AND STATUS AS A *HICCUP* SOLDIER.
I HATE TO THINK THIS IS WHAT PASSES FOR A MEMBER OF THE ROYAL GUARD.
WHAT BUSINESS IS IT OF YOURS?

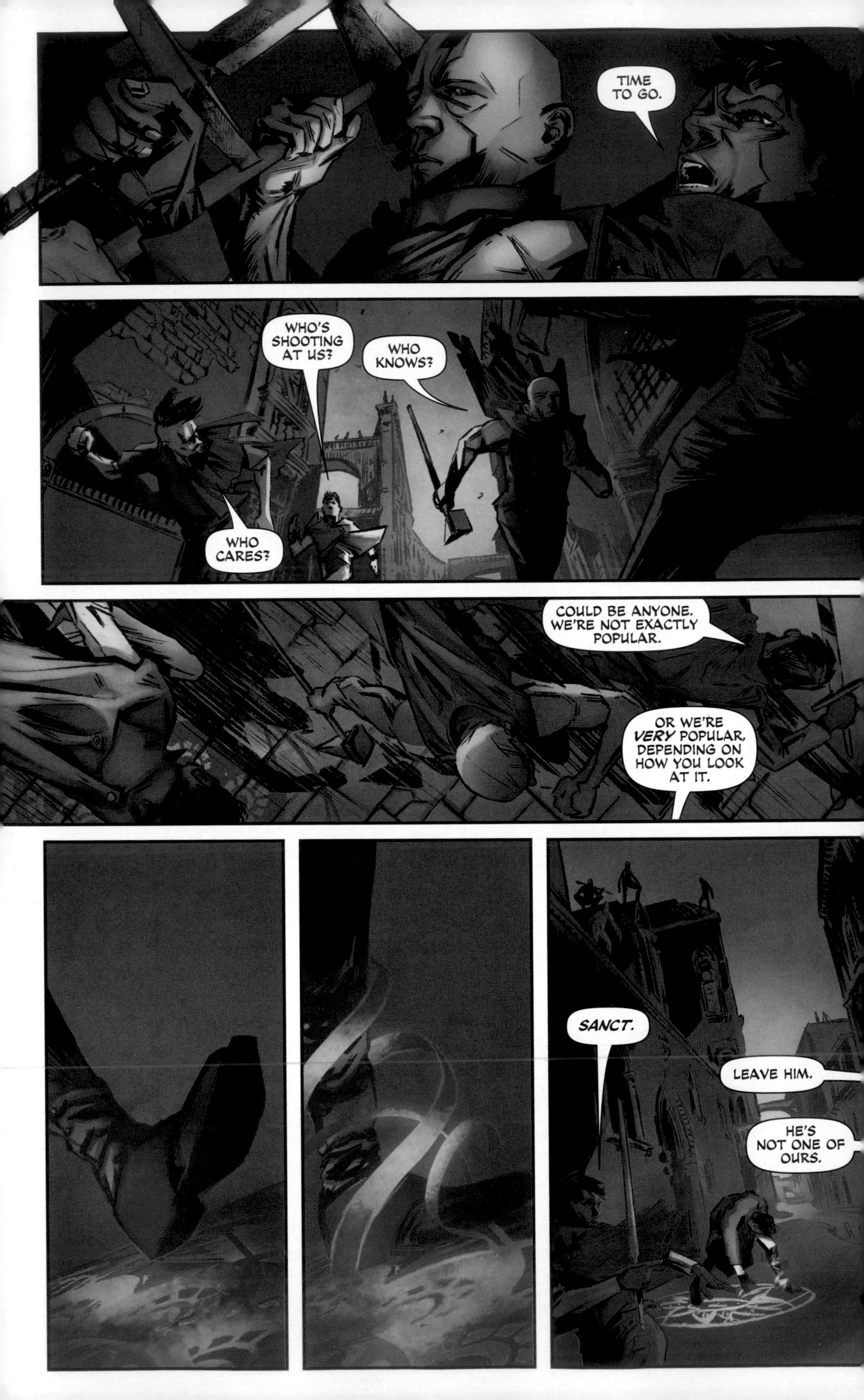
TIME TO GO.
WHO'S SHOOTING AT US?
WHO KNOWS?
WHO CARES?
COULD BE ANYONE. WE'RE NOT EXACTLY POPULAR.
OR WE'RE VERY POPULAR, DEPENDING ON HOW YOU LOOK AT IT.
SANCT.
LEAVE HIM.
HE'S NOT ONE OF OURS.

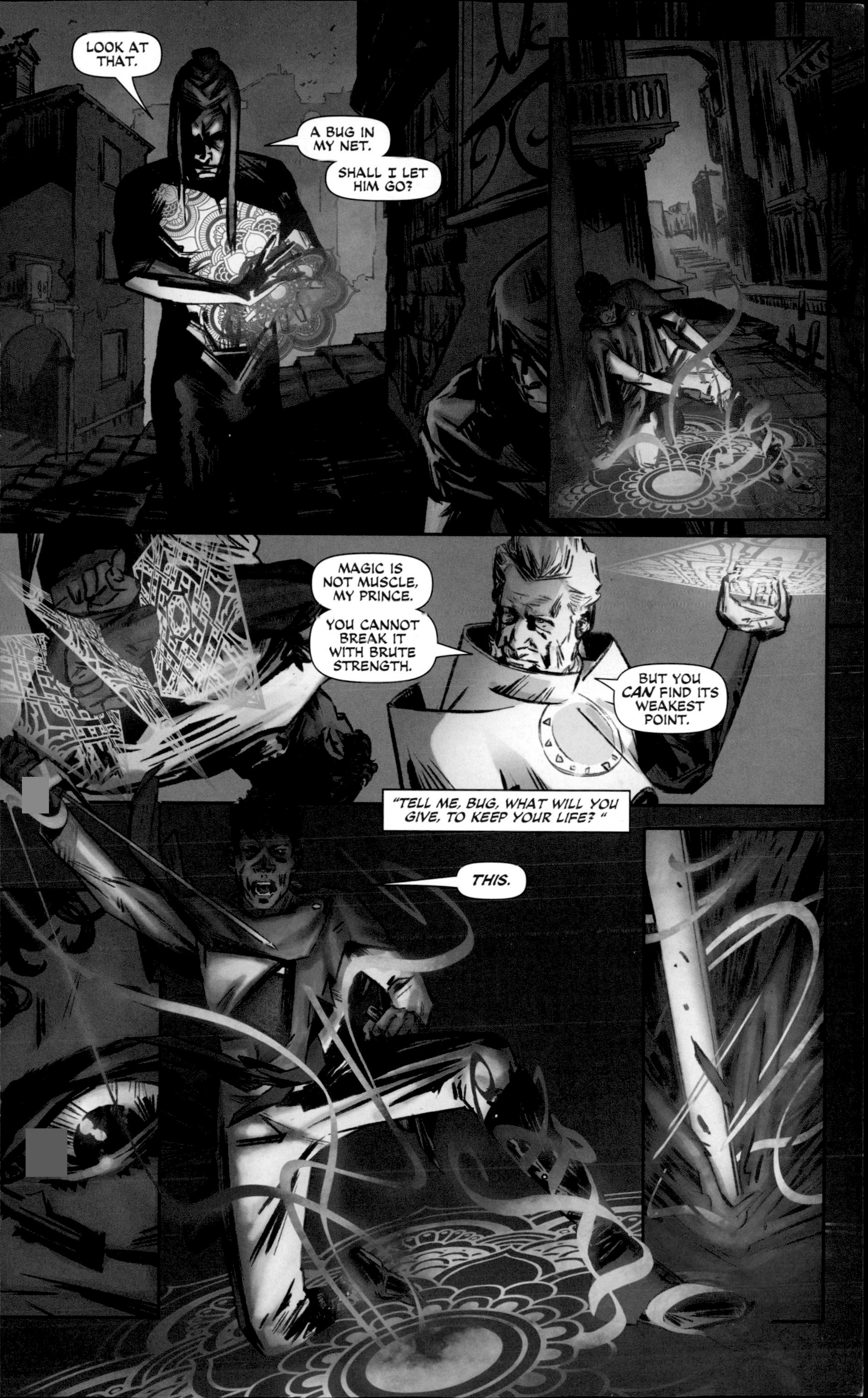
LOOK AT THAT.
A BUG IN MY NET.
SHALL I LET HIM GO?
MAGIC IS NOT MUSCLE, MY PRINCE.
YOU CANNOT BREAK IT WITH BRUTE STRENGTH.
BUT YOU CAN FIND ITS WEAKEST POINT.
"TELL ME, BUG, WHAT WILL YOU GIVE, TO KEEP YOUR LIFE? "
THIS.

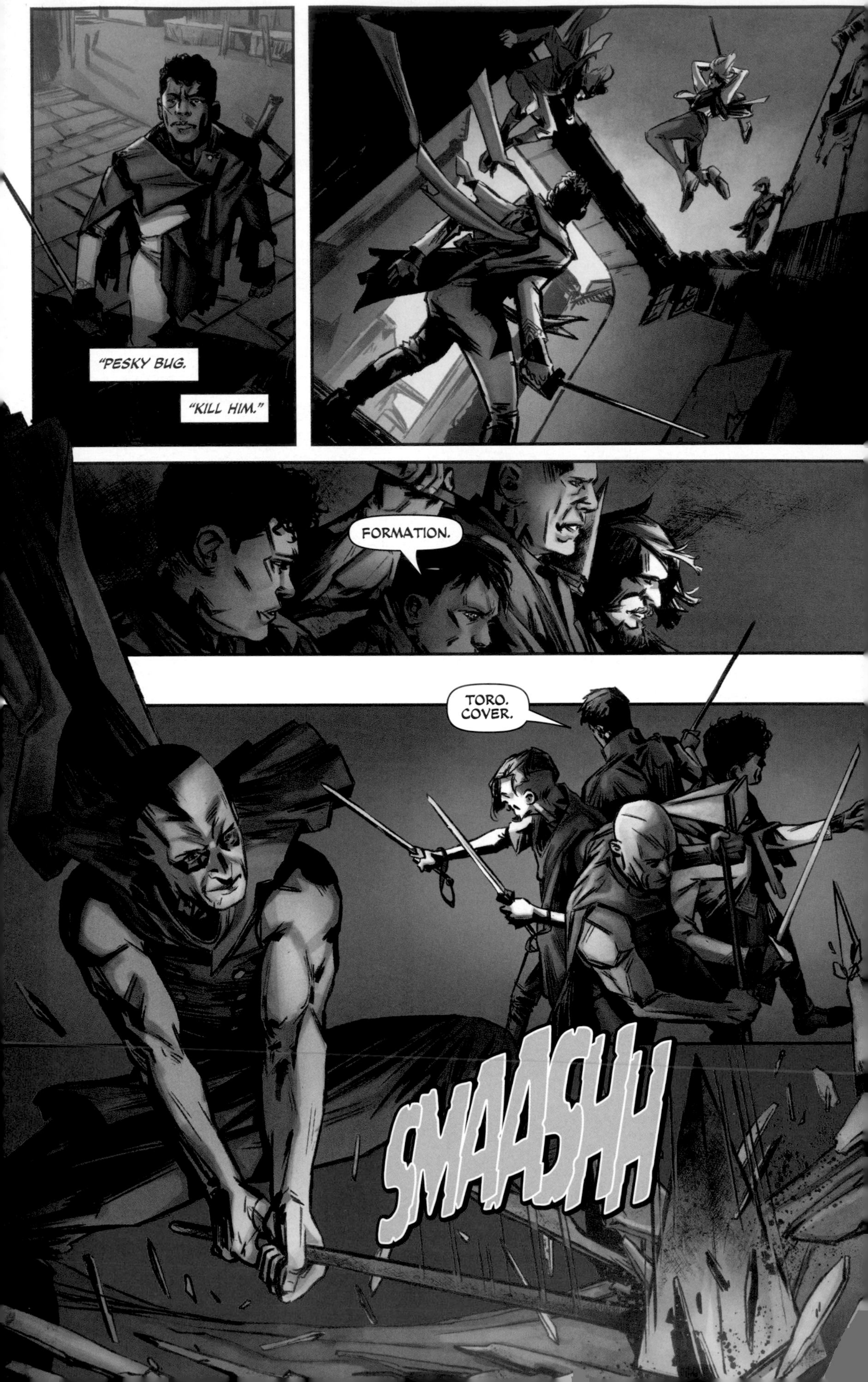
"PESKY BUG.
"KILL HIM."
FORMATION.
TORO. COVER.
SMAASHH

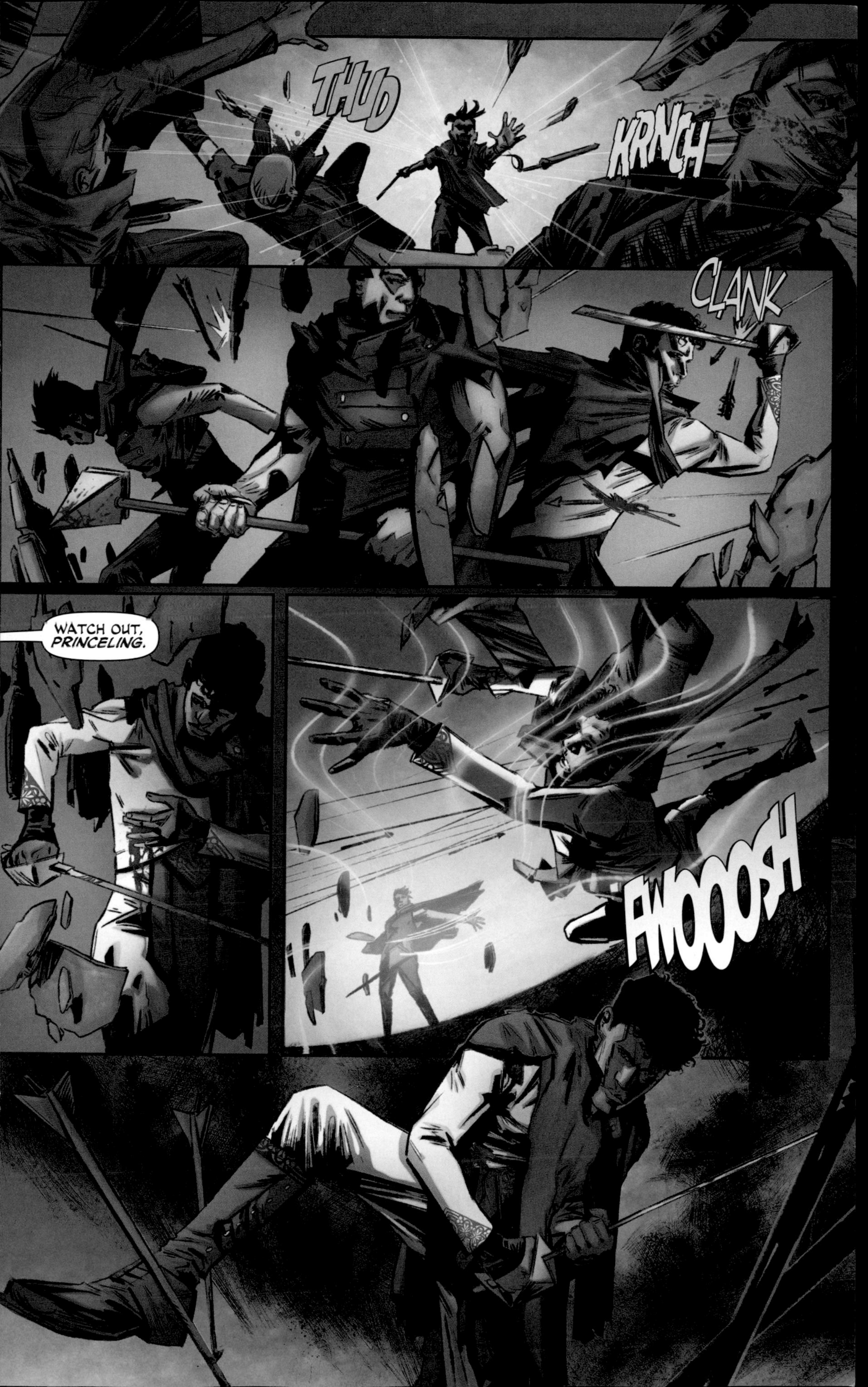
THUD
KRNCH
CLANK
WATCH OUT, PRINCELING.
FWOOOSH

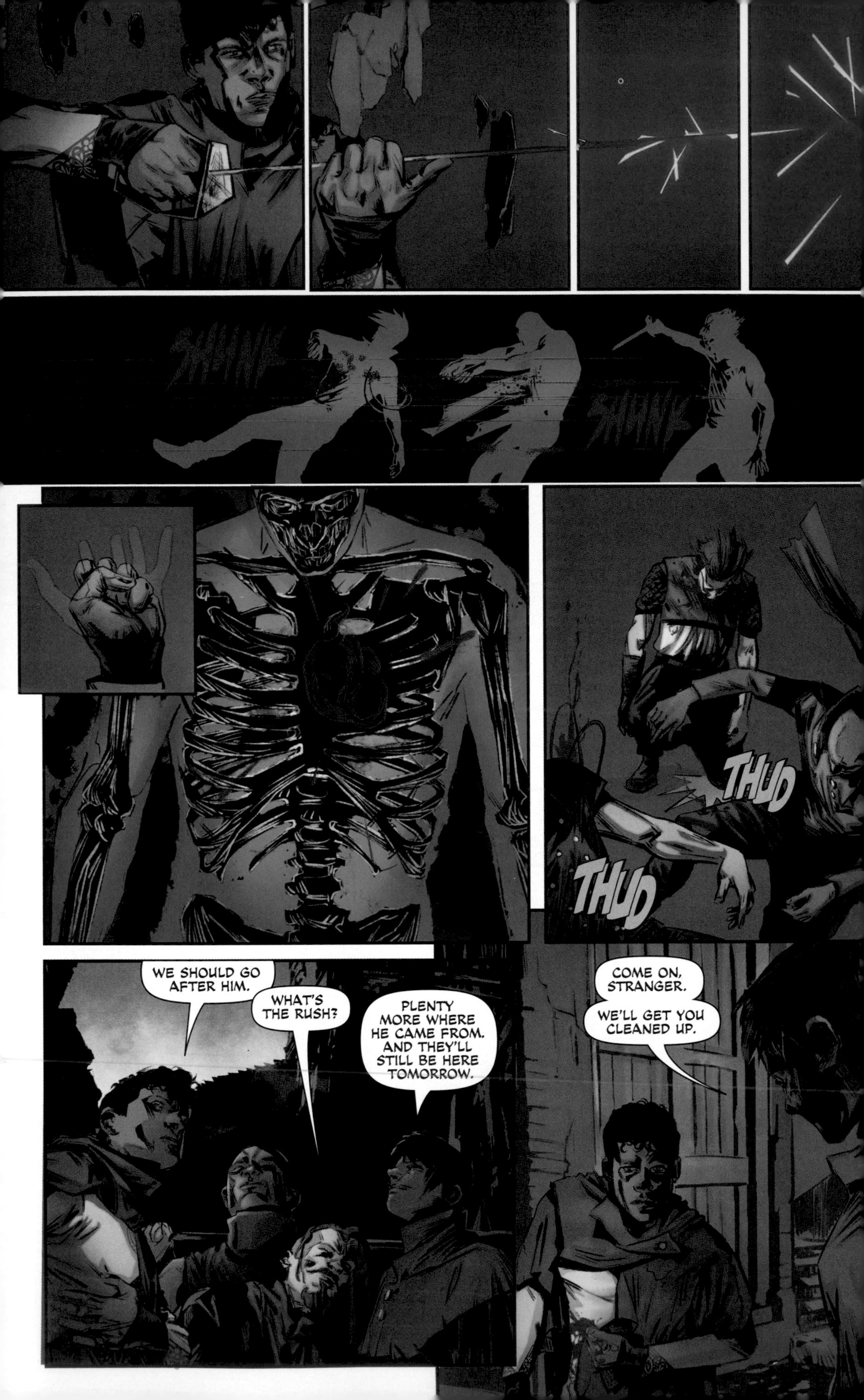
SHUNK
SHUNK
THUD
THUD
WE SHOULD GO AFTER HIM.
WHAT'S THE RUSH?
PLENTY MORE WHERE HE CAME FROM. AND THEY'LL STILL BE HERE TOMORROW.
COME ON, STRANGER.
WE'LL GET YOU CLEANED UP.

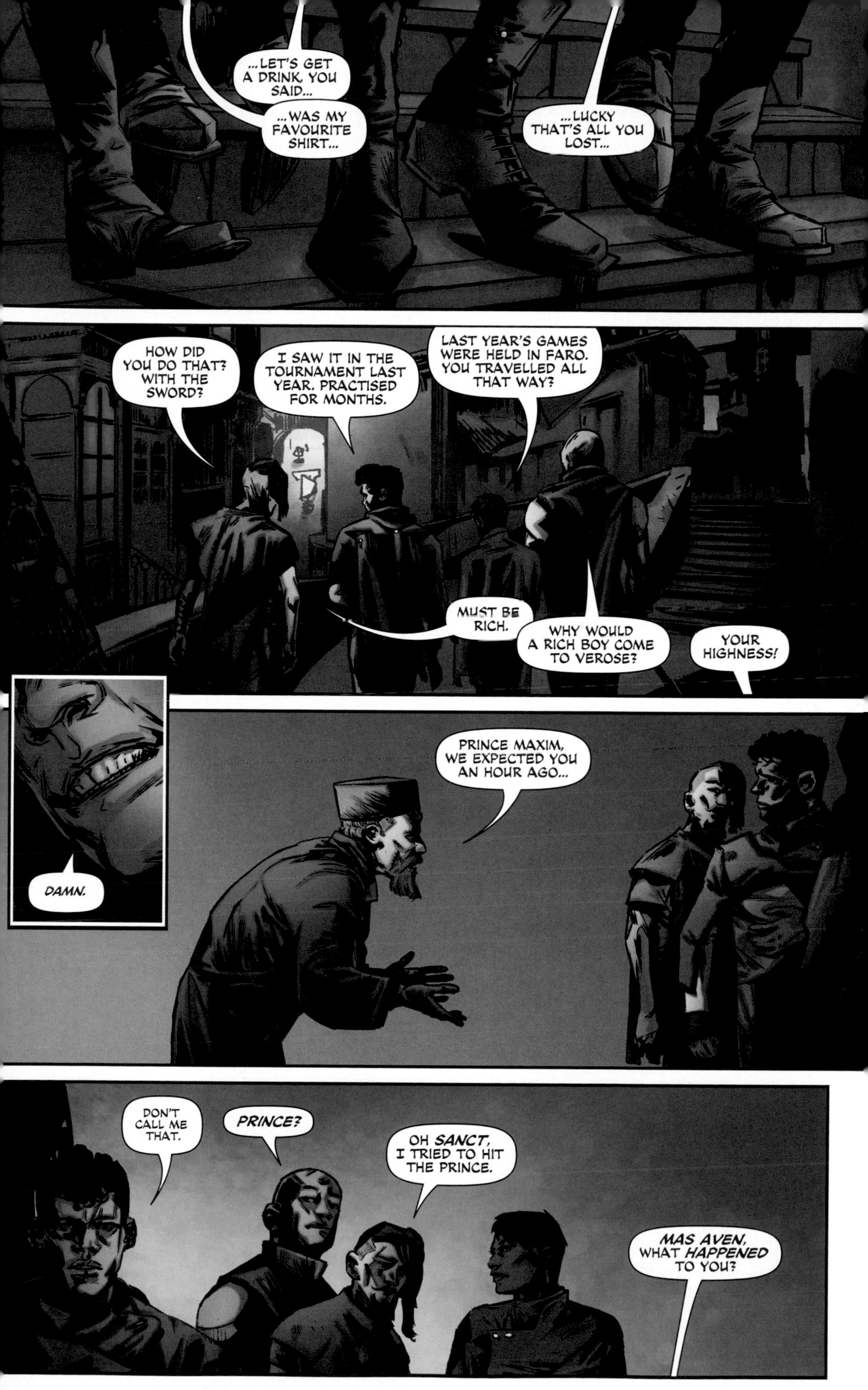
...LET'S GET A DRINK, YOU SAID...
...WAS MY FAVOURITE SHIRT...
...LUCKY THAT'S ALL YOU LOST...
HOW DID YOU DO THAT? WITH THE SWORD?
I SAW IT IN THE TOURNAMENT LAST YEAR. PRACTISED FOR MONTHS.
LAST YEAR'S GAMES WERE HELD IN FARO. YOU TRAVELLED ALL THAT WAY?
MUST BE RICH.
WHY WOULD A RICH BOY COME TO VEROSE?
YOUR HIGHNESS!
DAMN.
PRINCE MAXIM, WE EXPECTED YOU AN HOUR AGO...
DON'T CALL ME THAT.
PRINCE?
OH SANCT, I TRIED TO HIT THE PRINCE.
MAS AVEN, WHAT HAPPENED TO YOU?

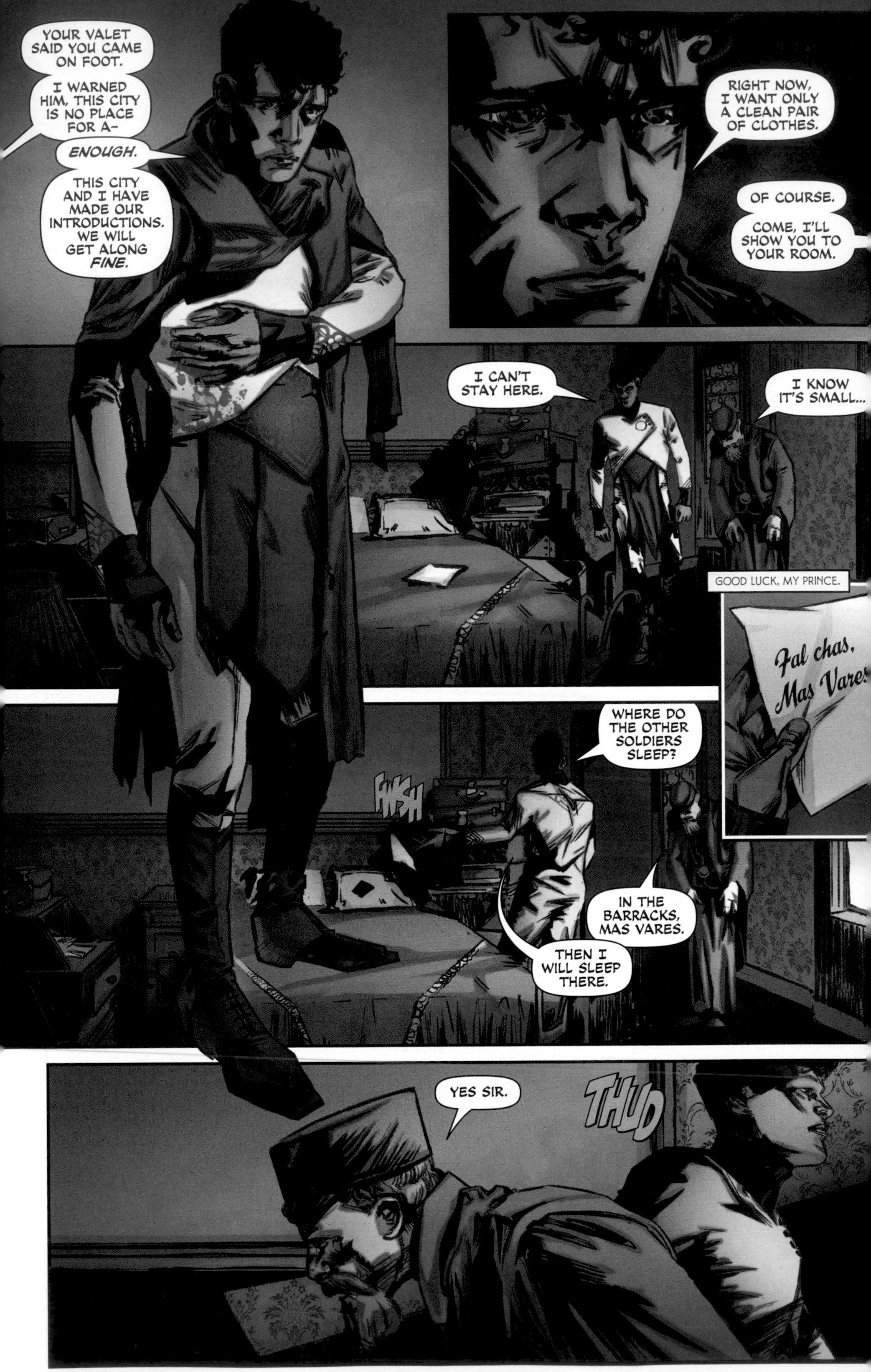
YOUR VALET SAID YOU CAME ON FOOT.
I WARNED HIM, THIS CITY IS NO PLACE FOR A-
ENOUGH.
THIS CITY AND I HAVE MADE OUR INTRODUCTIONS. WE WILL GET ALONG FINE.
RIGHT NOW, I WANT ONLY A CLEAN PAIR OF CLOTHES.
OF COURSE.
COME, I'LL SHOW YOU TO YOUR ROOM.
I CAN'T STAY HERE.
I KNOW IT'S SMALL...
GOOD LUCK, MY PRINCE.
Fal chas, Mas Vares
WHERE DO THE OTHER SOLDIERS SLEEP?
FWSH
IN THE BARRACKS, MAS VARES.
THEN I WILL SLEEP THERE.
YES SIR.
THUD

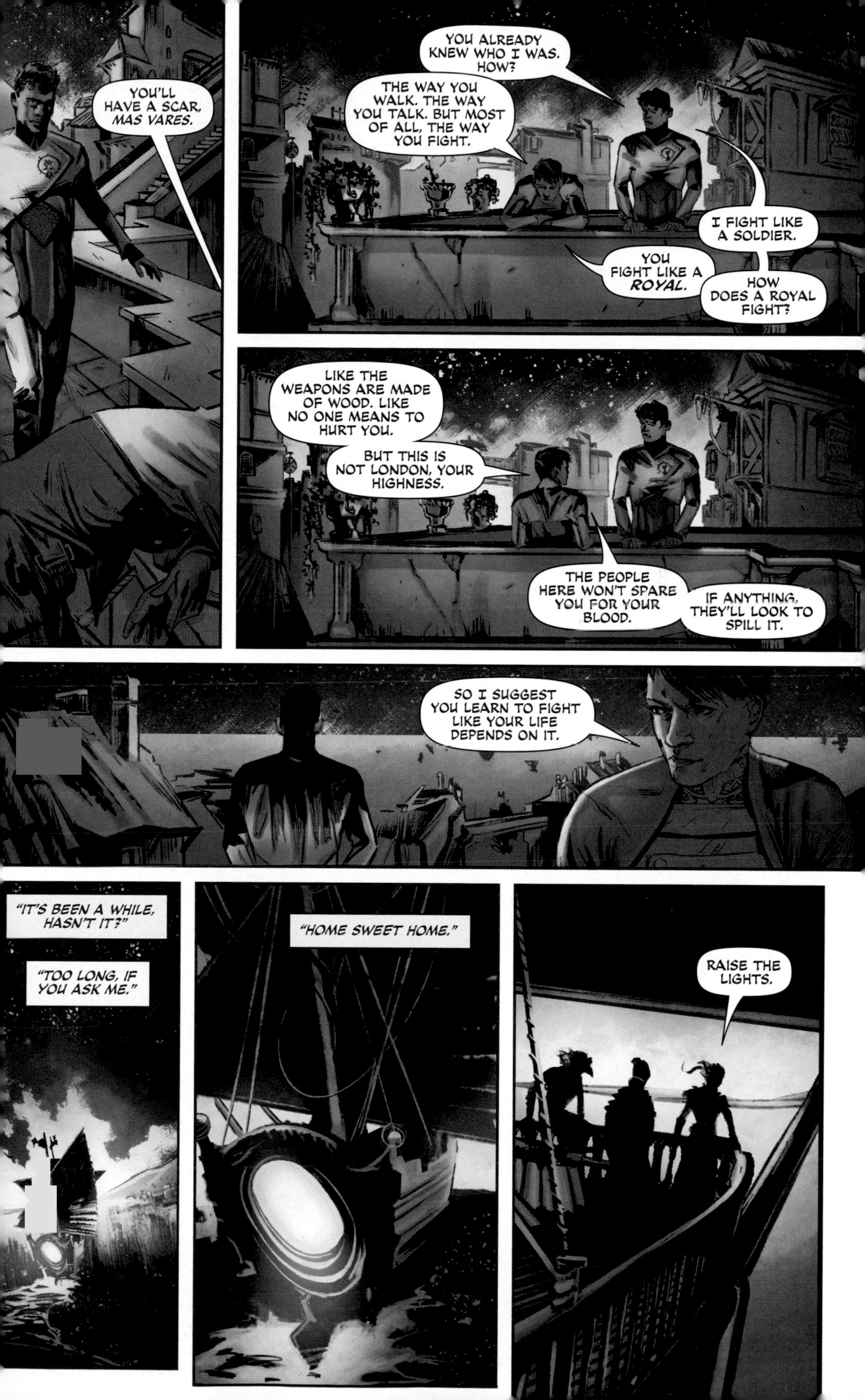
YOU'LL HAVE A SCAR, MAS VARES.
YOU ALREADY KNEW WHO I WAS. HOW?
THE WAY YOU WALK. THE WAY YOU TALK. BUT MOST OF ALL, THE WAY YOU FIGHT.
I FIGHT LIKE A SOLDIER.
YOU FIGHT LIKE A ROYAL.
HOW DOES A ROYAL FIGHT?
LIKE THE WEAPONS ARE MADE OF WOOD. LIKE NO ONE MEANS TO HURT YOU.
BUT THIS IS NOT LONDON, YOUR HIGHNESS.
THE PEOPLE HERE WON'T SPARE YOU FOR YOUR BLOOD.
IF ANYTHING, THEY'LL LOOK TO SPILL IT.
SO I SUGGEST YOU LEARN TO FIGHT LIKE YOUR LIFE DEPENDS ON IT.
"IT'S BEEN A WHILE, HASN'T IT?"
"TOO LONG, IF YOU ASK ME."
"HOME SWEET HOME."
RAISE THE LIGHTS.

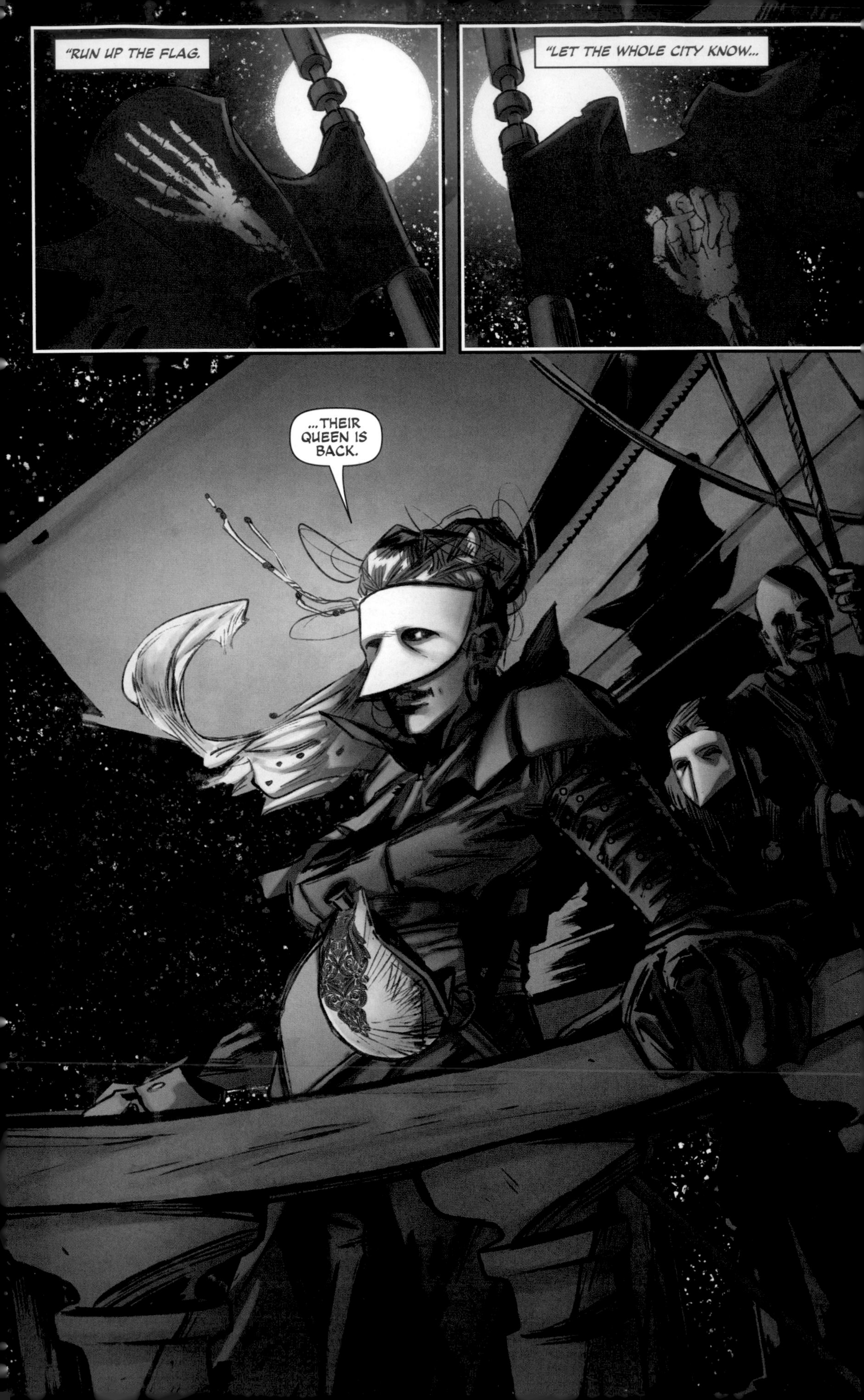
"RUN UP THE FLAG.
"LET THE WHOLE CITY KNOW...
...THEIR QUEEN IS BACK.

#2

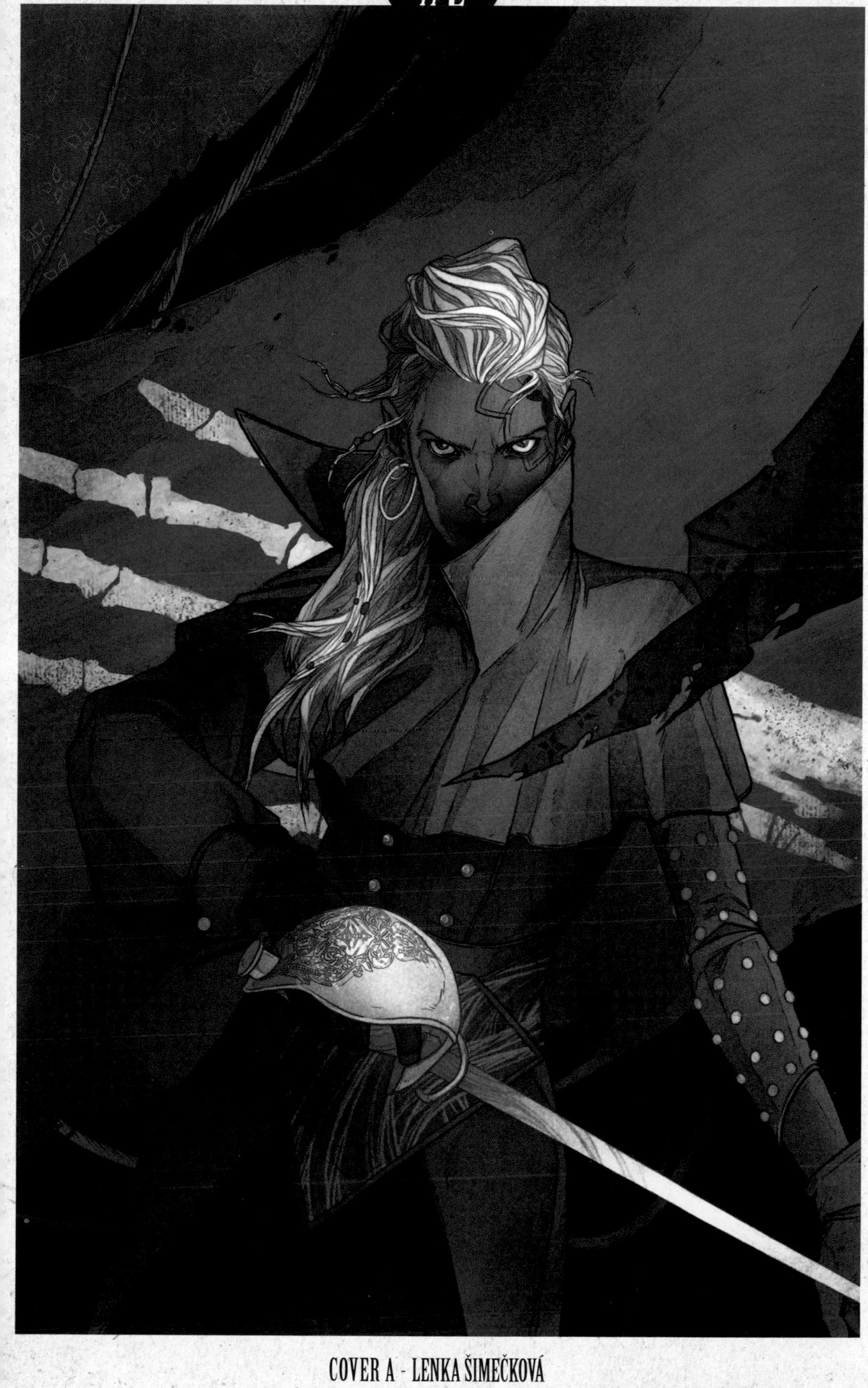

COVER A - LENKA ŠIMEČKOVÁ

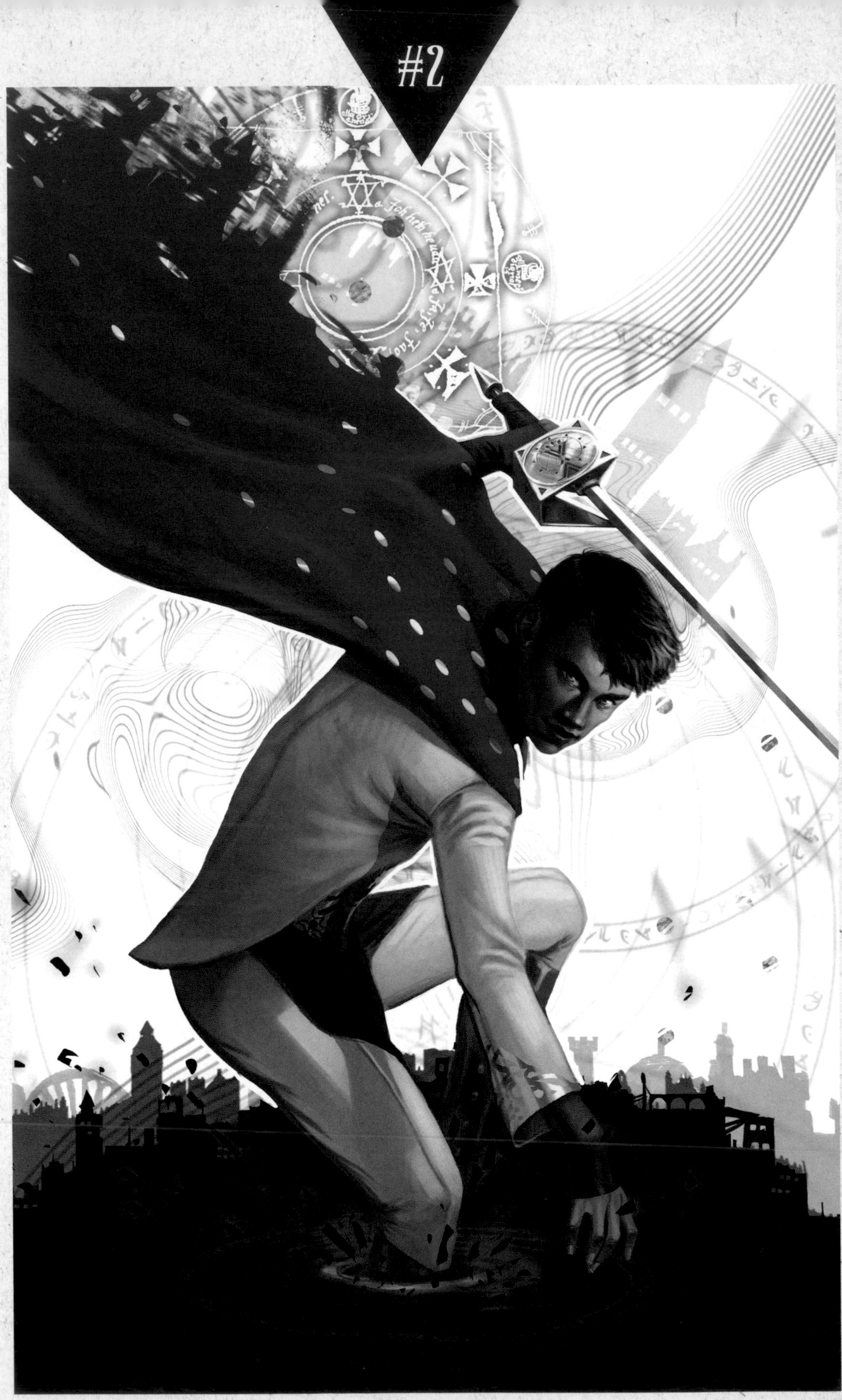
#2

COVER B - CLAUDIA IANNICIELLO

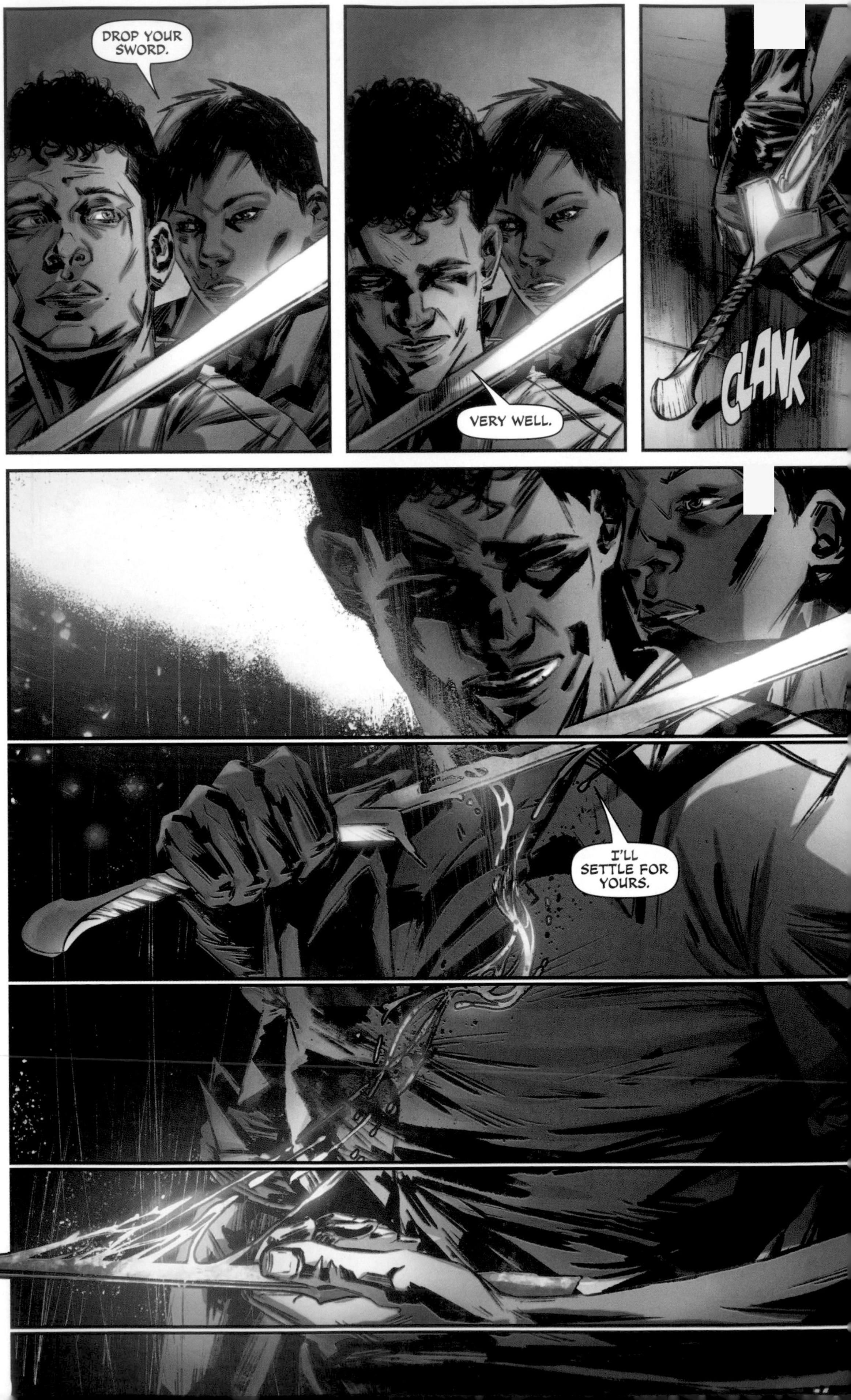
DROP YOUR SWORD.
VERY WELL.
CLANK
I'LL SETTLE FOR YOURS.

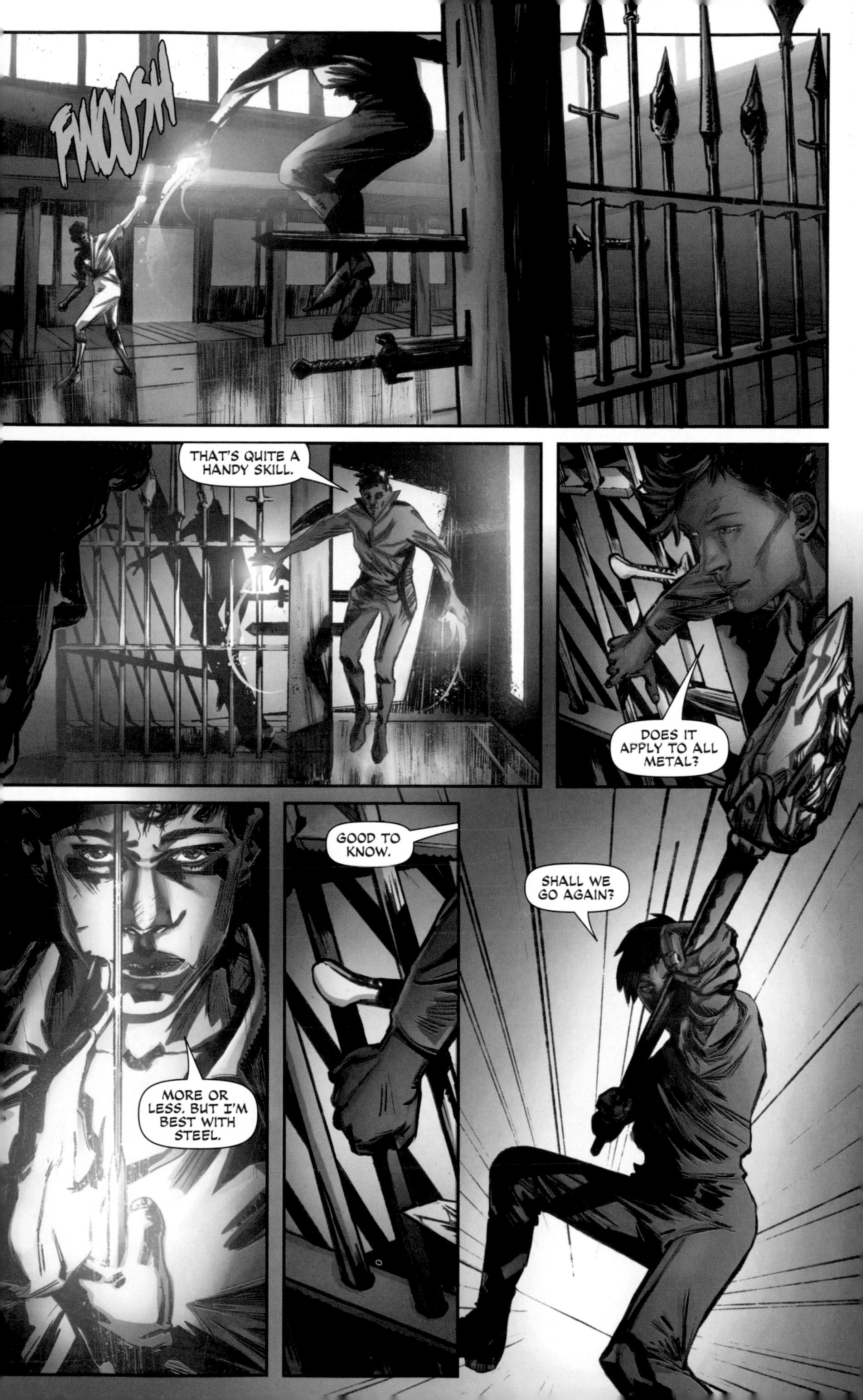
FWOOSH
THAT'S QUITE A HANDY SKILL.
DOES IT APPLY TO ALL METAL?
MORE OR LESS. BUT I'M BEST WITH STEEL.
GOOD TO KNOW.
SHALL WE GO AGAIN?

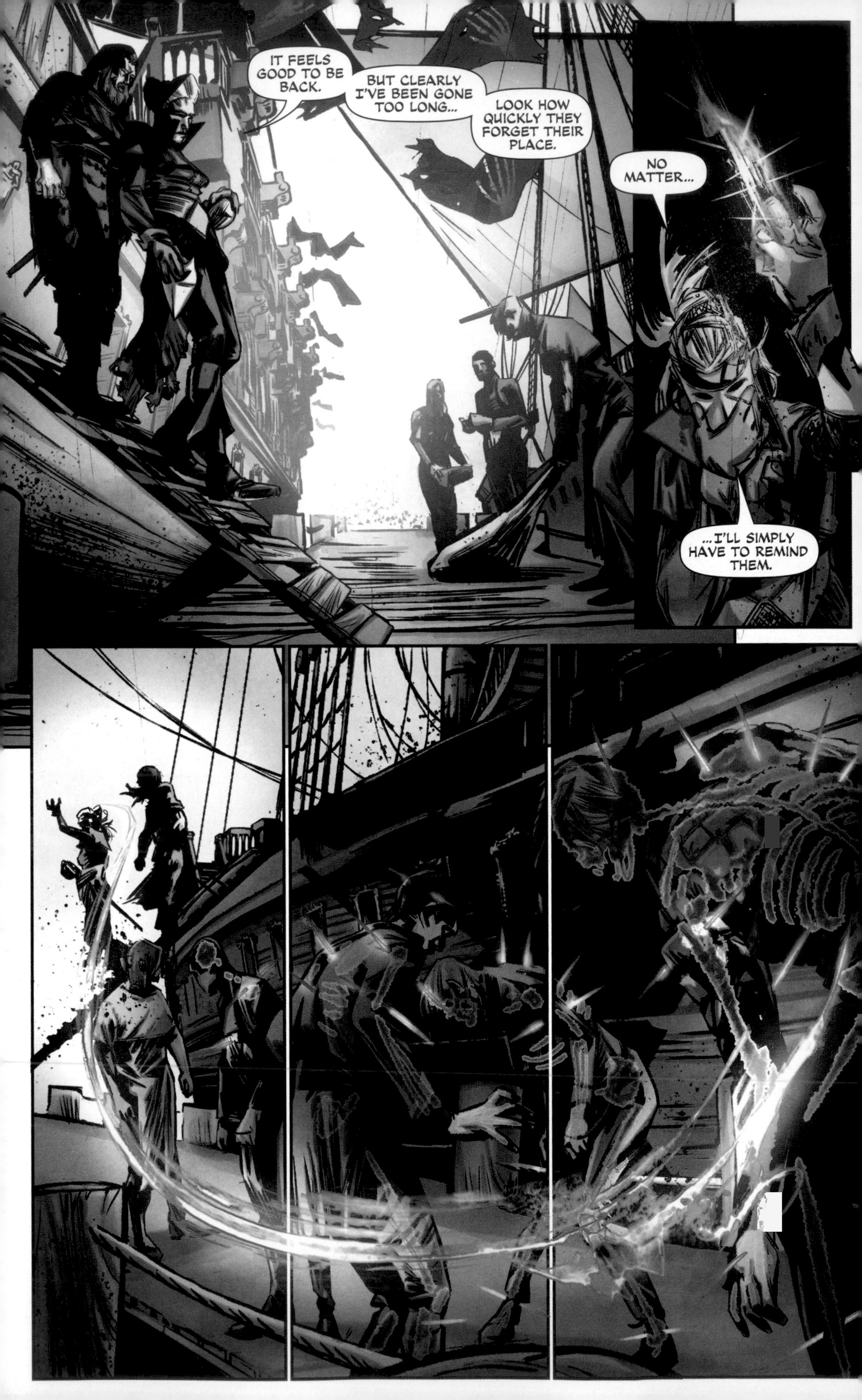
IT FEELS GOOD TO BE BACK.
BUT CLEARLY I'VE BEEN GONE TOO LONG...
LOOK HOW QUICKLY THEY FORGET THEIR PLACE.
NO MATTER...
...I'LL SIMPLY HAVE TO REMIND THEM.

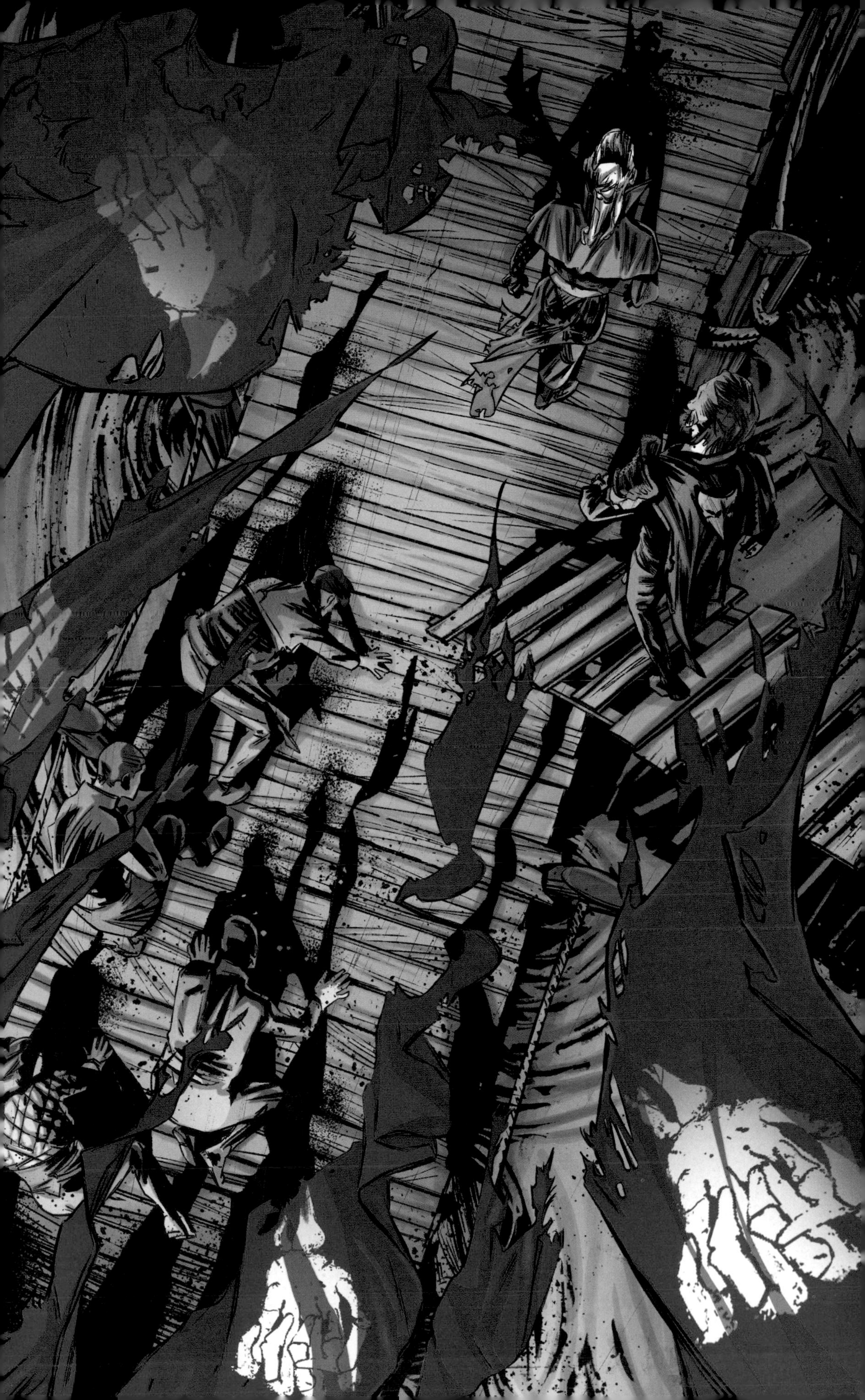

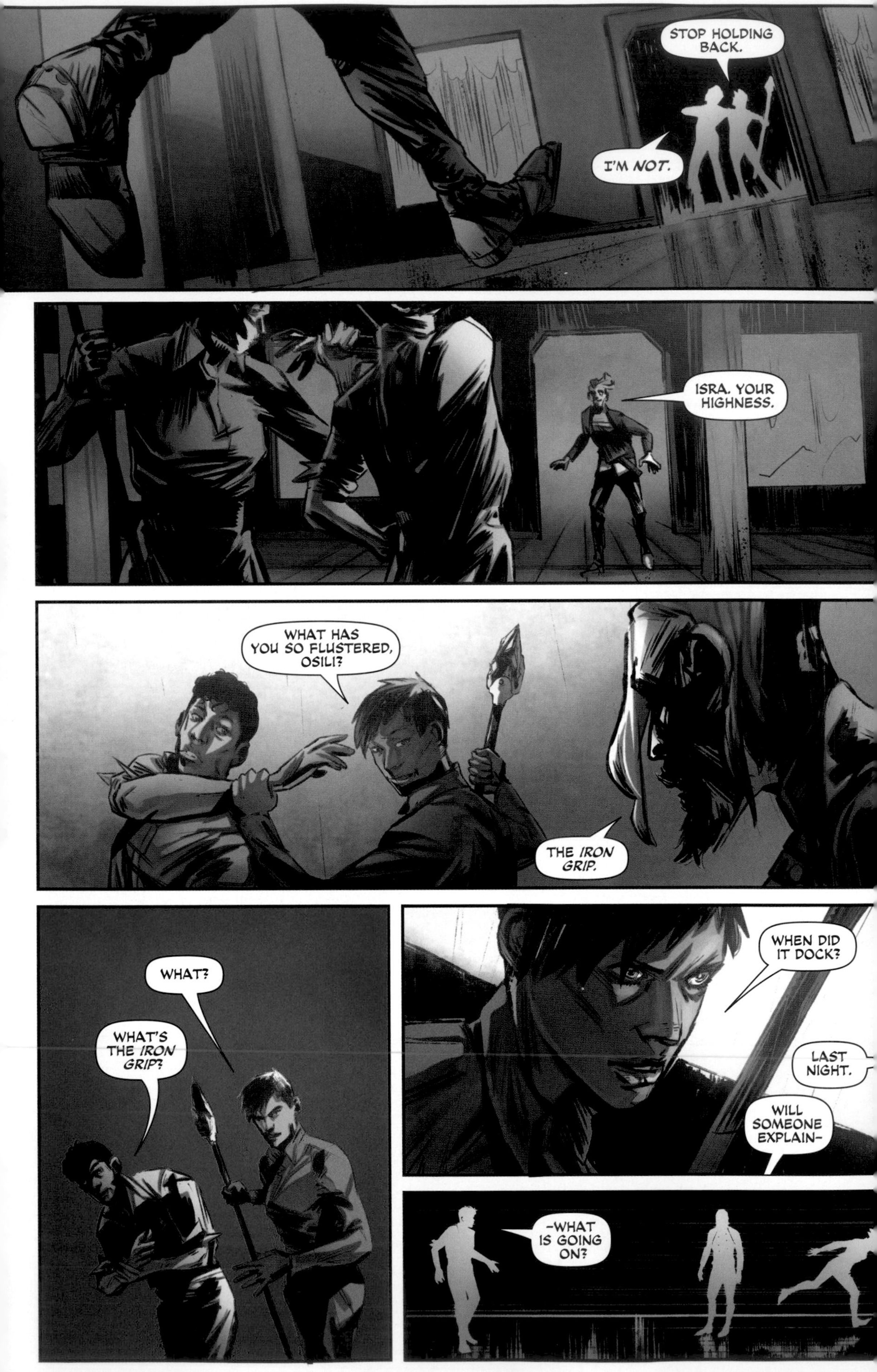
STOP HOLDING BACK.
I'M *NOT.*
ISRA. YOUR HIGHNESS.
WHAT HAS YOU SO FLUSTERED, OSILI?
THE *IRON GRIP.*
WHAT?
WHAT'S THE *IRON GRIP?*
WHEN DID IT DOCK?
LAST NIGHT.
WILL SOMEONE EXPLAIN–
–WHAT IS GOING ON?

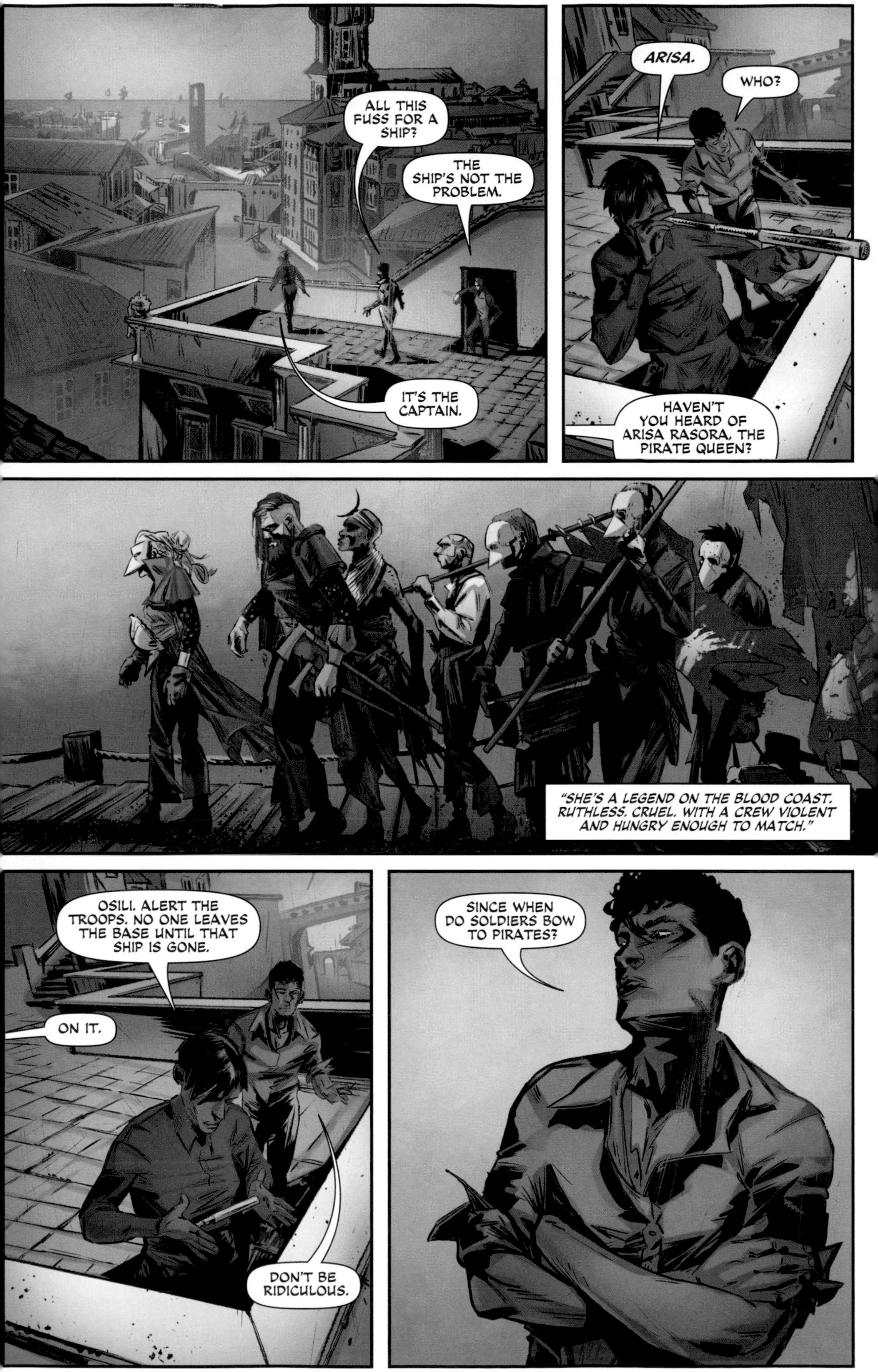
ALL THIS FUSS FOR A SHIP?
THE SHIP'S NOT THE PROBLEM.
IT'S THE CAPTAIN.
ARISA.
WHO?
HAVEN'T YOU HEARD OF ARISA RASORA, THE PIRATE QUEEN?
"SHE'S A LEGEND ON THE BLOOD COAST. RUTHLESS. CRUEL. WITH A CREW VIOLENT AND HUNGRY ENOUGH TO MATCH."
OSILI. ALERT THE TROOPS. NO ONE LEAVES THE BASE UNTIL THAT SHIP IS GONE.
ON IT.
DON'T BE RIDICULOUS.
SINCE WHEN DO SOLDIERS BOW TO PIRATES?

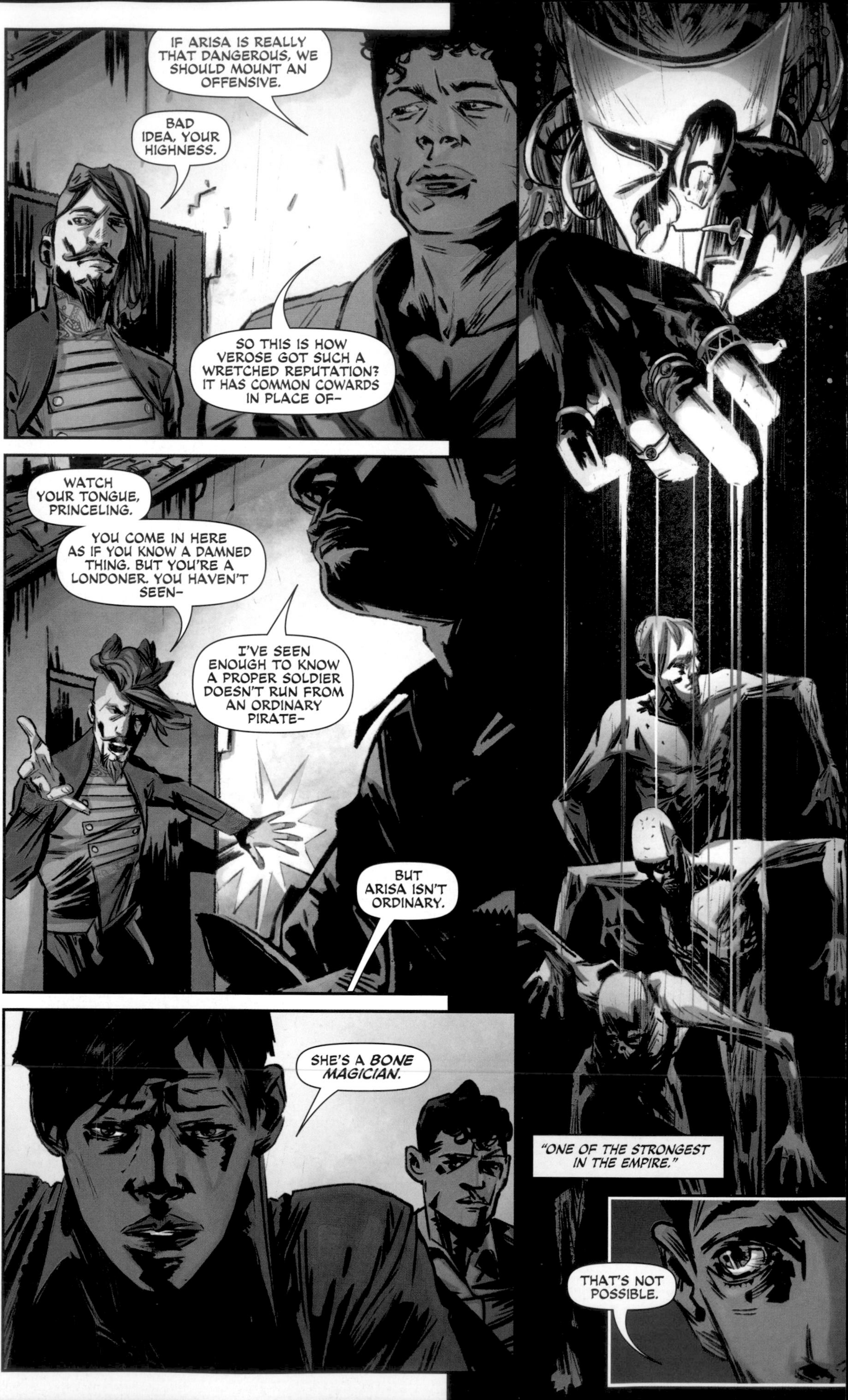
IF ARISA IS REALLY THAT DANGEROUS, WE SHOULD MOUNT AN OFFENSIVE.
BAD IDEA, YOUR HIGHNESS.
SO THIS IS HOW VEROSE GOT SUCH A WRETCHED REPUTATION? IT HAS COMMON COWARDS IN PLACE OF–
WATCH YOUR TONGUE, PRINCELING.
YOU COME IN HERE AS IF YOU KNOW A DAMNED THING. BUT YOU'RE A LONDONER. YOU HAVEN'T SEEN–
I'VE SEEN ENOUGH TO KNOW A PROPER SOLDIER DOESN'T RUN FROM AN ORDINARY PIRATE–
BUT ARISA ISN'T ORDINARY.
SHE'S A *BONE MAGICIAN.*
"ONE OF THE STRONGEST IN THE EMPIRE."
THAT'S NOT POSSIBLE.

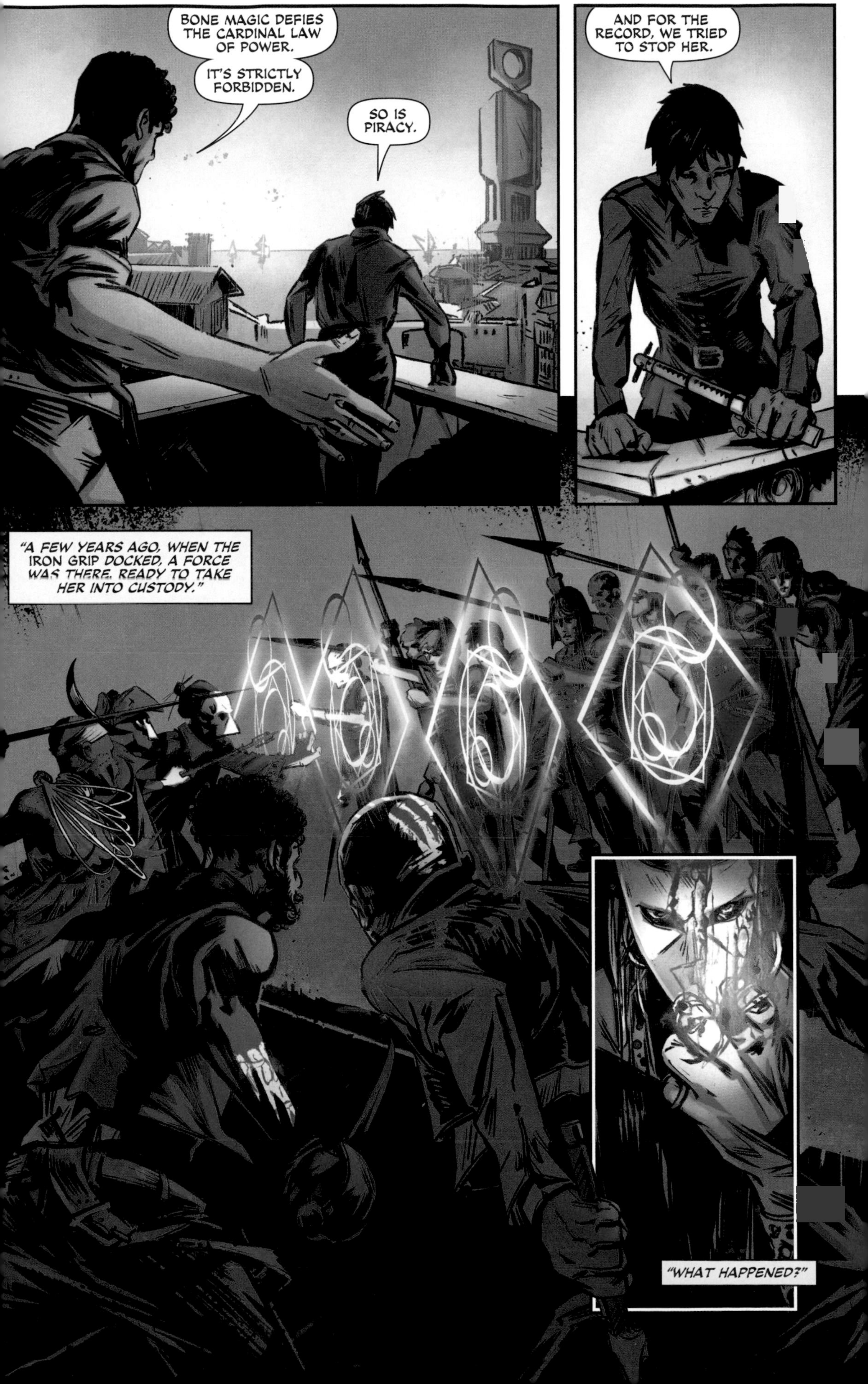
BONE MAGIC DEFIES THE CARDINAL LAW OF POWER.
IT'S STRICTLY FORBIDDEN.
SO IS PIRACY.
AND FOR THE RECORD, WE TRIED TO STOP HER.
"A FEW YEARS AGO, WHEN THE IRON GRIP DOCKED, A FORCE WAS THERE, READY TO TAKE HER INTO CUSTODY."
"WHAT HAPPENED?"

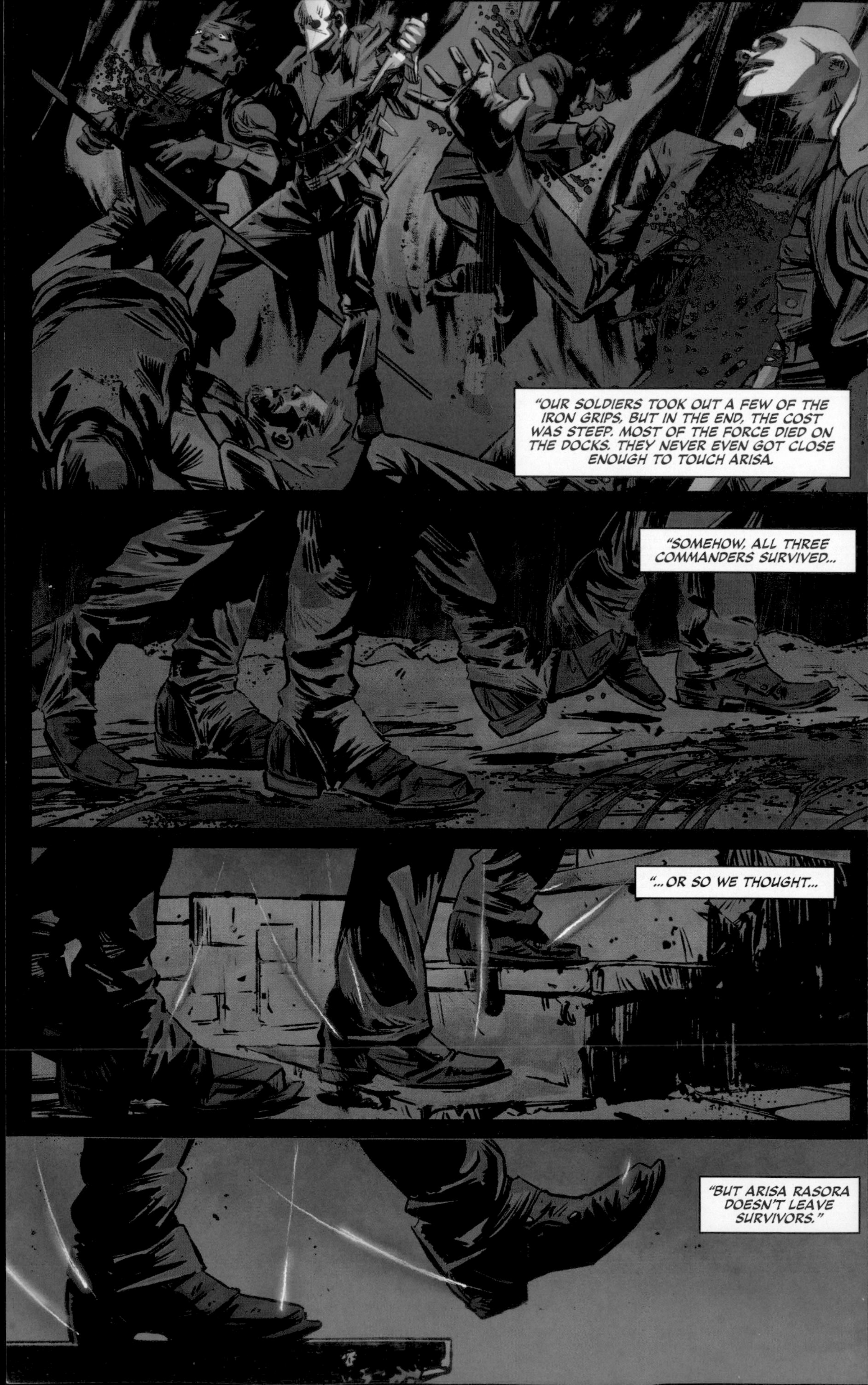
"OUR SOLDIERS TOOK OUT A FEW OF THE IRON GRIPS, BUT IN THE END, THE COST WAS STEEP. MOST OF THE FORCE DIED ON THE DOCKS. THEY NEVER EVEN GOT CLOSE ENOUGH TO TOUCH ARISA.
"SOMEHOW, ALL THREE COMMANDERS SURVIVED...
"...OR SO WE THOUGHT...
"BUT ARISA RASORA DOESN'T LEAVE SURVIVORS."

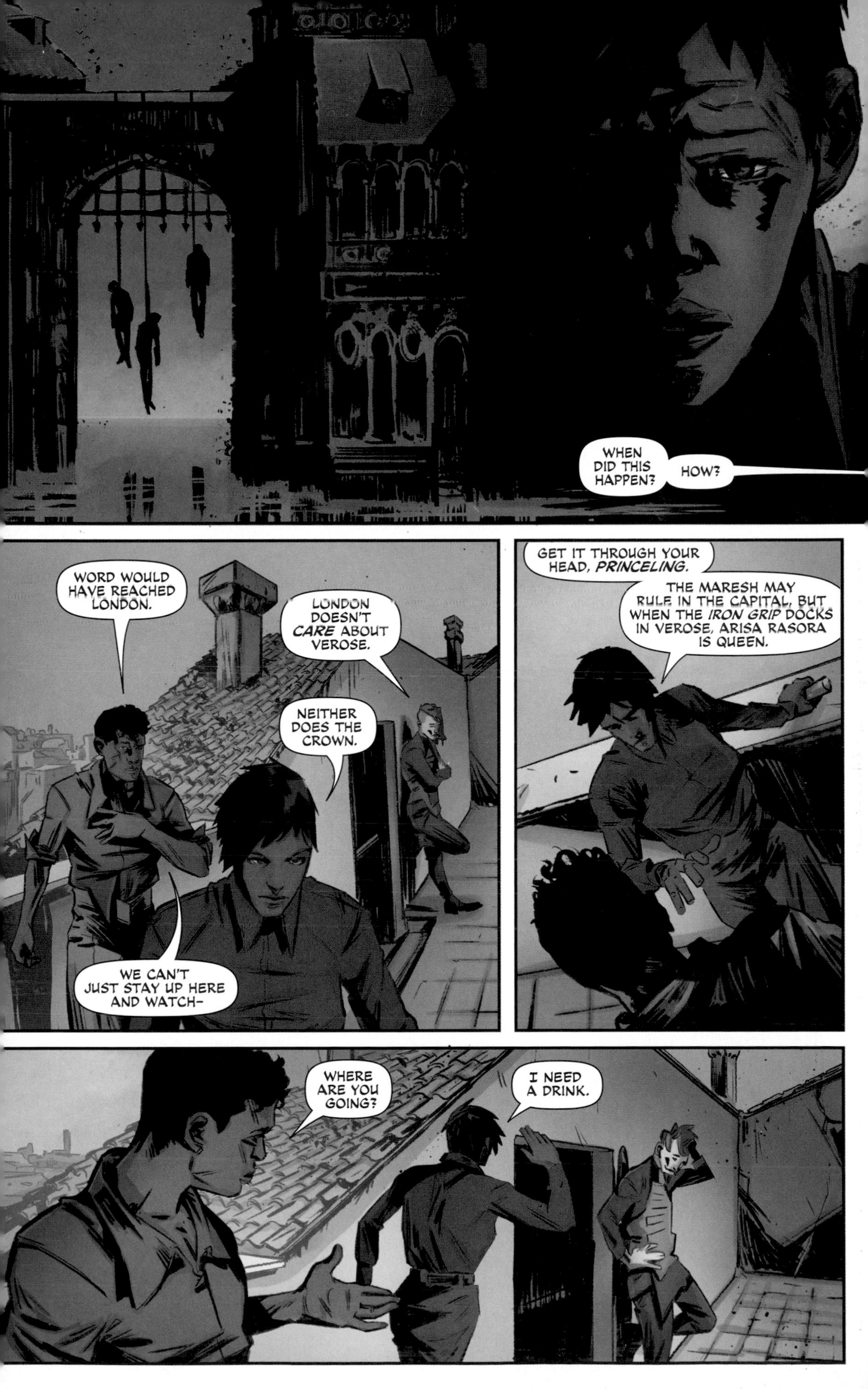
WHEN DID THIS HAPPEN?
HOW?
WORD WOULD HAVE REACHED LONDON.
LONDON DOESN'T *CARE* ABOUT VEROSE.
NEITHER DOES THE CROWN.
WE CAN'T JUST STAY UP HERE AND WATCH-
GET IT THROUGH YOUR HEAD, *PRINCELING.*
THE MARESH MAY RULE IN THE CAPITAL, BUT WHEN THE *IRON GRIP* DOCKS IN VEROSE, ARISA RASORA IS QUEEN.
WHERE ARE YOU GOING?
I NEED A DRINK.

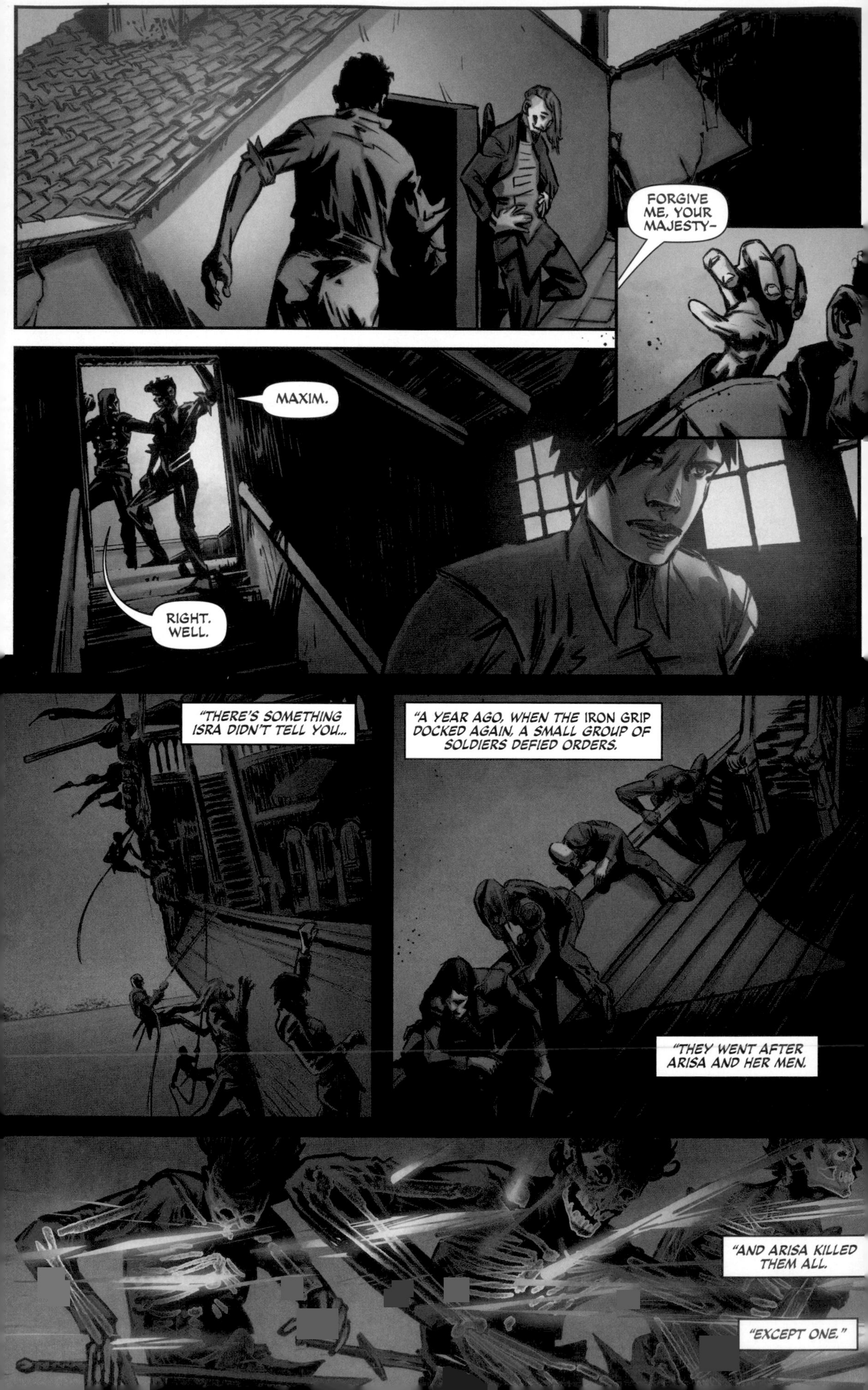
FORGIVE ME, YOUR MAJESTY-
MAXIM.
RIGHT. WELL.
"THERE'S SOMETHING ISRA DIDN'T TELL YOU...
"A YEAR AGO, WHEN THE IRON GRIP DOCKED AGAIN, A SMALL GROUP OF SOLDIERS DEFIED ORDERS.
"THEY WENT AFTER ARISA AND HER MEN.
"AND ARISA KILLED THEM ALL.
"EXCEPT ONE."

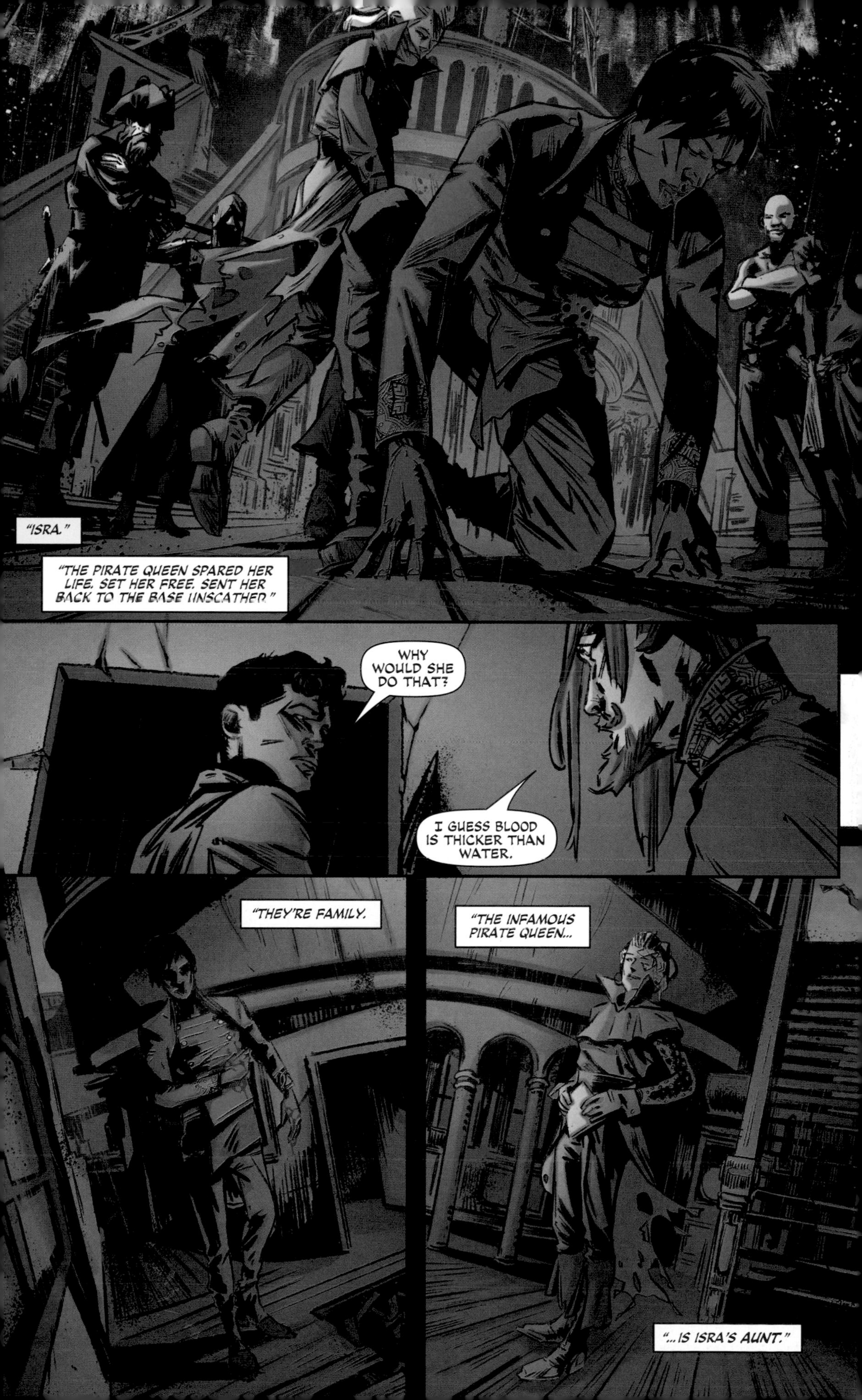
"ISRA."
"THE PIRATE QUEEN SPARED HER LIFE. SET HER FREE. SENT HER BACK TO THE BASE UNSCATHED."
WHY WOULD SHE DO THAT?
I GUESS BLOOD IS THICKER THAN WATER.
"THEY'RE FAMILY.
"THE INFAMOUS PIRATE QUEEN...
"...IS ISRA'S AUNT."

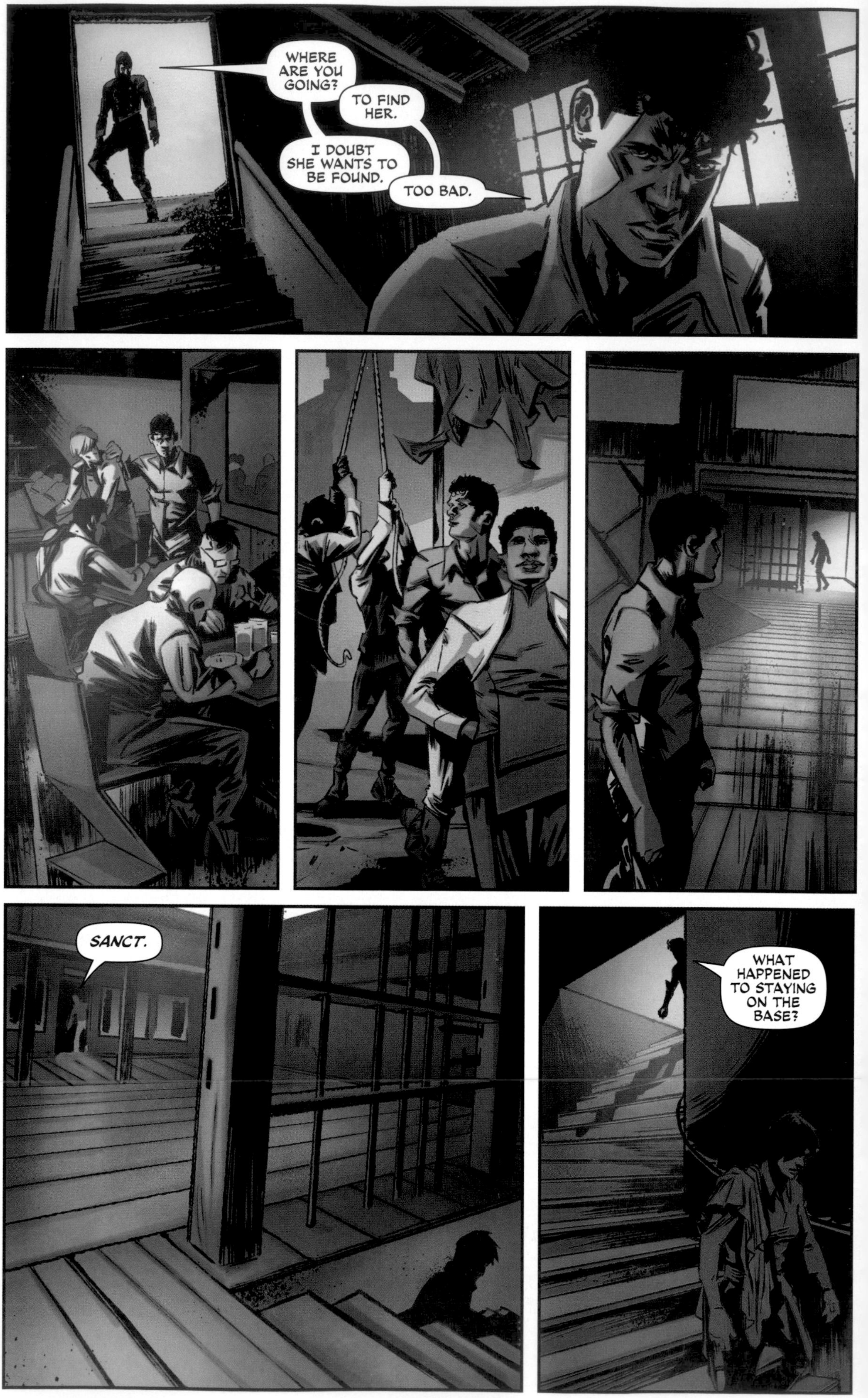
WHERE ARE YOU GOING?
TO FIND HER.
I DOUBT SHE WANTS TO BE FOUND.
TOO BAD.
SANCT.
WHAT HAPPENED TO STAYING ON THE BASE?

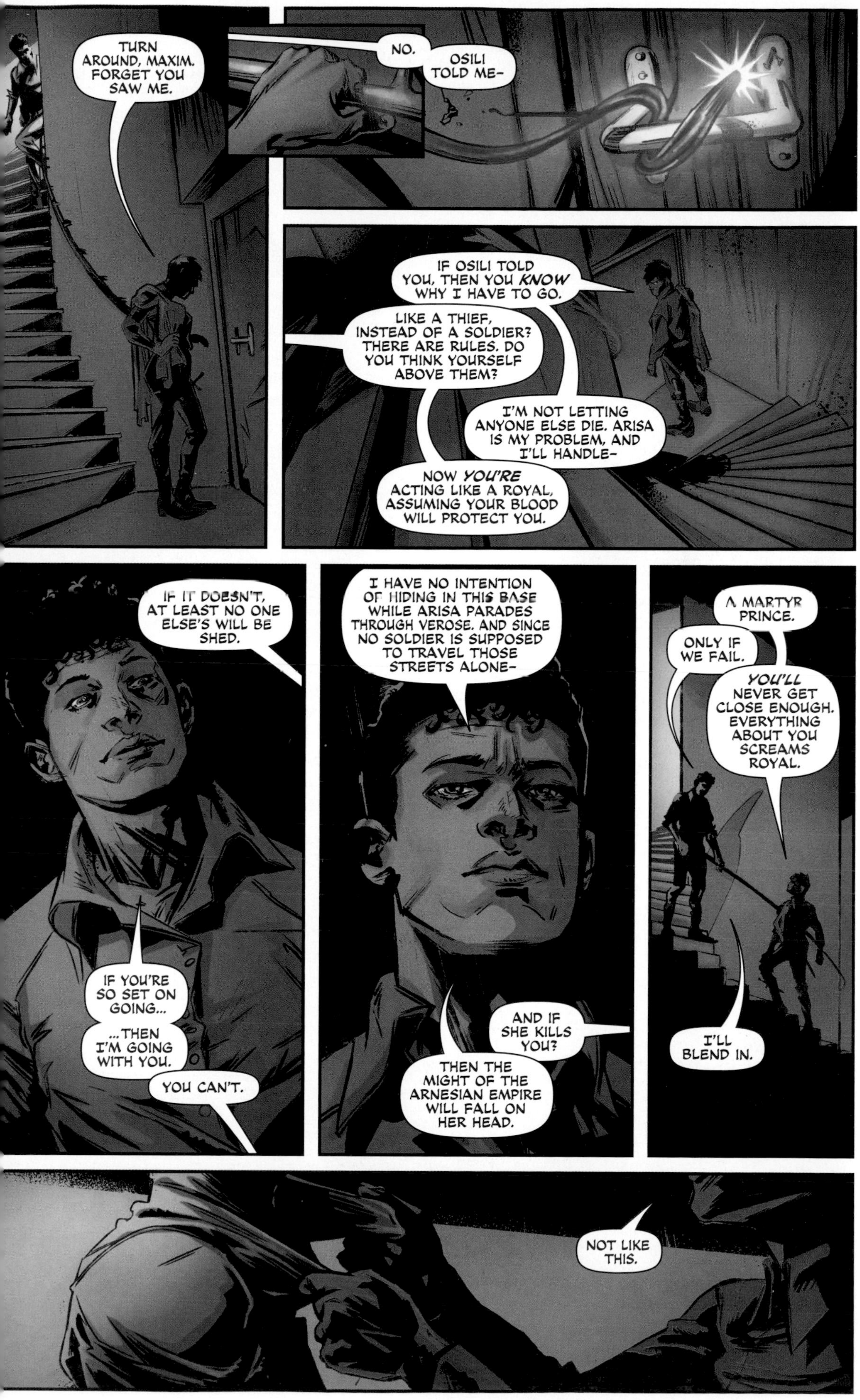
TURN AROUND, MAXIM. FORGET YOU SAW ME.
NO.
OSILI TOLD ME-
IF OSILI TOLD YOU, THEN YOU KNOW WHY I HAVE TO GO.
LIKE A THIEF, INSTEAD OF A SOLDIER? THERE ARE RULES. DO YOU THINK YOURSELF ABOVE THEM?
I'M NOT LETTING ANYONE ELSE DIE. ARISA IS MY PROBLEM, AND I'LL HANDLE-
NOW YOU'RE ACTING LIKE A ROYAL, ASSUMING YOUR BLOOD WILL PROTECT YOU.
IF IT DOESN'T, AT LEAST NO ONE ELSE'S WILL BE SHED.
IF YOU'RE SO SET ON GOING...
...THEN I'M GOING WITH YOU.
YOU CAN'T.
I HAVE NO INTENTION OF HIDING IN THIS BASE WHILE ARISA PARADES THROUGH VEROSE. AND SINCE NO SOLDIER IS SUPPOSED TO TRAVEL THOSE STREETS ALONE-
AND IF SHE KILLS YOU?
THEN THE MIGHT OF THE ARNESIAN EMPIRE WILL FALL ON HER HEAD.
A MARTYR PRINCE.
ONLY IF WE FAIL.
YOU'LL NEVER GET CLOSE ENOUGH. EVERYTHING ABOUT YOU SCREAMS ROYAL.
I'LL BLEND IN.
NOT LIKE THIS.

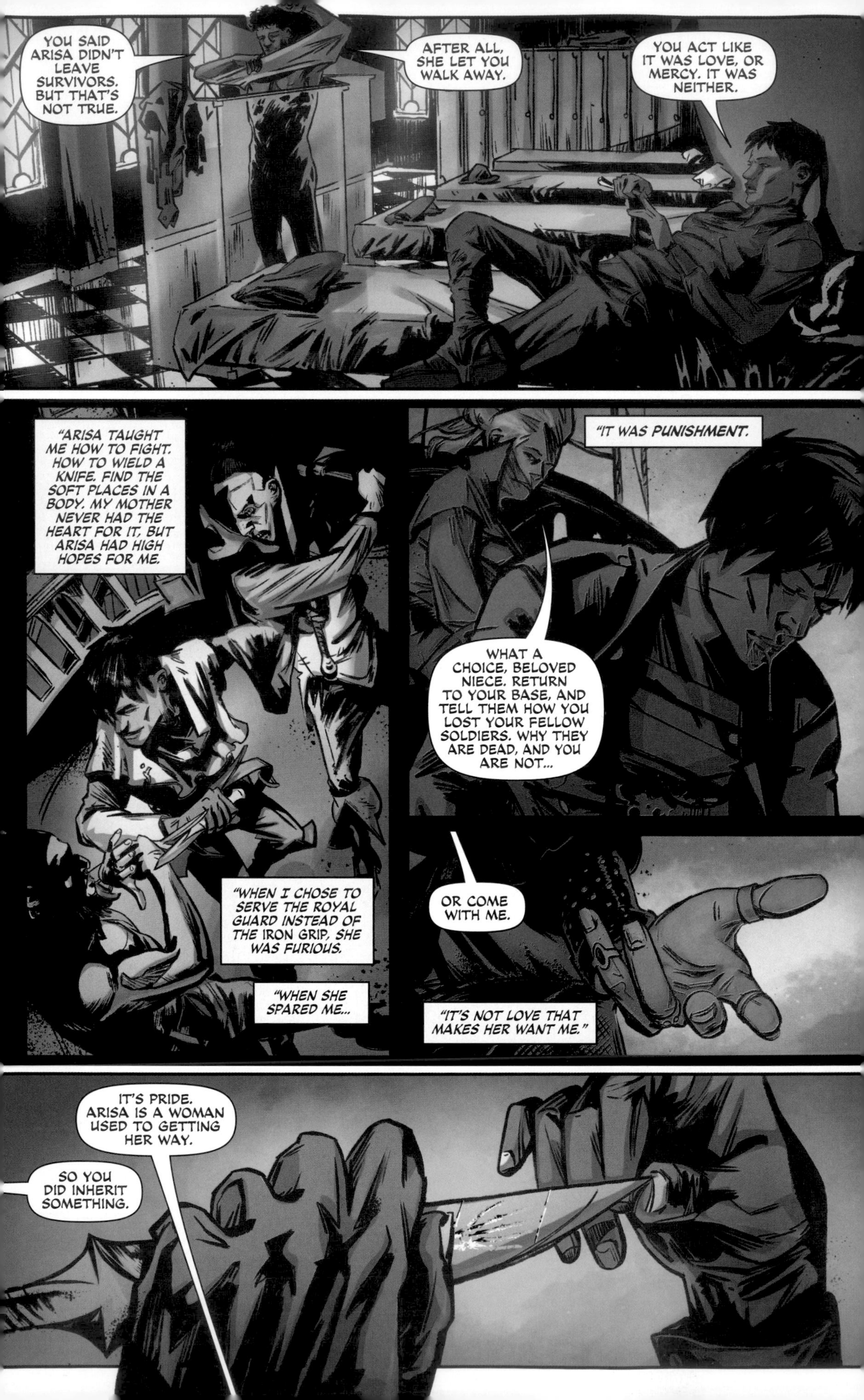
YOU SAID ARISA DIDN'T LEAVE SURVIVORS. BUT THAT'S NOT TRUE.
AFTER ALL, SHE LET YOU WALK AWAY.
YOU ACT LIKE IT WAS LOVE, OR MERCY. IT WAS NEITHER.
"ARISA TAUGHT ME HOW TO FIGHT. HOW TO WIELD A KNIFE. FIND THE SOFT PLACES IN A BODY. MY MOTHER NEVER HAD THE HEART FOR IT, BUT ARISA HAD HIGH HOPES FOR ME.
"WHEN I CHOSE TO SERVE THE ROYAL GUARD INSTEAD OF THE IRON GRIP, SHE WAS FURIOUS.
"WHEN SHE SPARED ME...
"IT WAS PUNISHMENT.
WHAT A CHOICE, BELOVED NIECE. RETURN TO YOUR BASE, AND TELL THEM HOW YOU LOST YOUR FELLOW SOLDIERS. WHY THEY ARE DEAD, AND YOU ARE NOT...
OR COME WITH ME.
"IT'S NOT LOVE THAT MAKES HER WANT ME."
IT'S PRIDE. ARISA IS A WOMAN USED TO GETTING HER WAY.
SO YOU DID INHERIT SOMETHING.

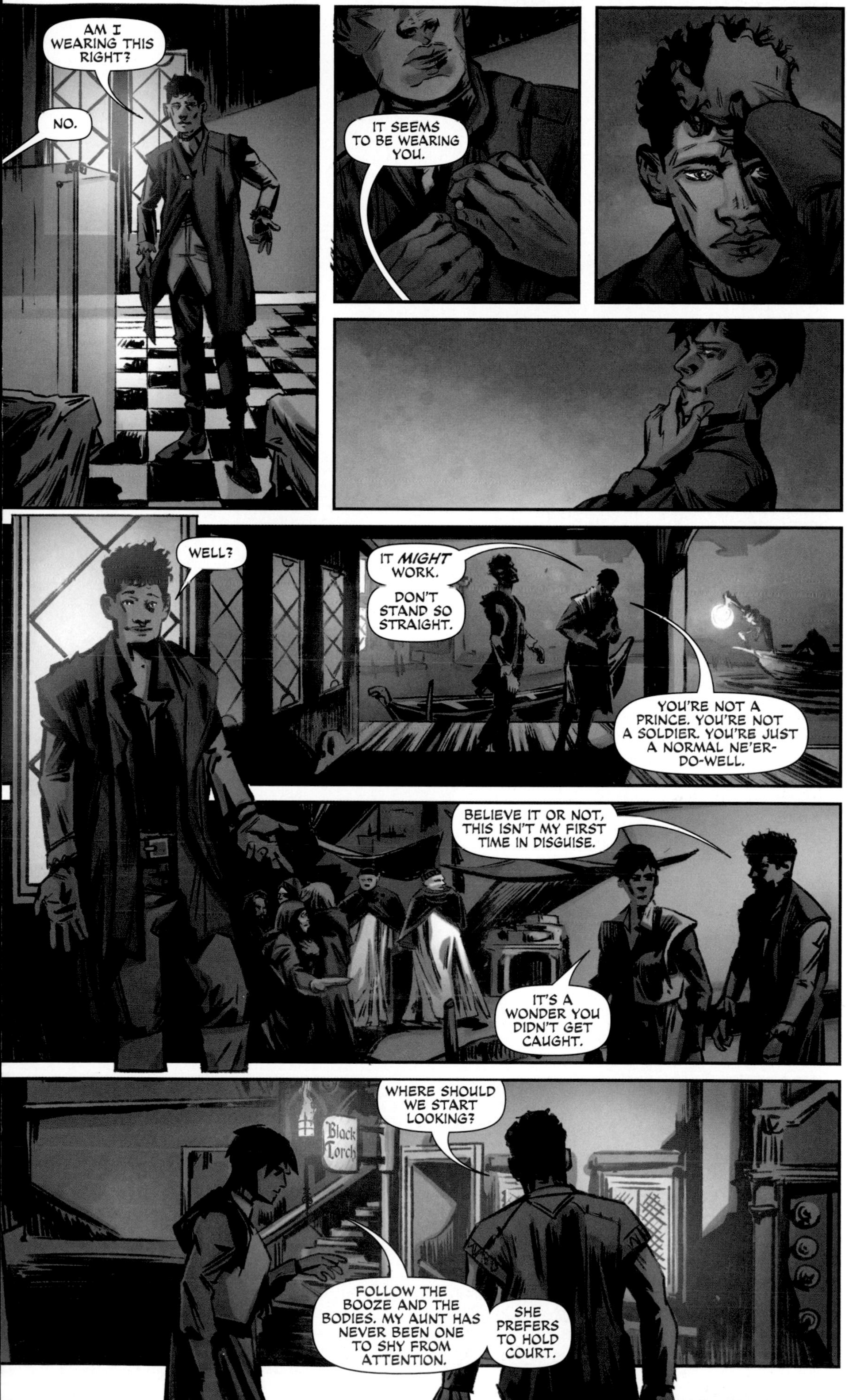
AM I WEARING THIS RIGHT?
NO.
IT SEEMS TO BE WEARING YOU.
WELL?
IT *MIGHT* WORK.
DON'T STAND SO STRAIGHT.
YOU'RE NOT A PRINCE. YOU'RE NOT A SOLDIER. YOU'RE JUST A NORMAL NE'ER-DO-WELL.
BELIEVE IT OR NOT, THIS ISN'T MY FIRST TIME IN DISGUISE.
IT'S A WONDER YOU DIDN'T GET CAUGHT.
Black Torch
WHERE SHOULD WE START LOOKING?
FOLLOW THE BOOZE AND THE BODIES. MY AUNT HAS NEVER BEEN ONE TO SHY FROM ATTENTION.
SHE PREFERS TO HOLD COURT.

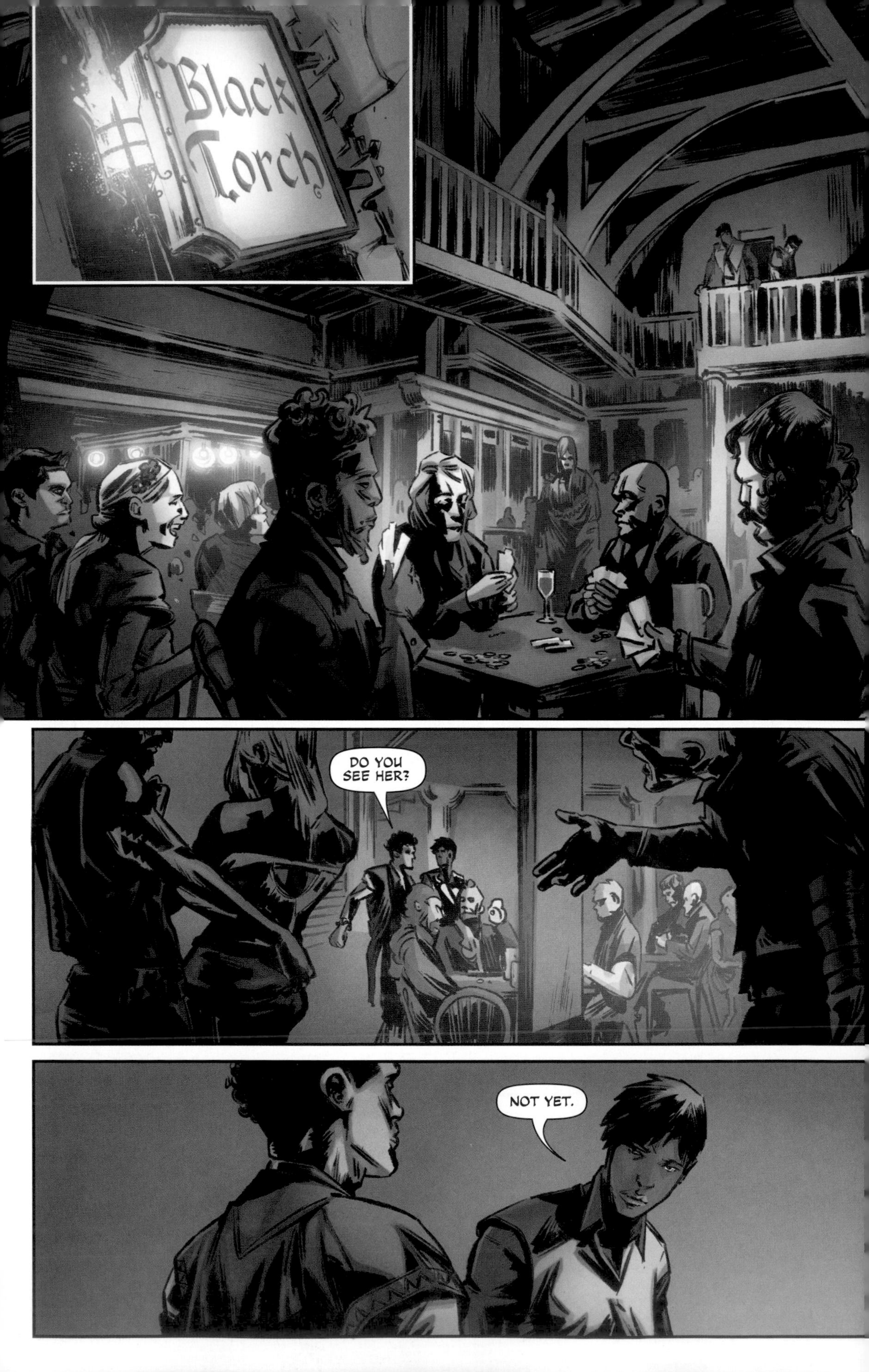
Black Torch
DO YOU SEE HER?
NOT YET.

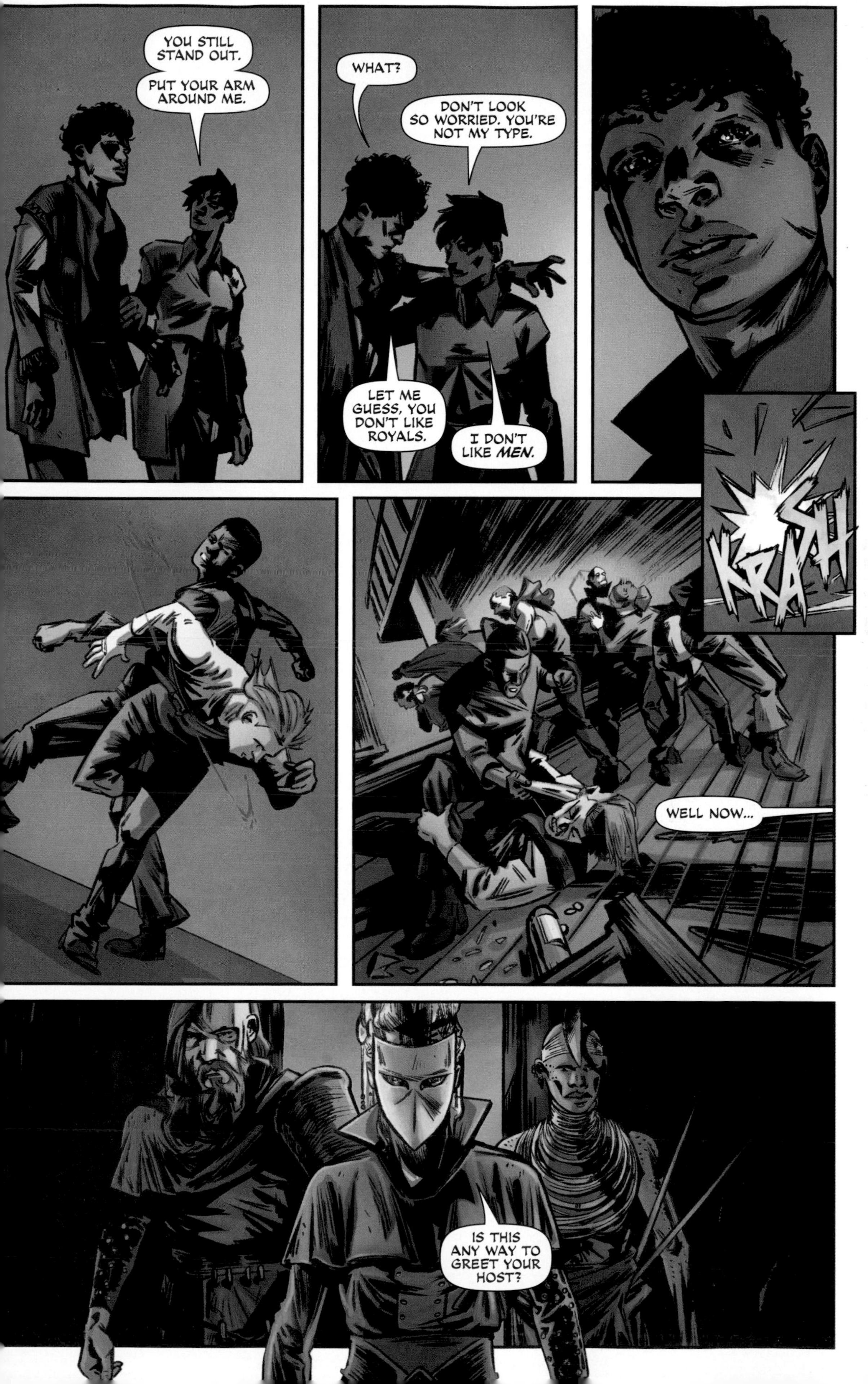
YOU STILL STAND OUT.
PUT YOUR ARM AROUND ME.
WHAT?
DON'T LOOK SO WORRIED. YOU'RE NOT MY TYPE.
LET ME GUESS, YOU DON'T LIKE ROYALS.
I DON'T LIKE *MEN*.
KRASH
WELL NOW...
IS THIS ANY WAY TO GREET YOUR HOST?

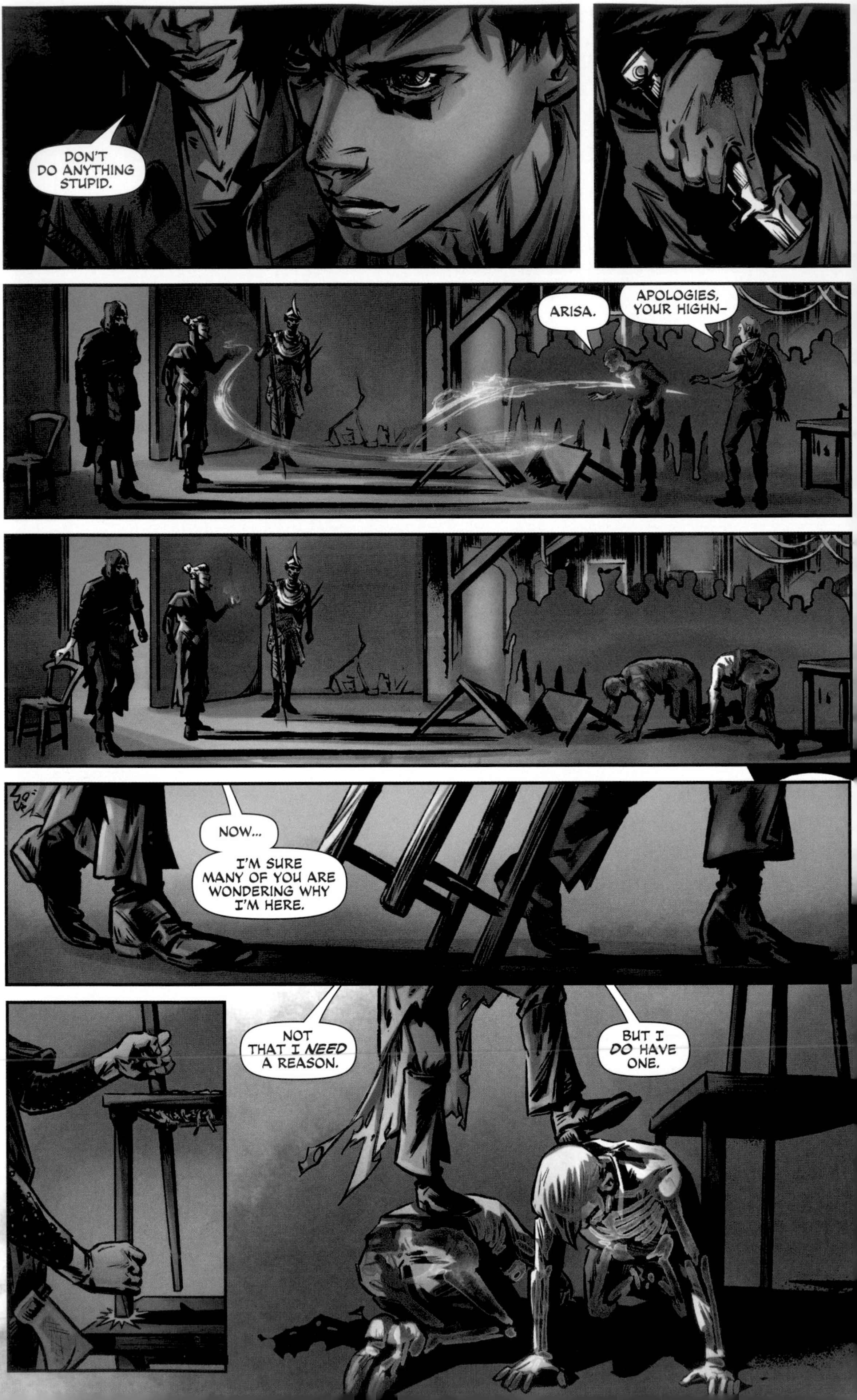
DON'T DO ANYTHING STUPID.
ARISA.
APOLOGIES, YOUR HIGHN-
NOW...
I'M SURE MANY OF YOU ARE WONDERING WHY I'M HERE.
NOT THAT I *NEED* A REASON.
BUT I *DO* HAVE ONE.

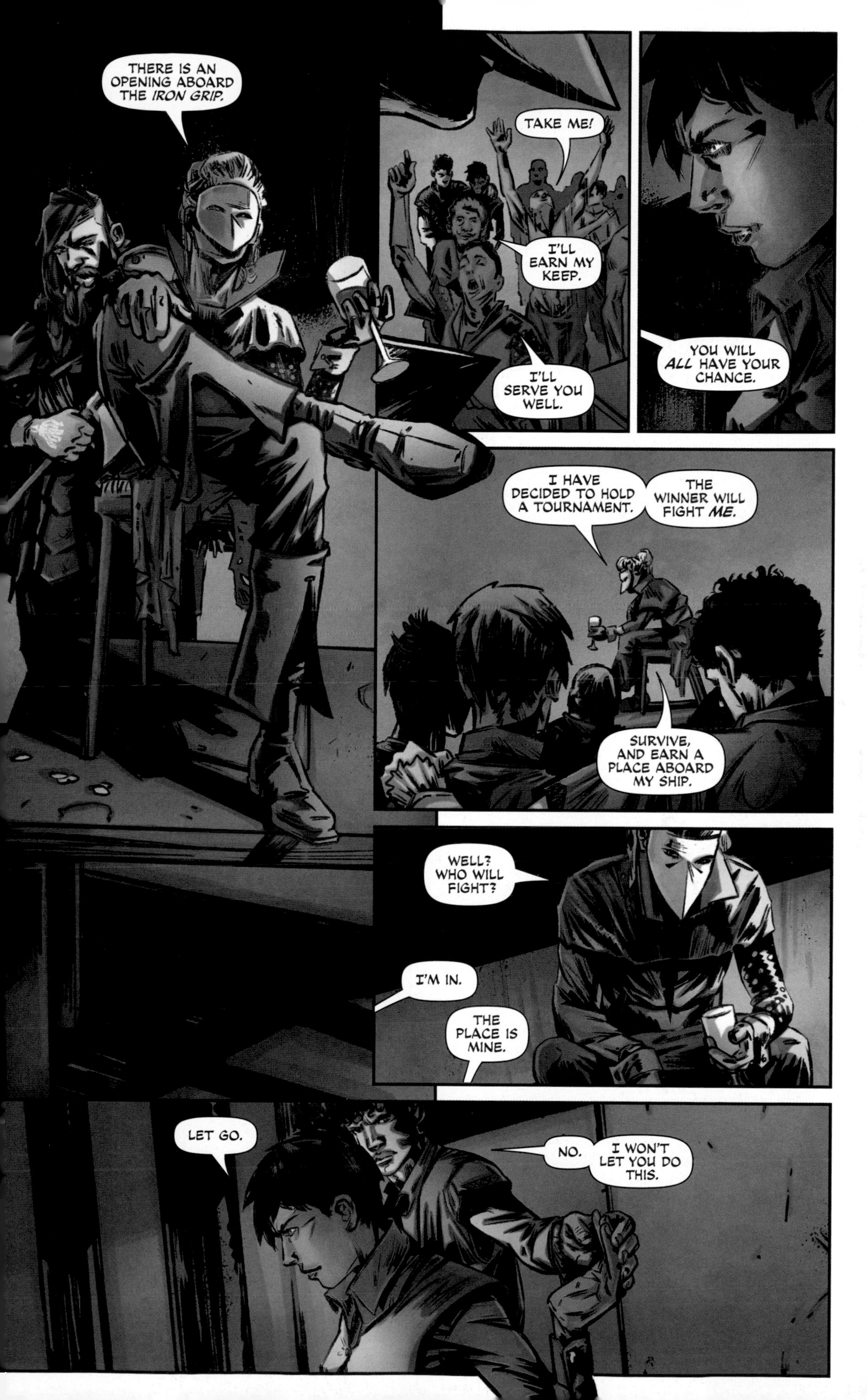
THERE IS AN OPENING ABOARD THE *IRON GRIP.*
TAKE ME!
I'LL EARN MY KEEP.
I'LL SERVE YOU WELL.
YOU WILL *ALL* HAVE YOUR CHANCE.
I HAVE DECIDED TO HOLD A TOURNAMENT.
THE WINNER WILL FIGHT *ME.*
SURVIVE, AND EARN A PLACE ABOARD MY SHIP.
WELL? WHO WILL FIGHT?
I'M IN.
THE PLACE IS MINE.
LET GO.
NO.
I WON'T LET YOU DO THIS.

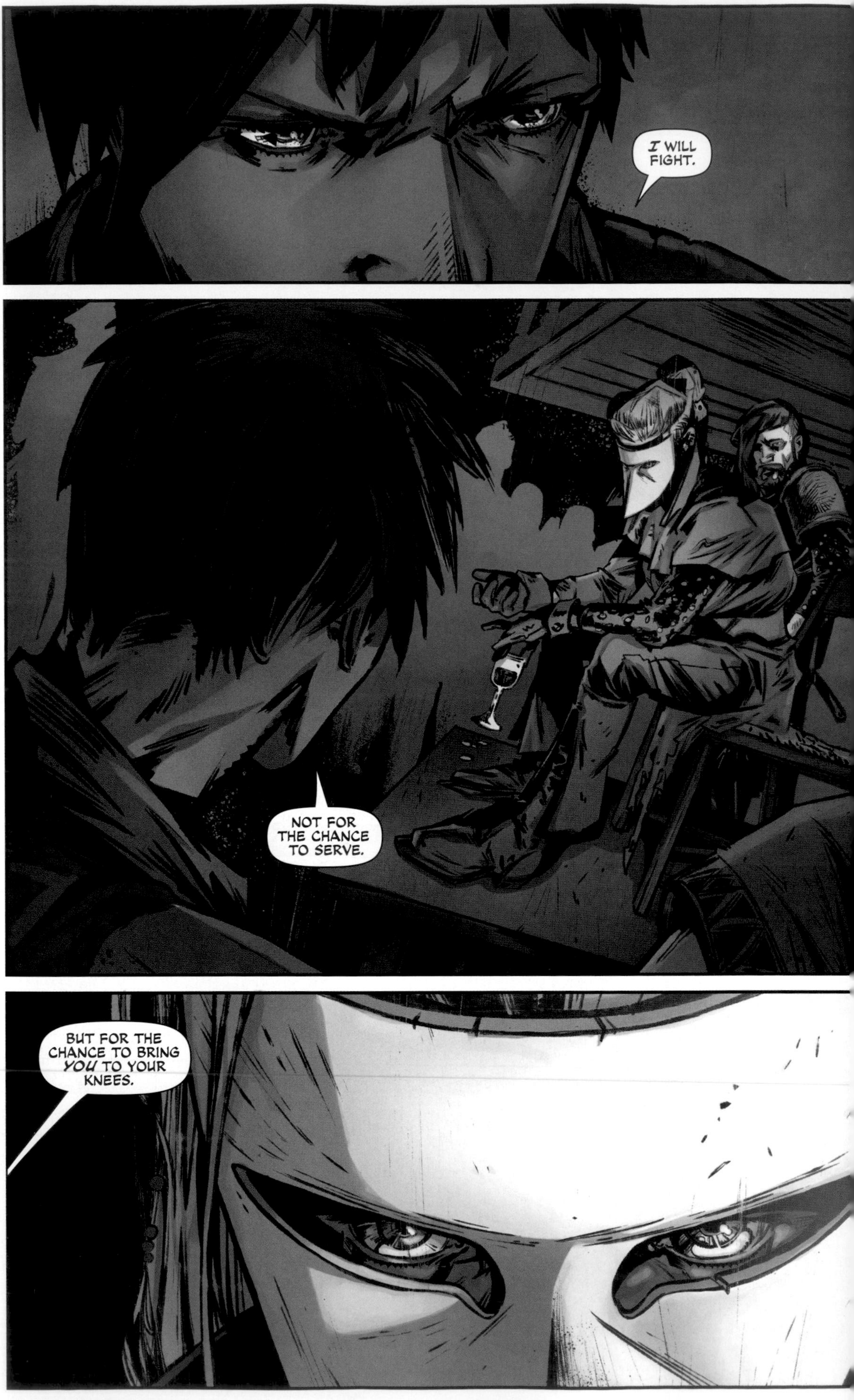
I WILL FIGHT.
NOT FOR THE CHANCE TO SERVE.
BUT FOR THE CHANCE TO BRING YOU TO YOUR KNEES.

#3

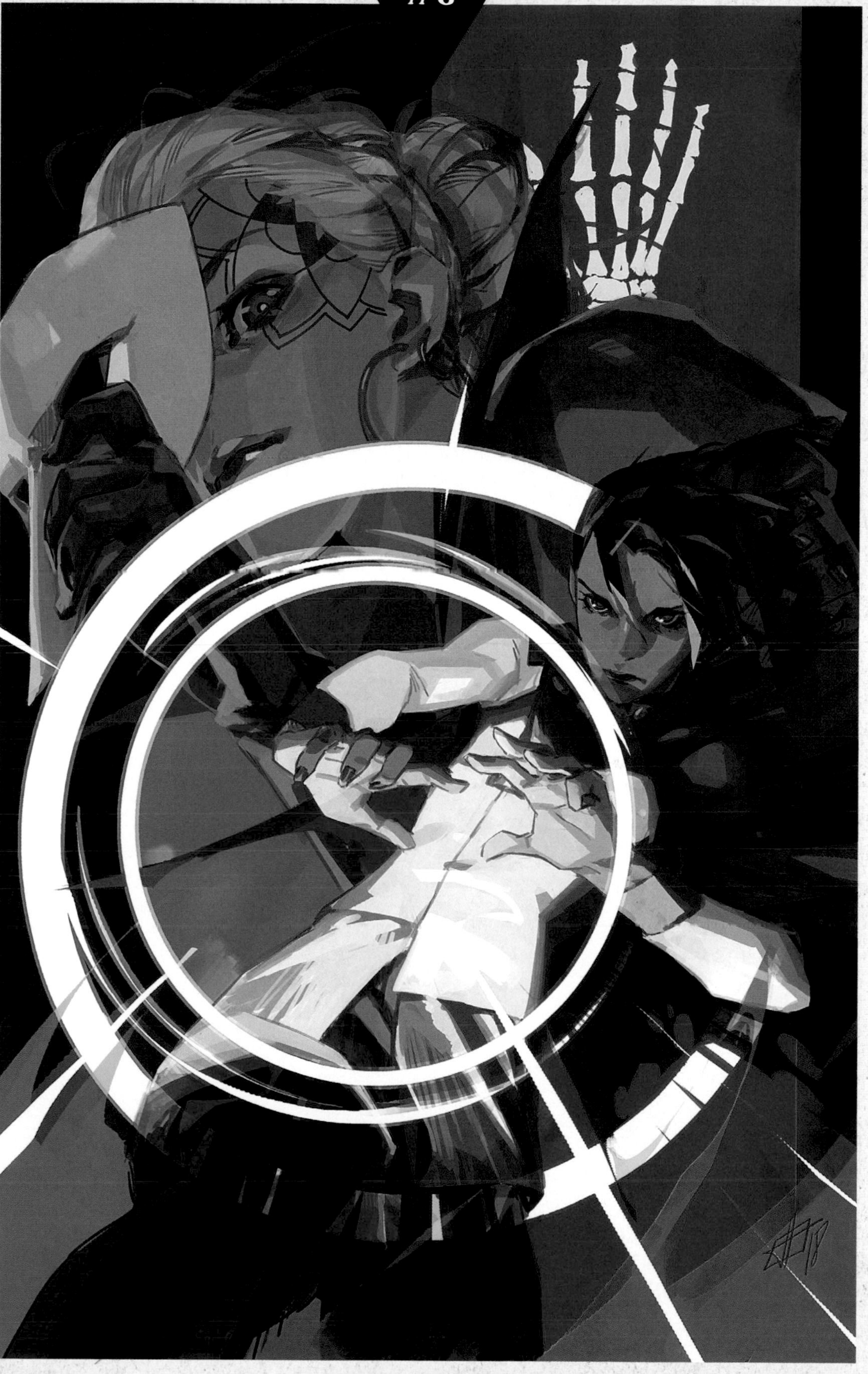

COVER A - TONI INFANTE

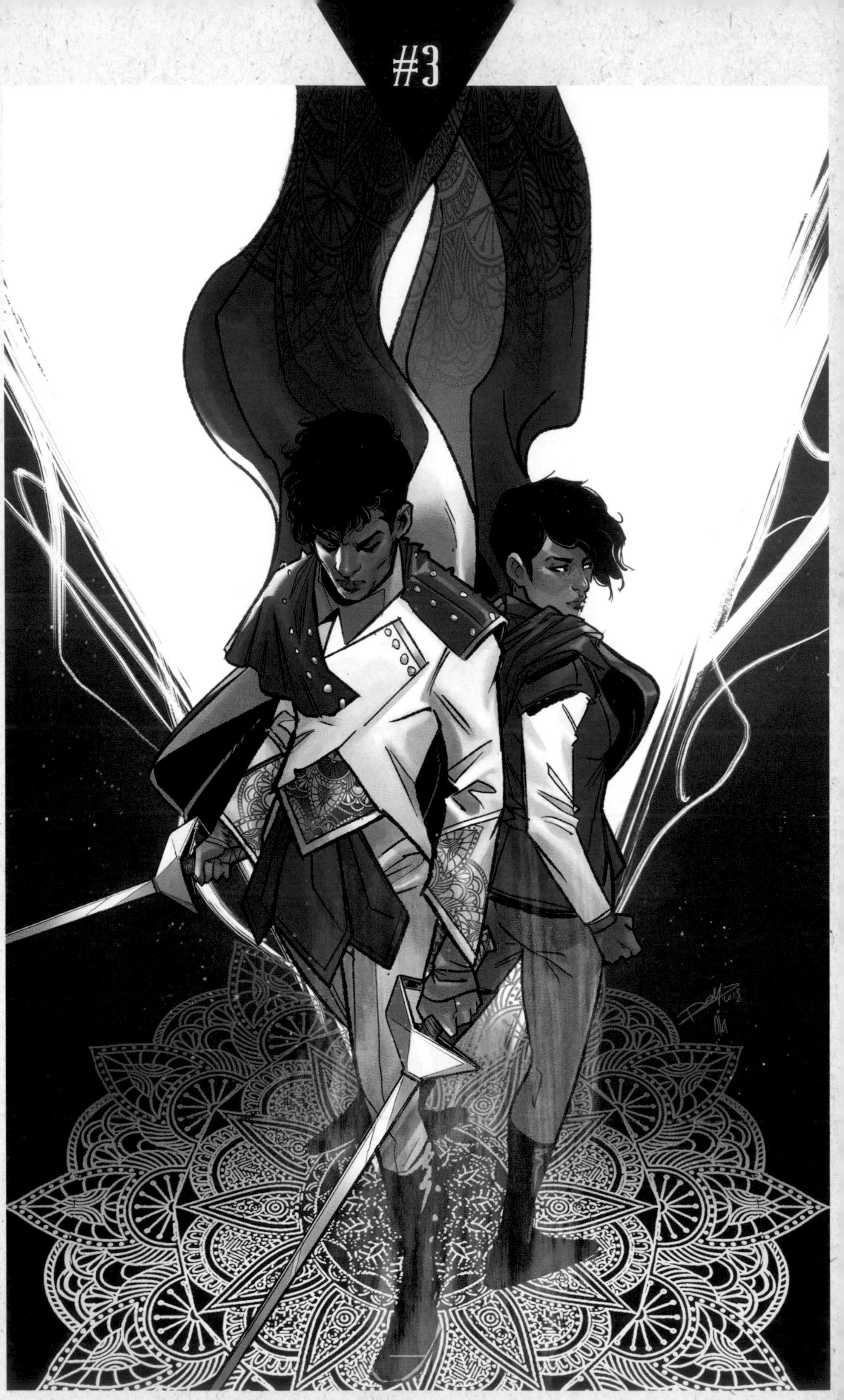
#3

COVER B - ROBERTA INGRANATA & WARNIA SAHADEWA

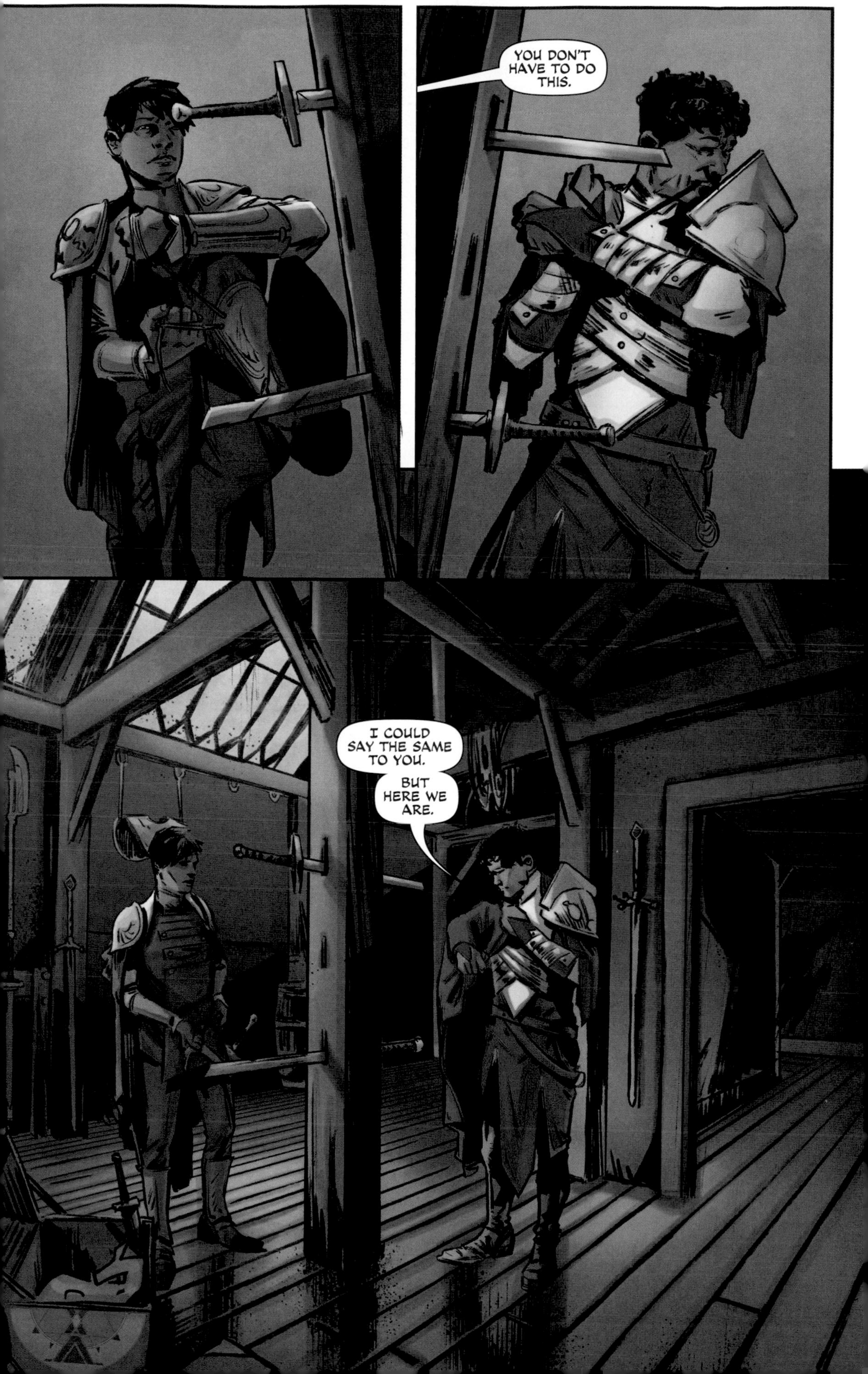
YOU DON'T HAVE TO DO THIS.
I COULD SAY THE SAME TO YOU.
BUT HERE WE ARE.

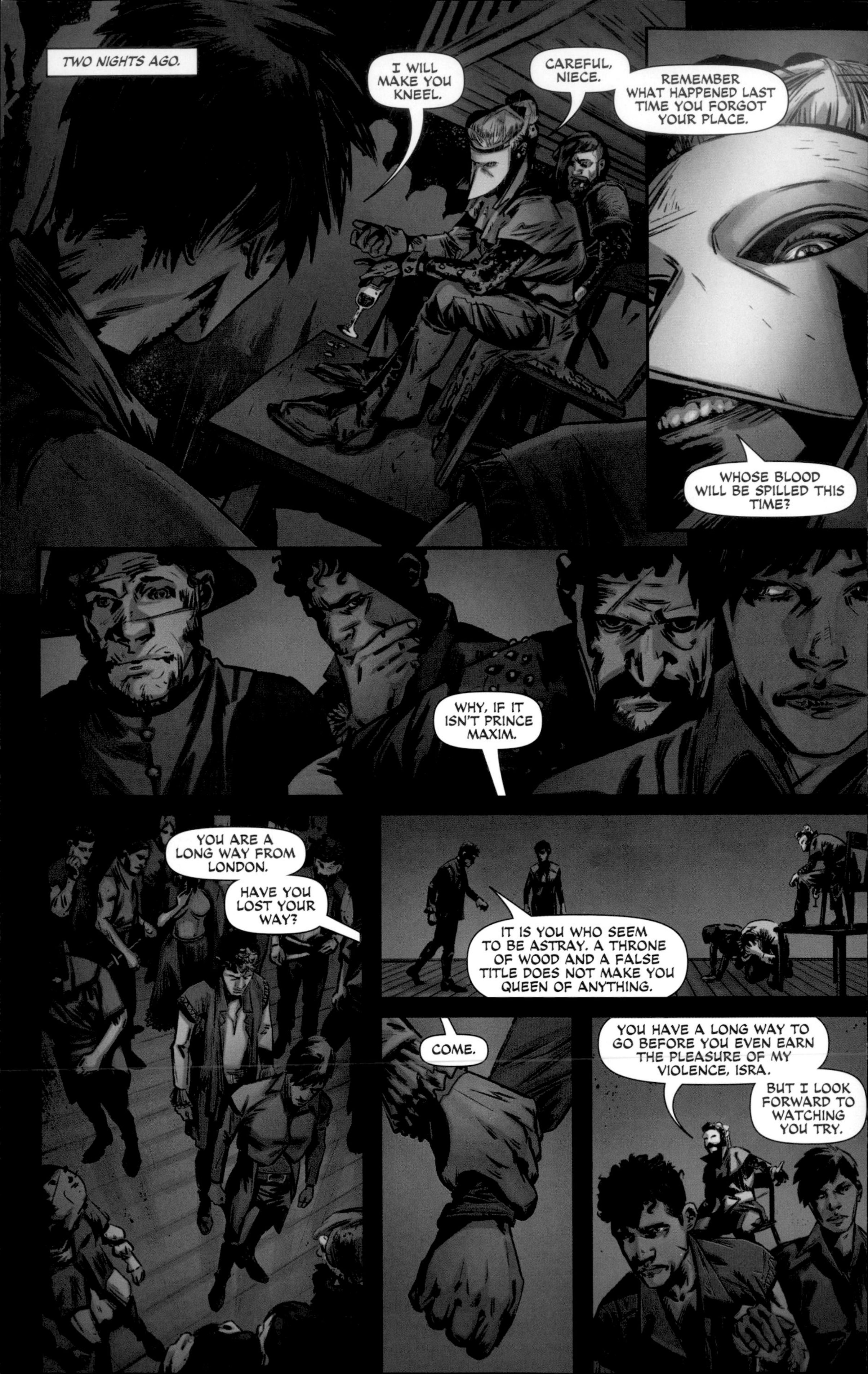
TWO NIGHTS AGO.
I WILL MAKE YOU KNEEL.
CAREFUL, NIECE.
REMEMBER WHAT HAPPENED LAST TIME YOU FORGOT YOUR PLACE.
WHOSE BLOOD WILL BE SPILLED THIS TIME?
WHY, IF IT ISN'T PRINCE MAXIM.
YOU ARE A LONG WAY FROM LONDON.
HAVE YOU LOST YOUR WAY?
IT IS YOU WHO SEEM TO BE ASTRAY. A THRONE OF WOOD AND A FALSE TITLE DOES NOT MAKE YOU QUEEN OF ANYTHING.
COME.
YOU HAVE A LONG WAY TO GO BEFORE YOU EVEN EARN THE PLEASURE OF MY VIOLENCE, ISRA.
BUT I LOOK FORWARD TO WATCHING YOU TRY.

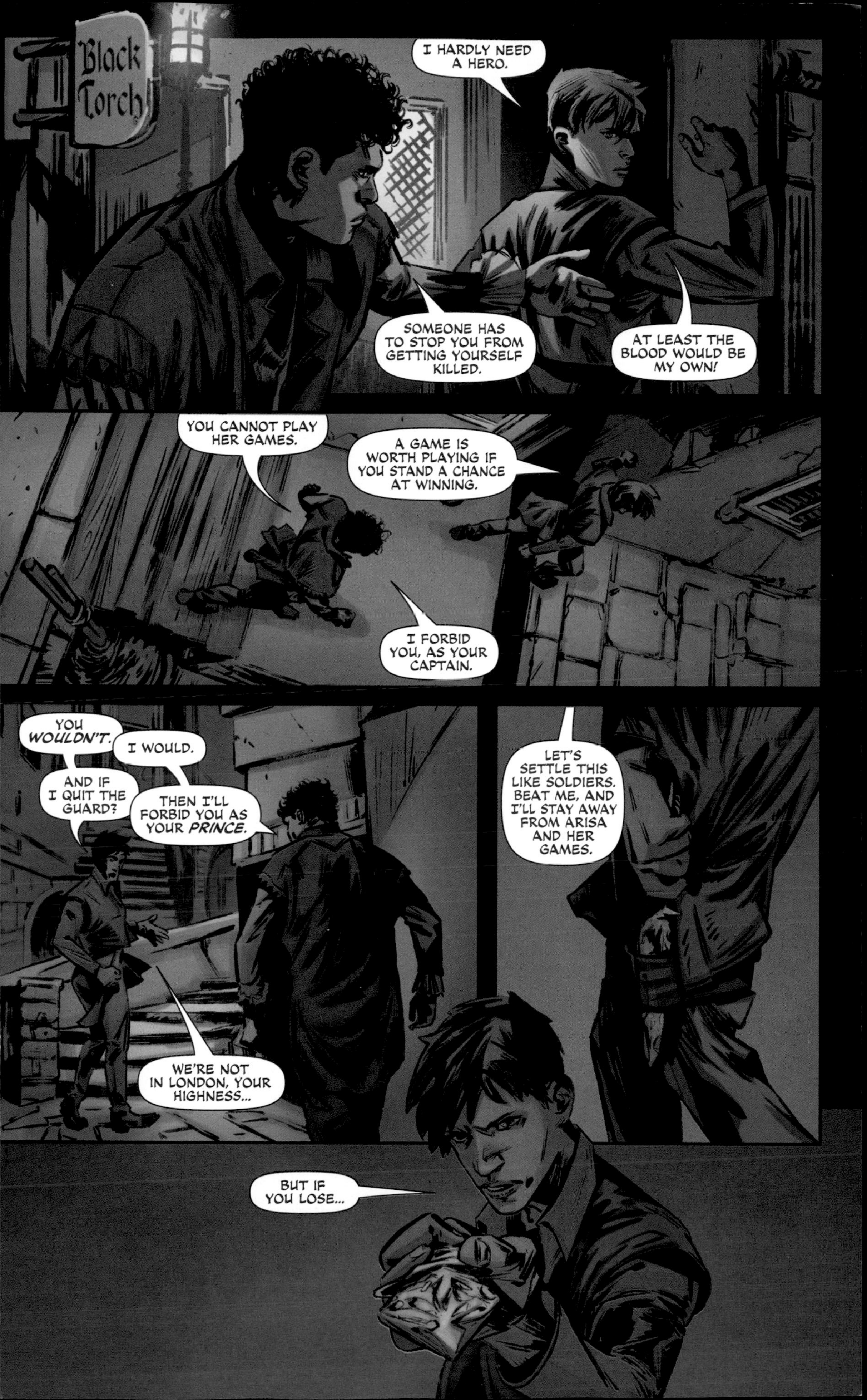
Black Torch
I HARDLY NEED A HERO.
SOMEONE HAS TO STOP YOU FROM GETTING YOURSELF KILLED.
AT LEAST THE BLOOD WOULD BE MY OWN!
YOU CANNOT PLAY HER GAMES.
A GAME IS WORTH PLAYING IF YOU STAND A CHANCE AT WINNING.
I FORBID YOU, AS YOUR CAPTAIN.
YOU WOULDN'T.
I WOULD.
AND IF I QUIT THE GUARD?
THEN I'LL FORBID YOU AS YOUR PRINCE.
WE'RE NOT IN LONDON, YOUR HIGHNESS...
LET'S SETTLE THIS LIKE SOLDIERS. BEAT ME, AND I'LL STAY AWAY FROM ARISA AND HER GAMES.
BUT IF YOU LOSE...

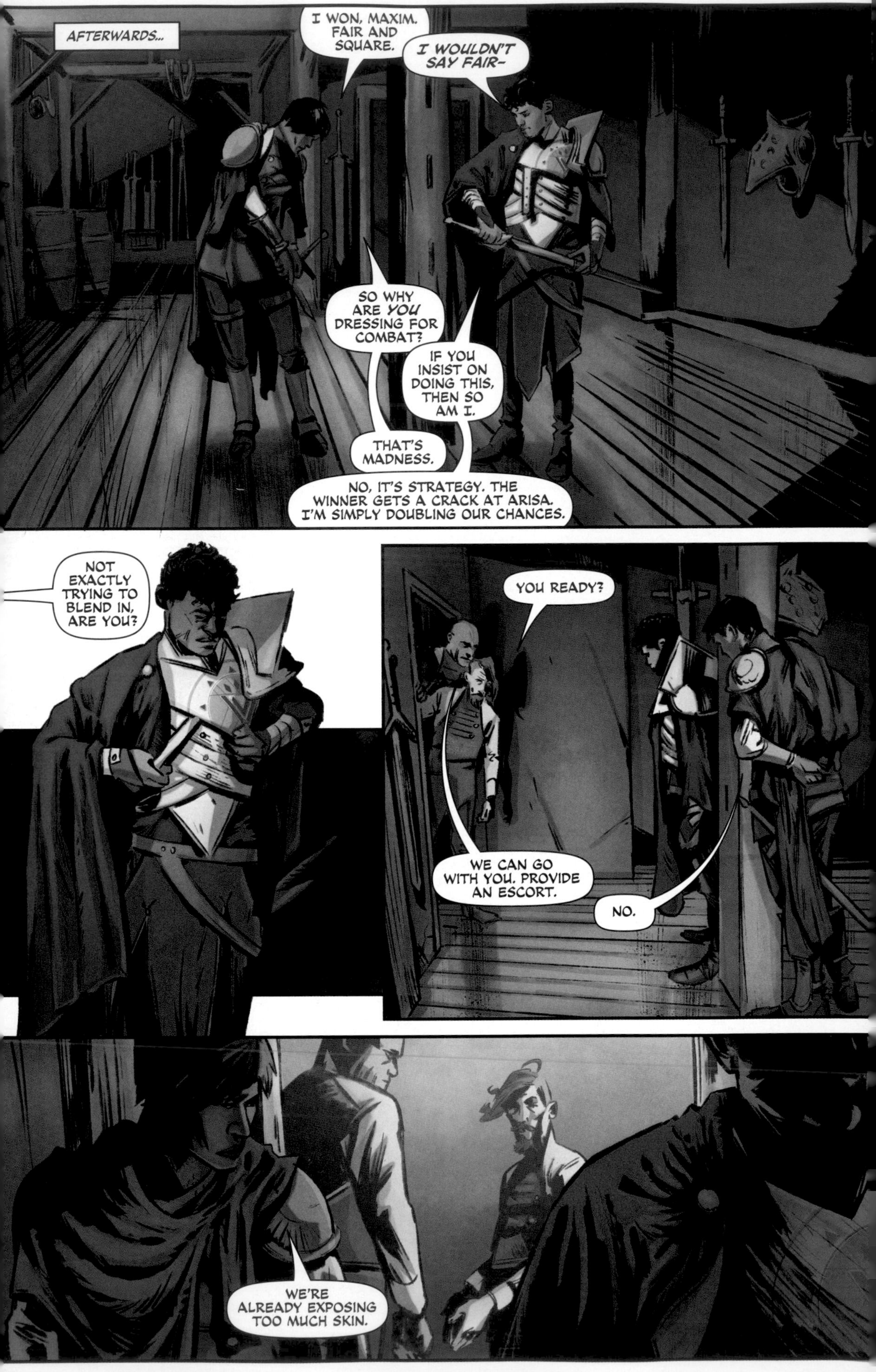
AFTERWARDS...
I WON, MAXIM. FAIR AND SQUARE.
I WOULDN'T SAY FAIR–
SO WHY ARE YOU DRESSING FOR COMBAT?
IF YOU INSIST ON DOING THIS, THEN SO AM I.
THAT'S MADNESS.
NO, IT'S STRATEGY. THE WINNER GETS A CRACK AT ARISA. I'M SIMPLY DOUBLING OUR CHANCES.
NOT EXACTLY TRYING TO BLEND IN, ARE YOU?
YOU READY?
WE CAN GO WITH YOU. PROVIDE AN ESCORT.
NO.
WE'RE ALREADY EXPOSING TOO MUCH SKIN.

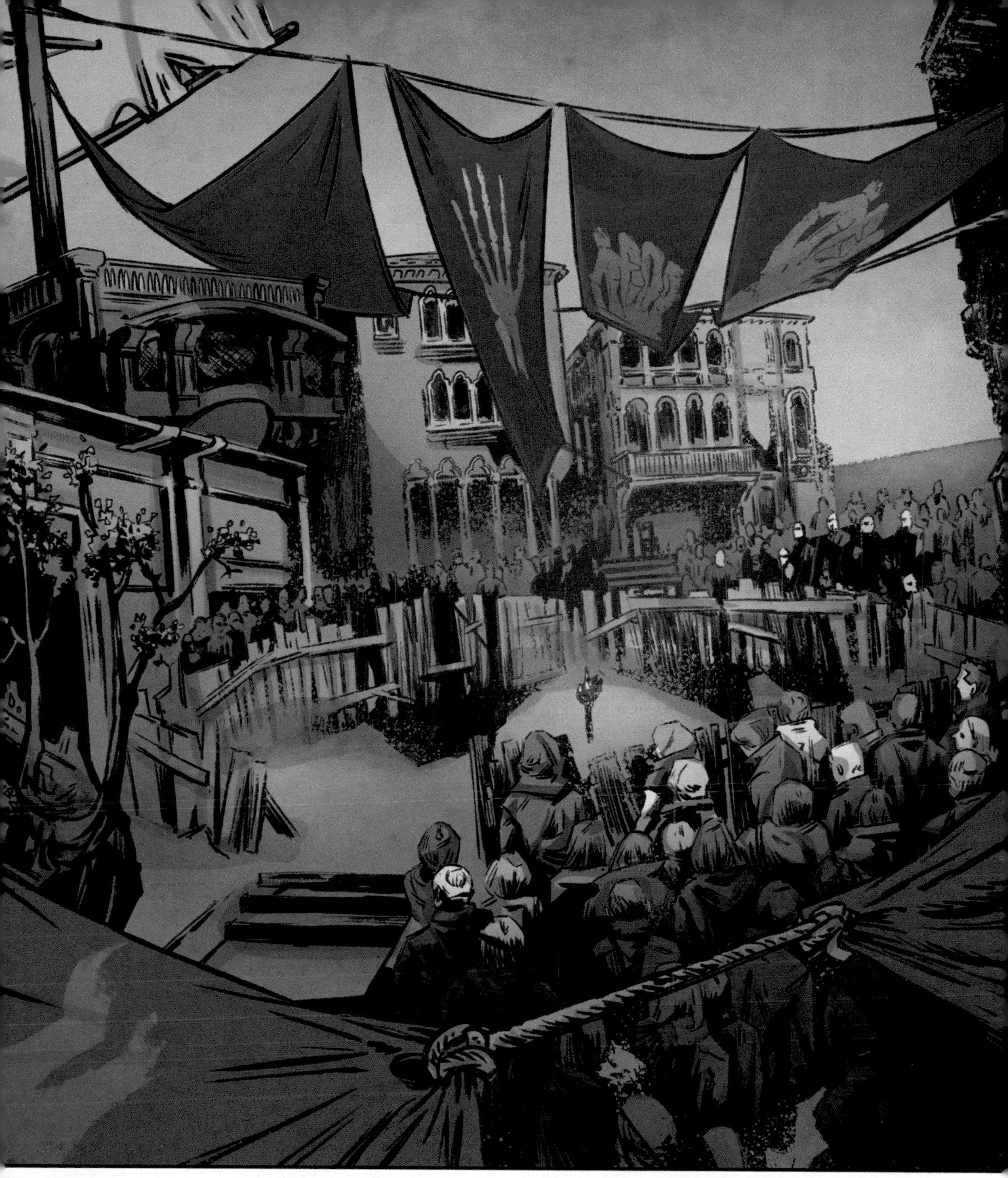

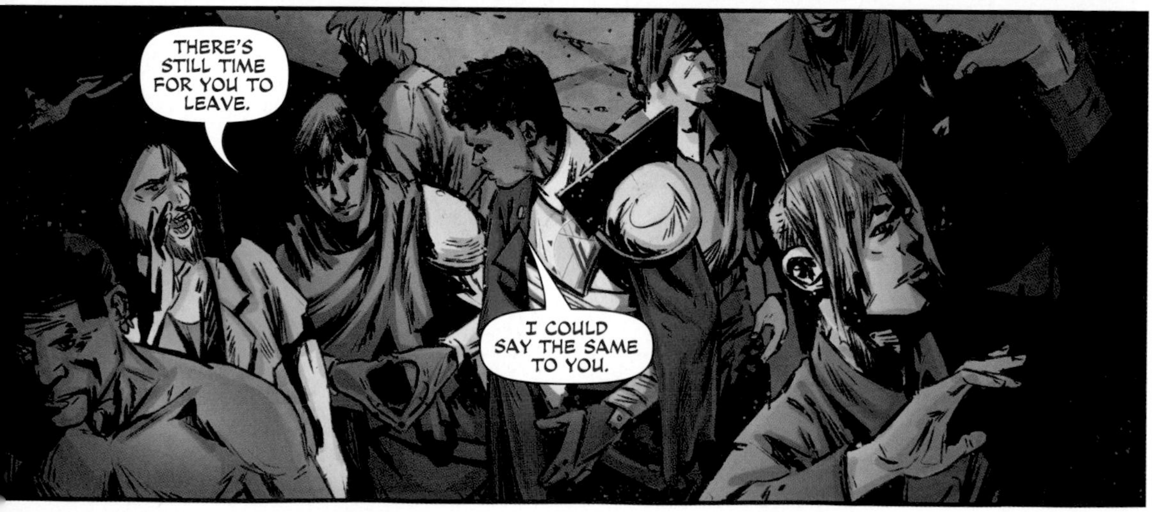
THERE'S STILL TIME FOR YOU TO LEAVE.
I COULD SAY THE SAME TO YOU.

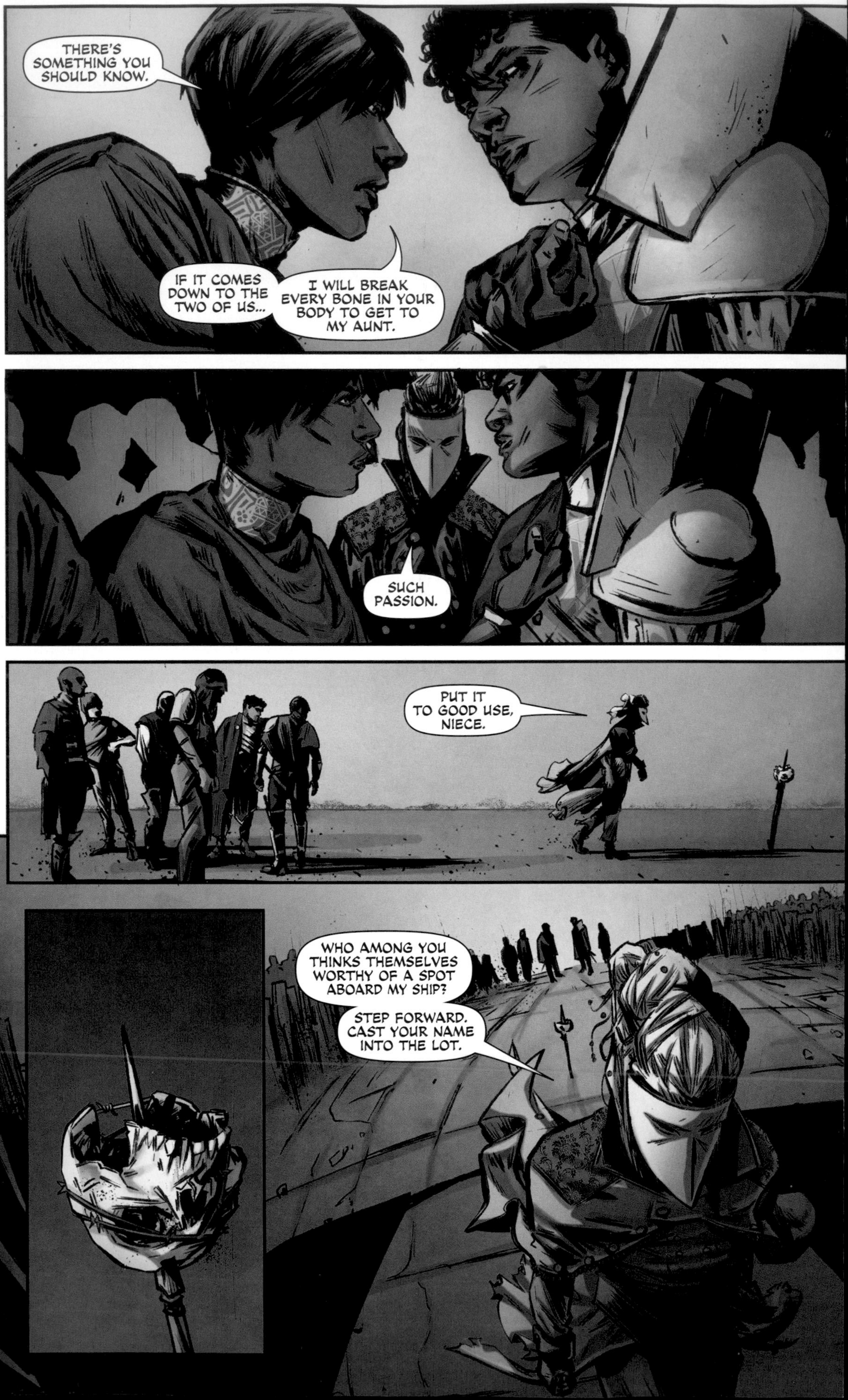
THERE'S SOMETHING YOU SHOULD KNOW.
IF IT COMES DOWN TO THE TWO OF US...
I WILL BREAK EVERY BONE IN YOUR BODY TO GET TO MY AUNT.
SUCH PASSION.
PUT IT TO GOOD USE, NIECE.
WHO AMONG YOU THINKS THEMSELVES WORTHY OF A SPOT ABOARD MY SHIP?
STEP FORWARD. CAST YOUR NAME INTO THE LOT.

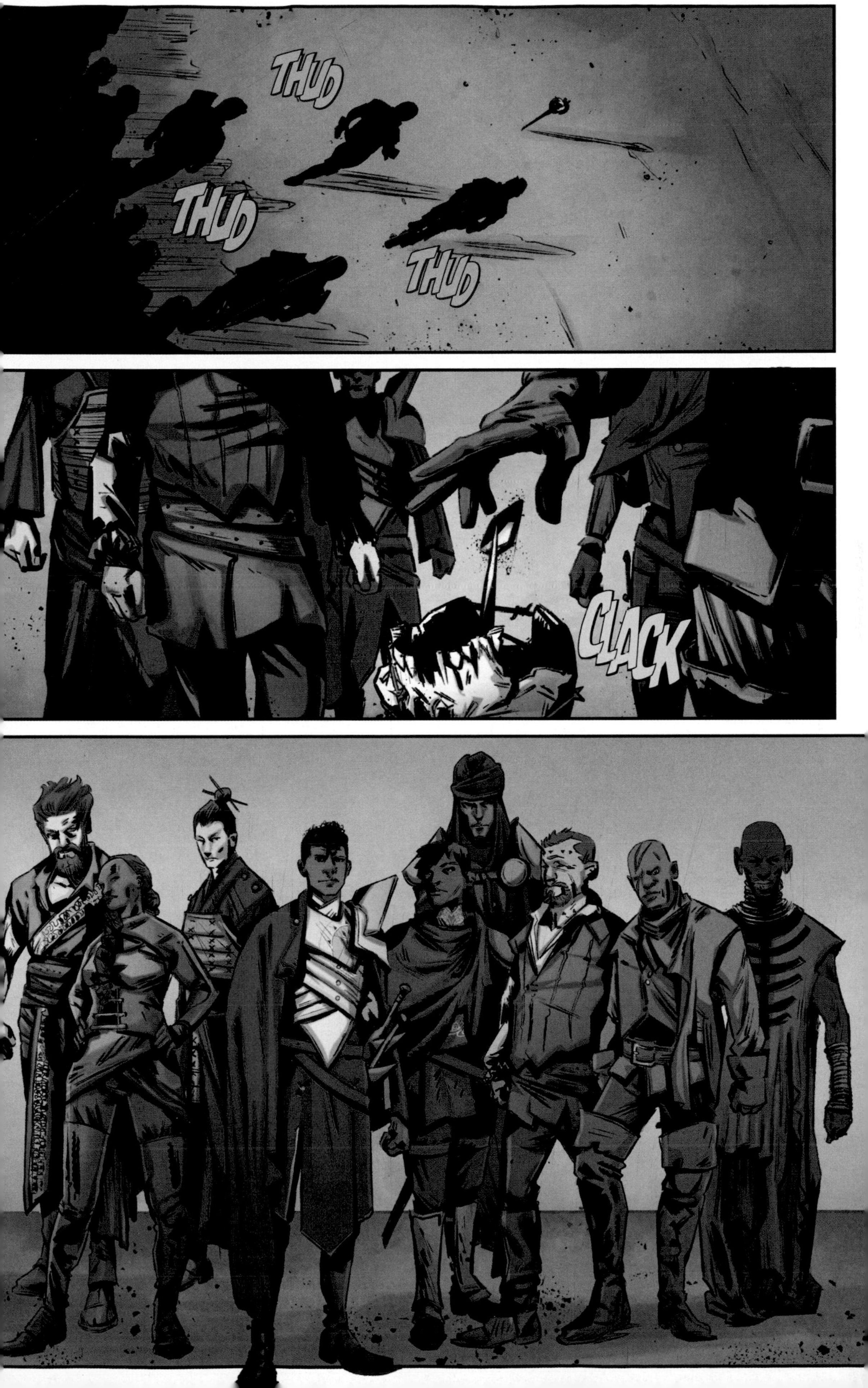
THUD
THUD
THUD
CLACK

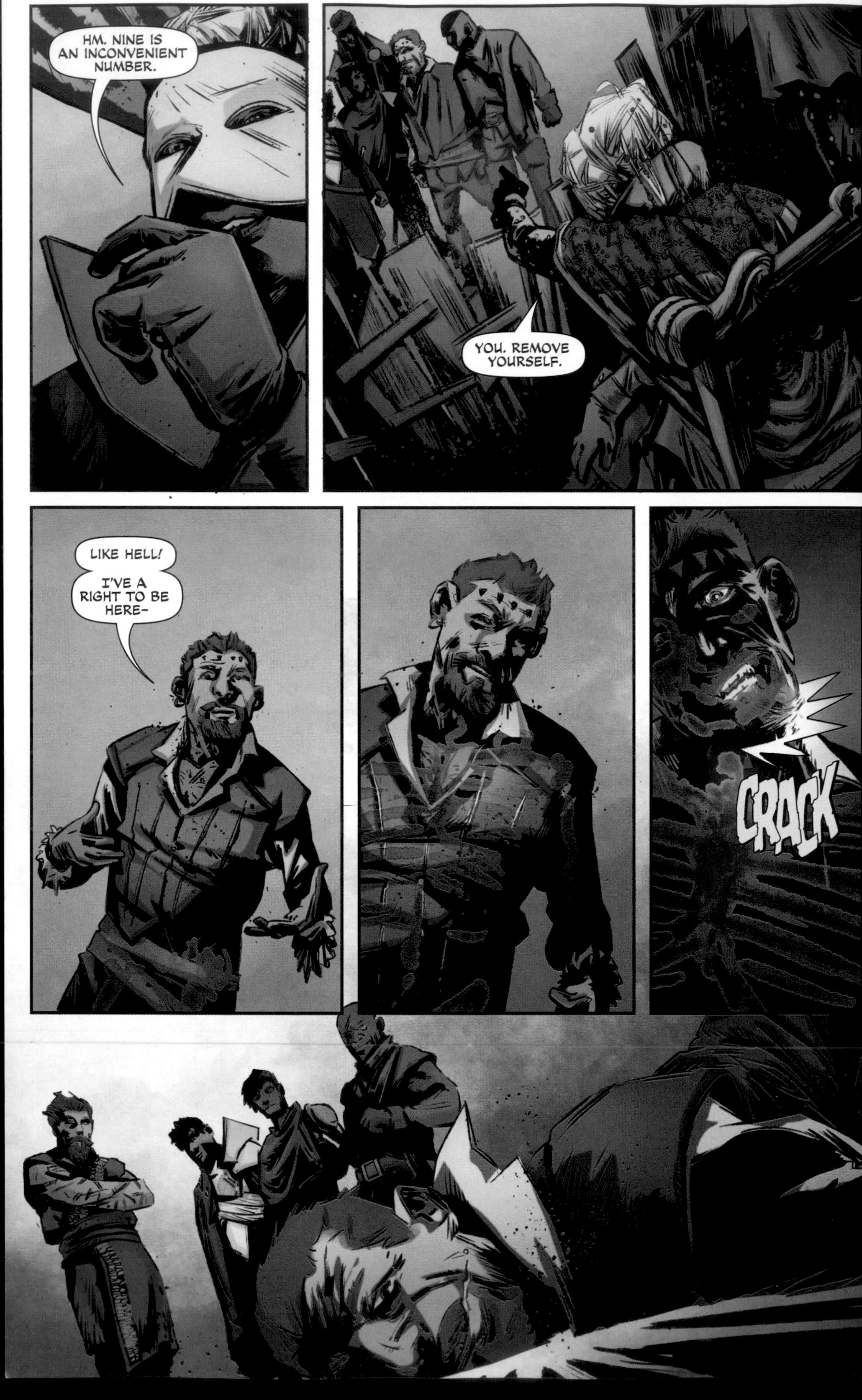
HM. NINE IS AN INCONVENIENT NUMBER.
YOU. REMOVE YOURSELF.
LIKE HELL!
I'VE A RIGHT TO BE HERE-
CRACK

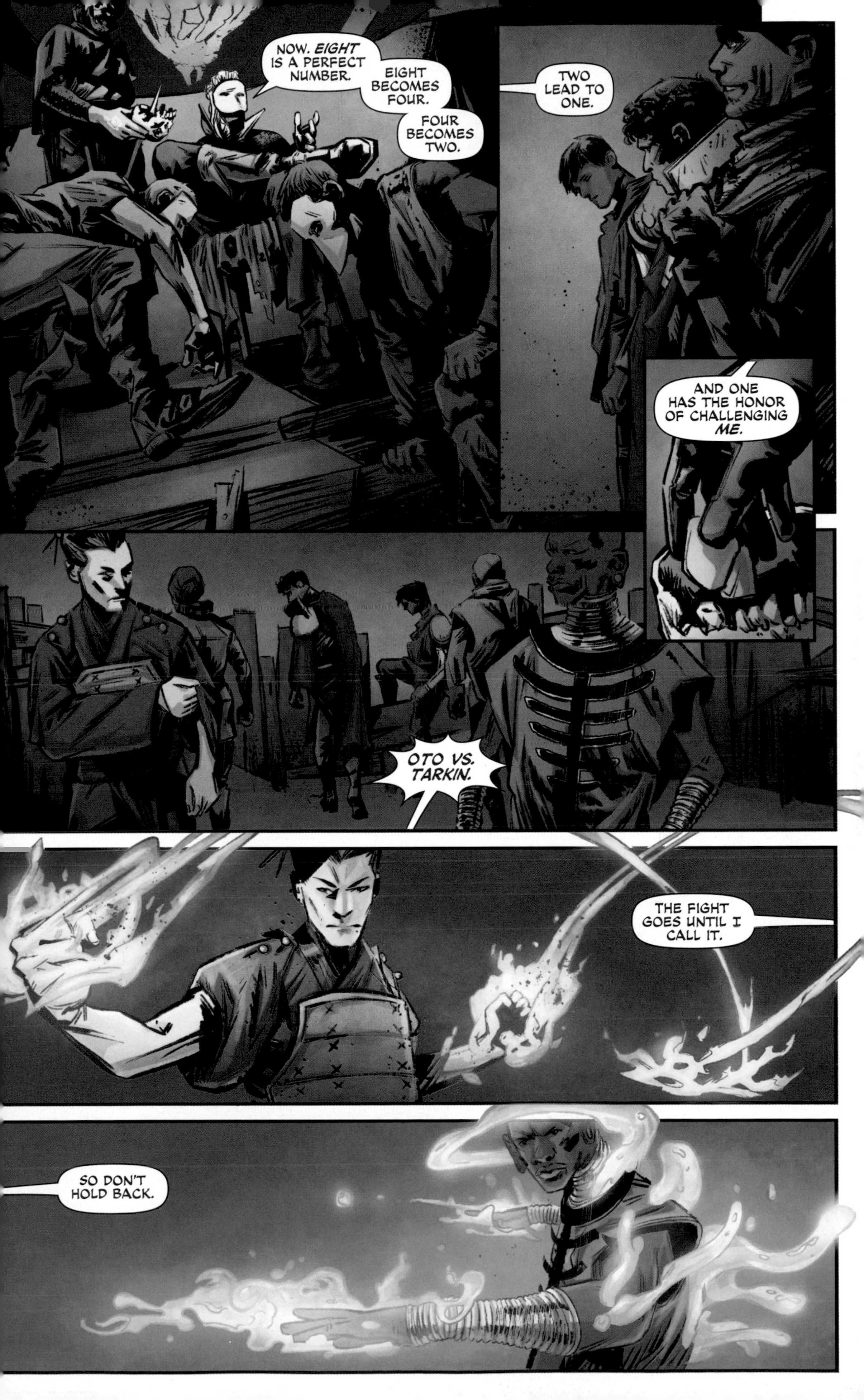
NOW. *EIGHT* IS A PERFECT NUMBER.
EIGHT BECOMES FOUR.
FOUR BECOMES TWO.
TWO LEAD TO ONE.
AND ONE HAS THE HONOR OF CHALLENGING *ME.*
OTO VS. TARKIN.
THE FIGHT GOES UNTIL I CALL IT.
SO DON'T HOLD BACK.

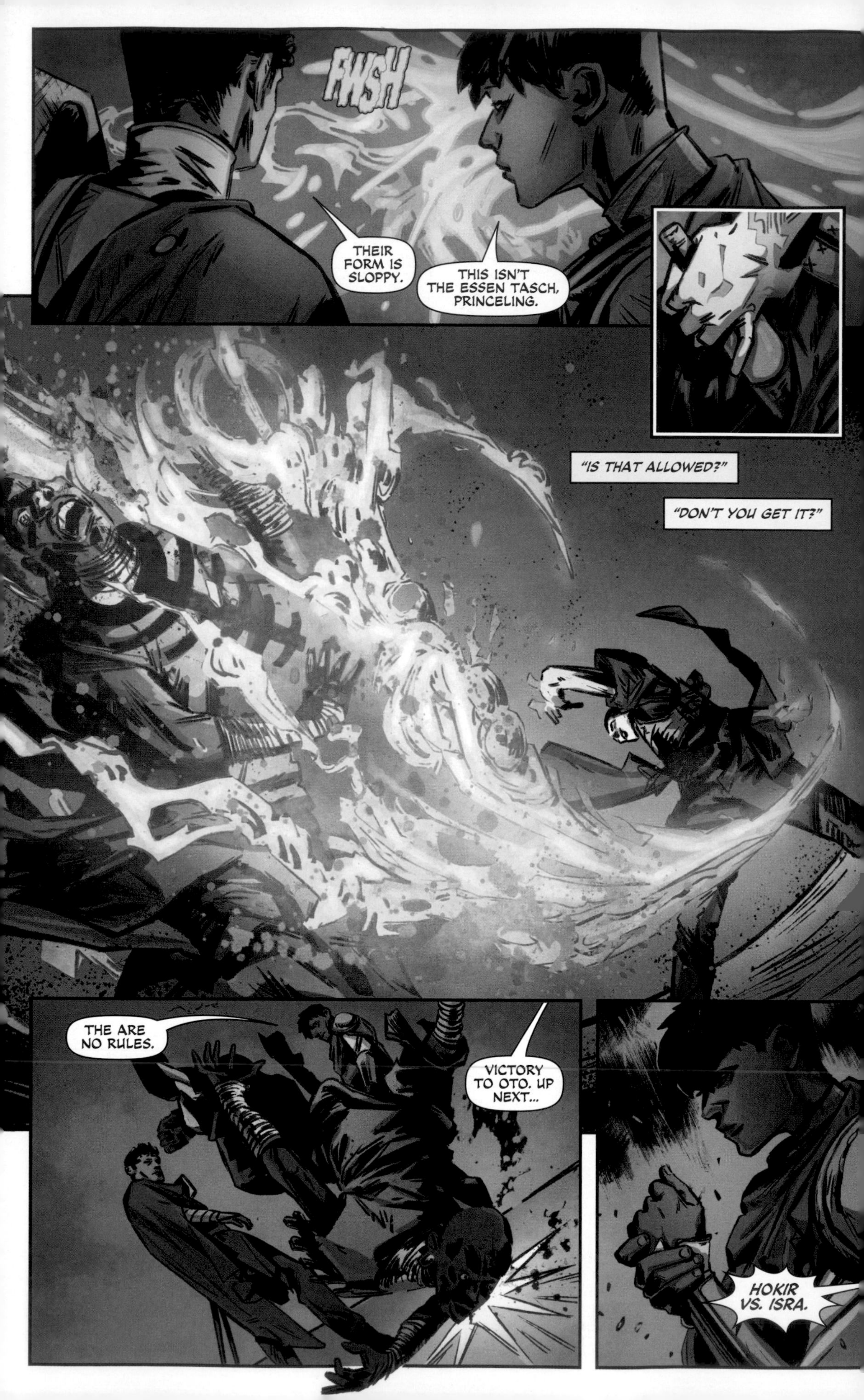
FWSH
THEIR FORM IS SLOPPY.
THIS ISN'T THE ESSEN TASCH, PRINCELING.
"IS THAT ALLOWED?"
"DON'T YOU GET IT?"
THE ARE NO RULES.
VICTORY TO OTO. UP NEXT...
HOKIR VS. ISRA.

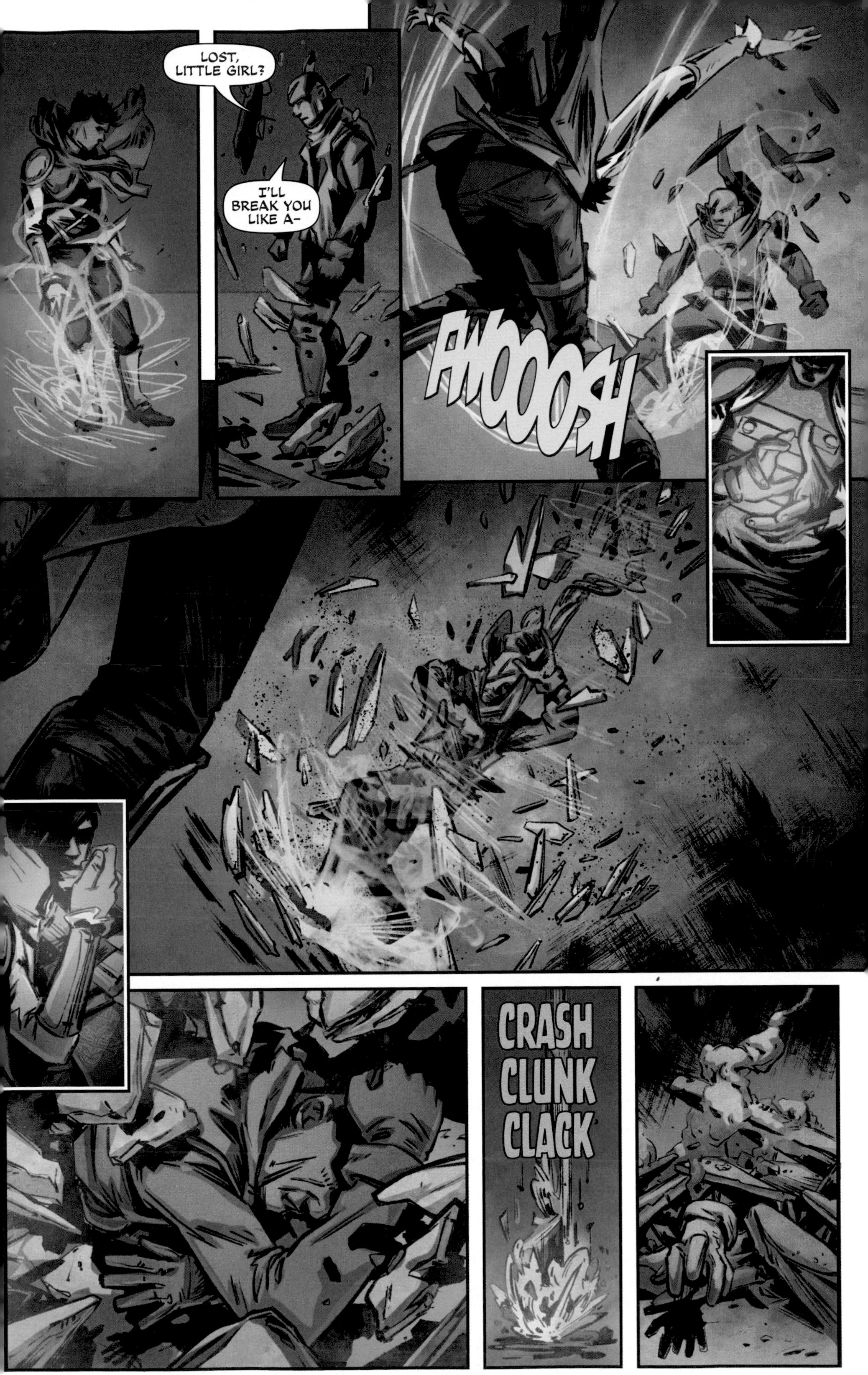
LOST, LITTLE GIRL?
I'LL BREAK YOU LIKE A-
FWOOOSH
CRASH
CLUNK
CLACK

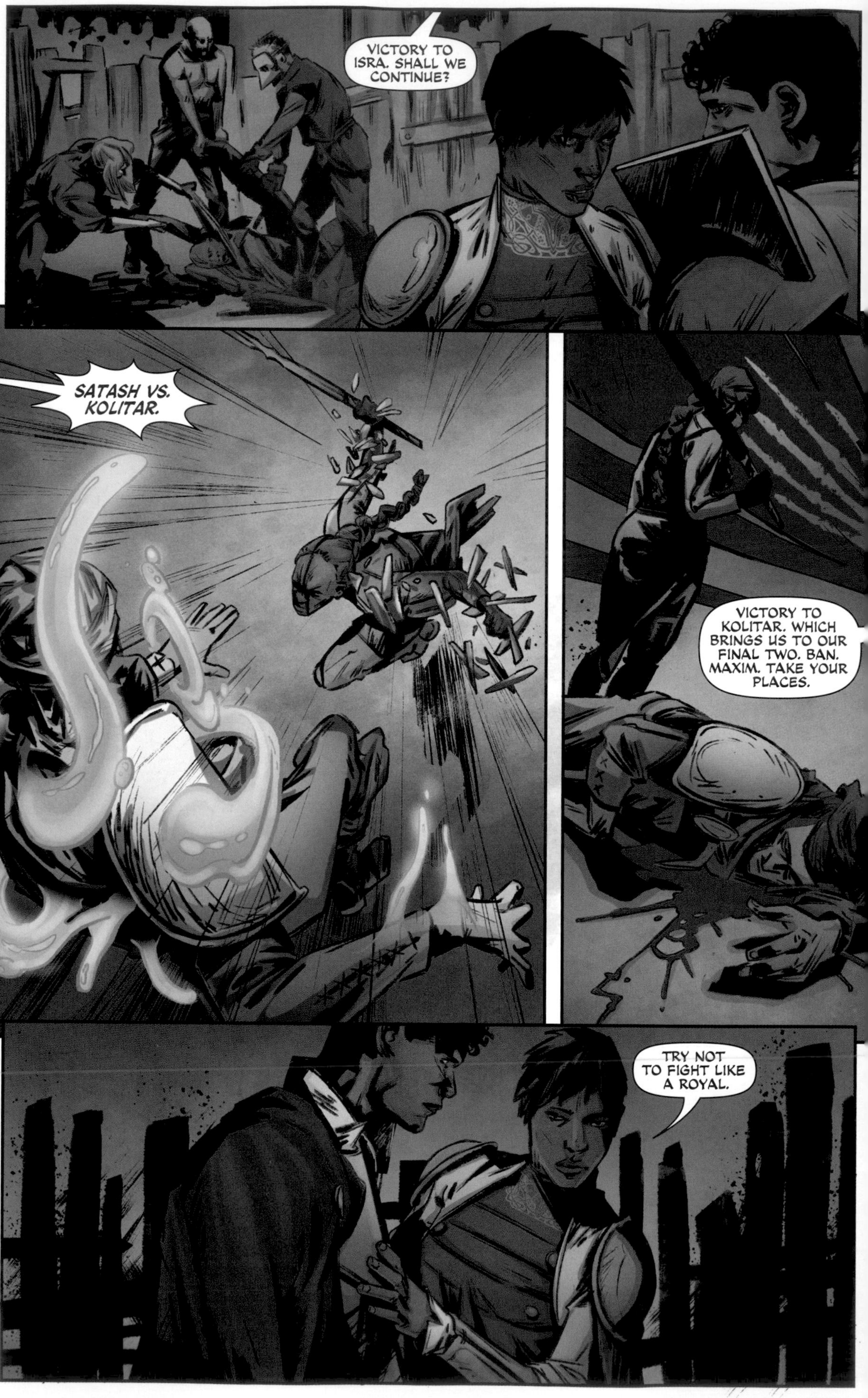
VICTORY TO ISRA. SHALL WE CONTINUE?
SATASH VS. KOLITAR.
VICTORY TO KOLITAR. WHICH BRINGS US TO OUR FINAL TWO. BAN. MAXIM. TAKE YOUR PLACES.
TRY NOT TO FIGHT LIKE A ROYAL.

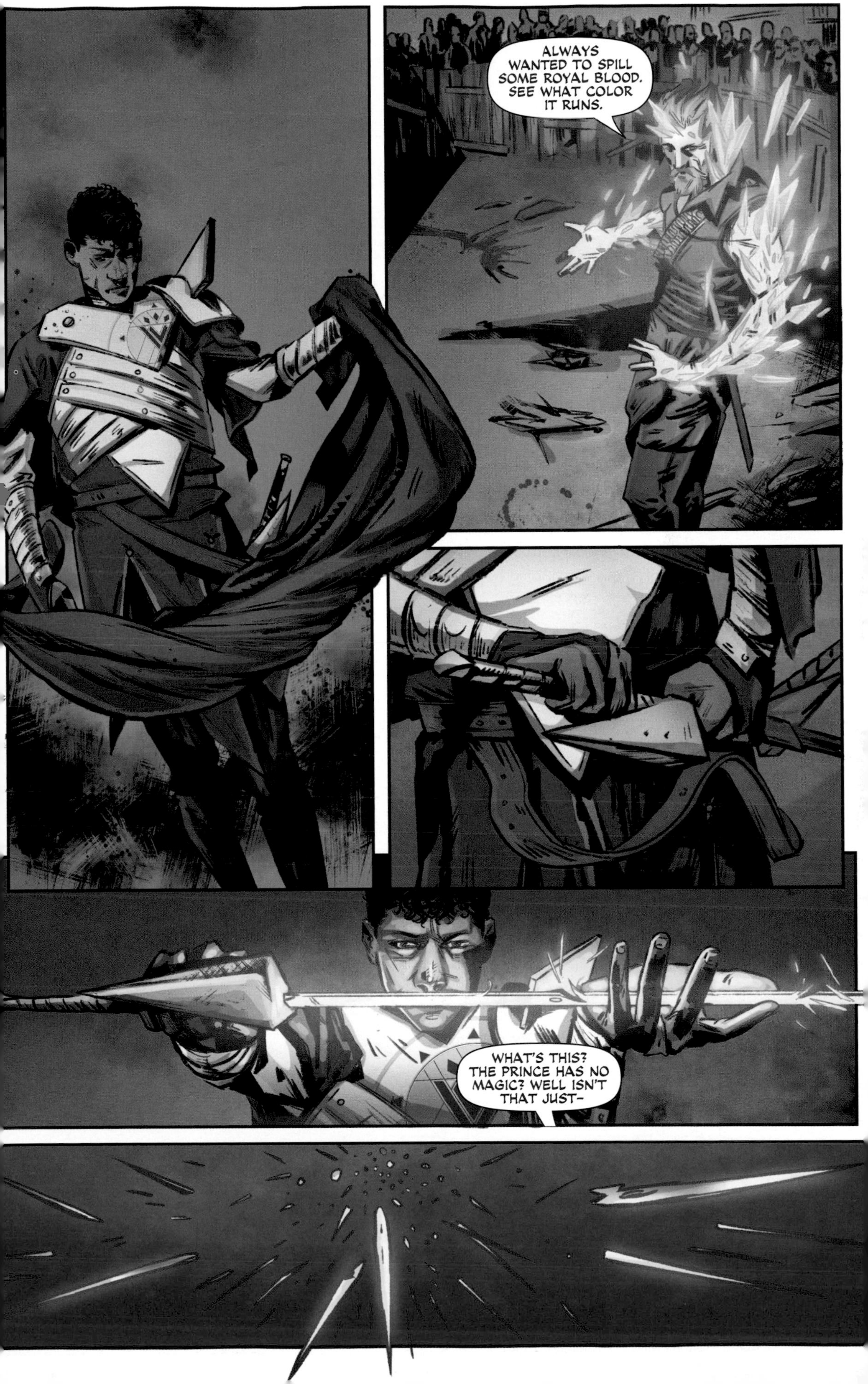
ALWAYS WANTED TO SPILL SOME ROYAL BLOOD. SEE WHAT COLOR IT RUNS.
WHAT'S THIS? THE PRINCE HAS NO MAGIC? WELL ISN'T THAT JUST–

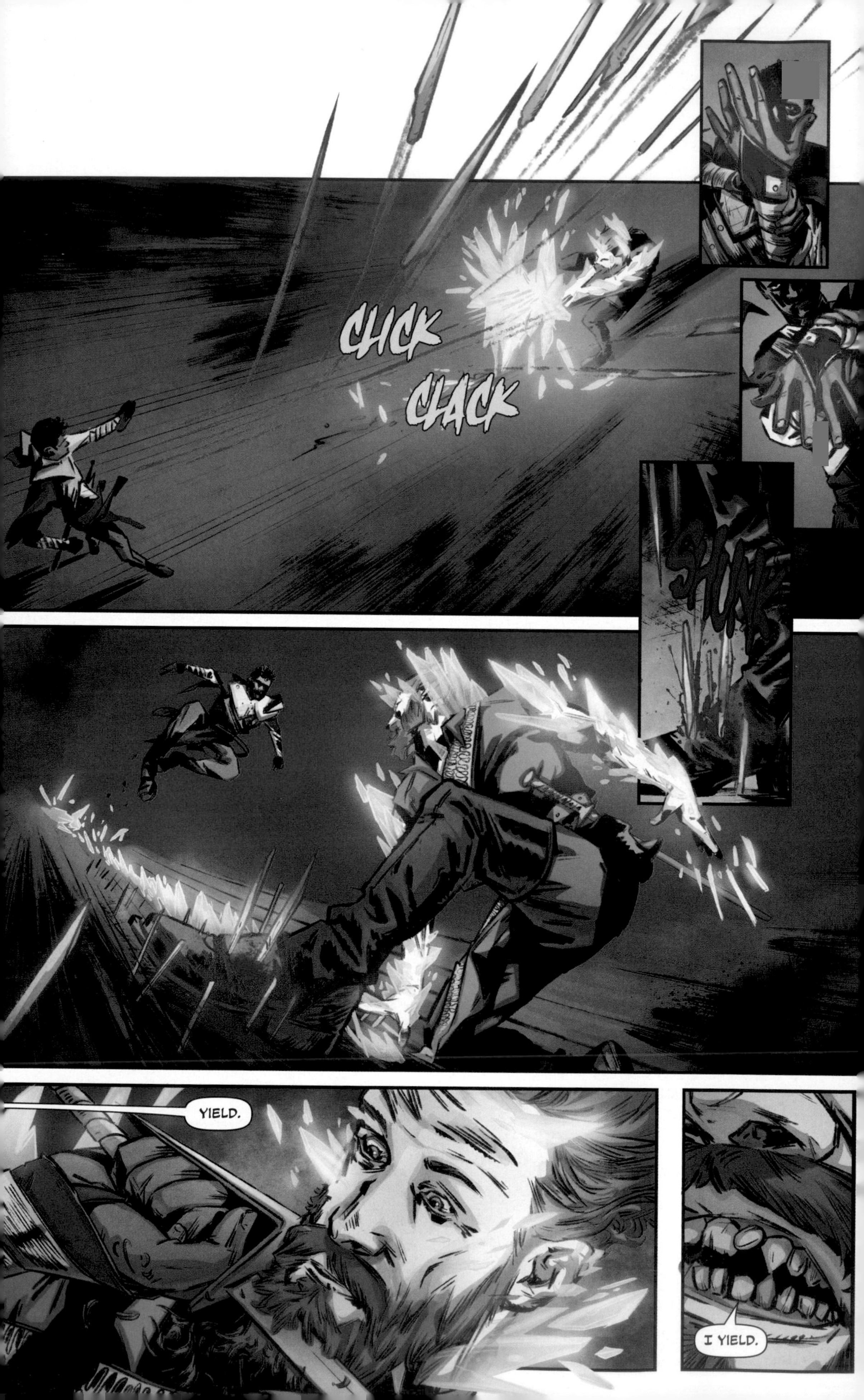
CLICK
CLACK
SHUNK
YIELD.
I YIELD.

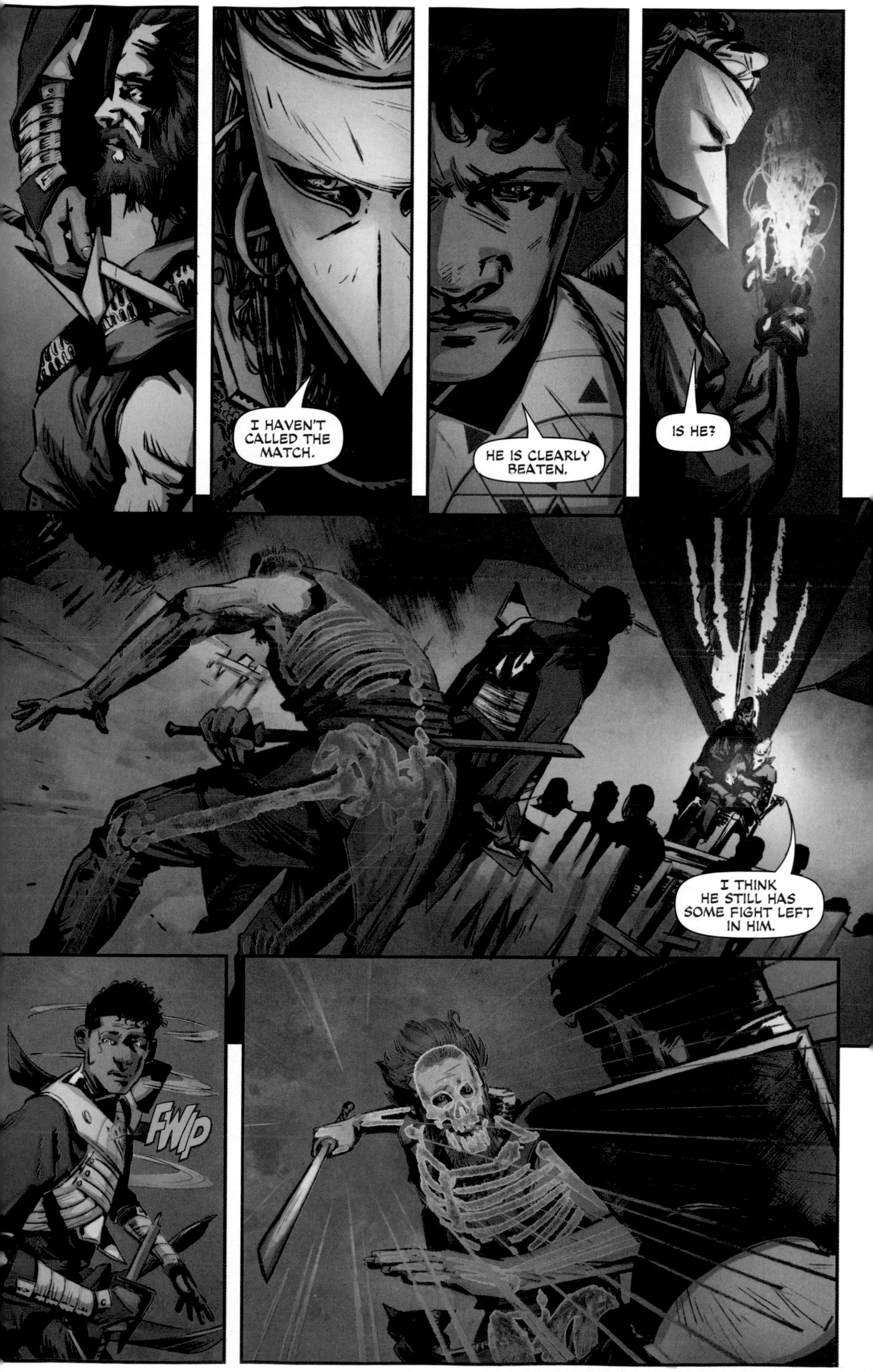
I HAVEN'T CALLED THE MATCH.
HE IS CLEARLY BEATEN.
IS HE?
I THINK HE STILL HAS SOME FIGHT LEFT IN HIM.
FWIP

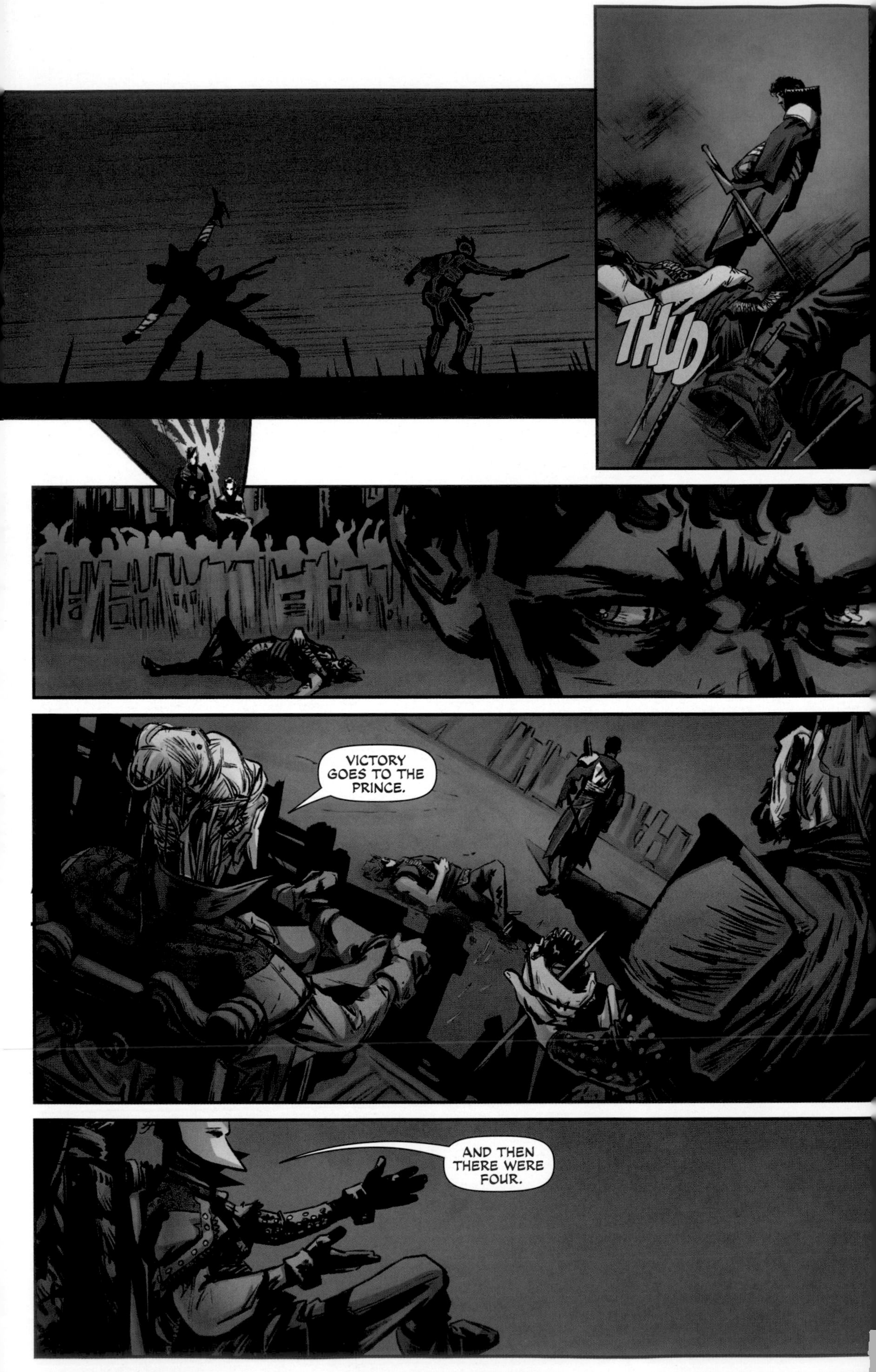
THUD
VICTORY GOES TO THE PRINCE.
AND THEN THERE WERE FOUR.

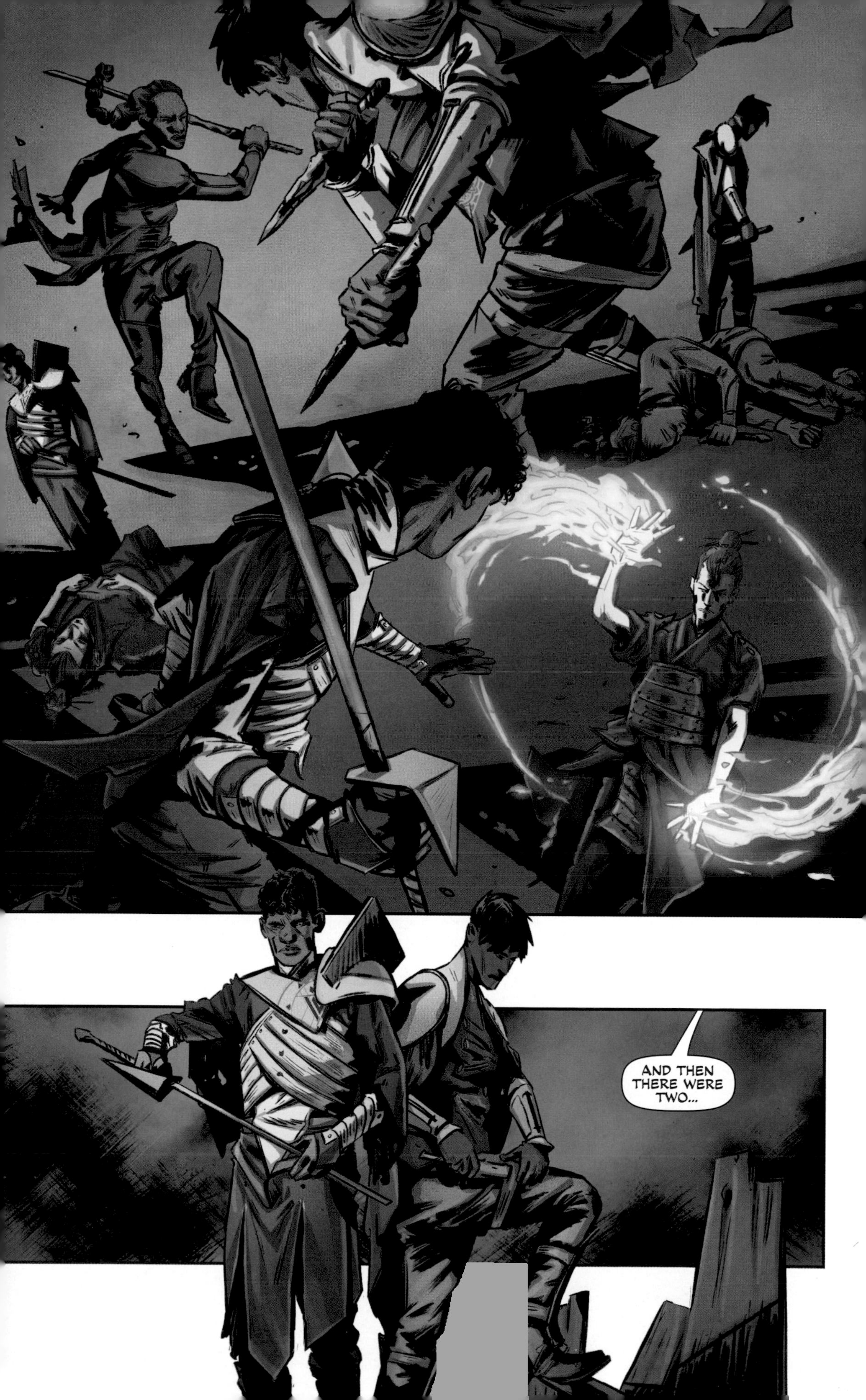
AND THEN
THERE WERE
TWO...

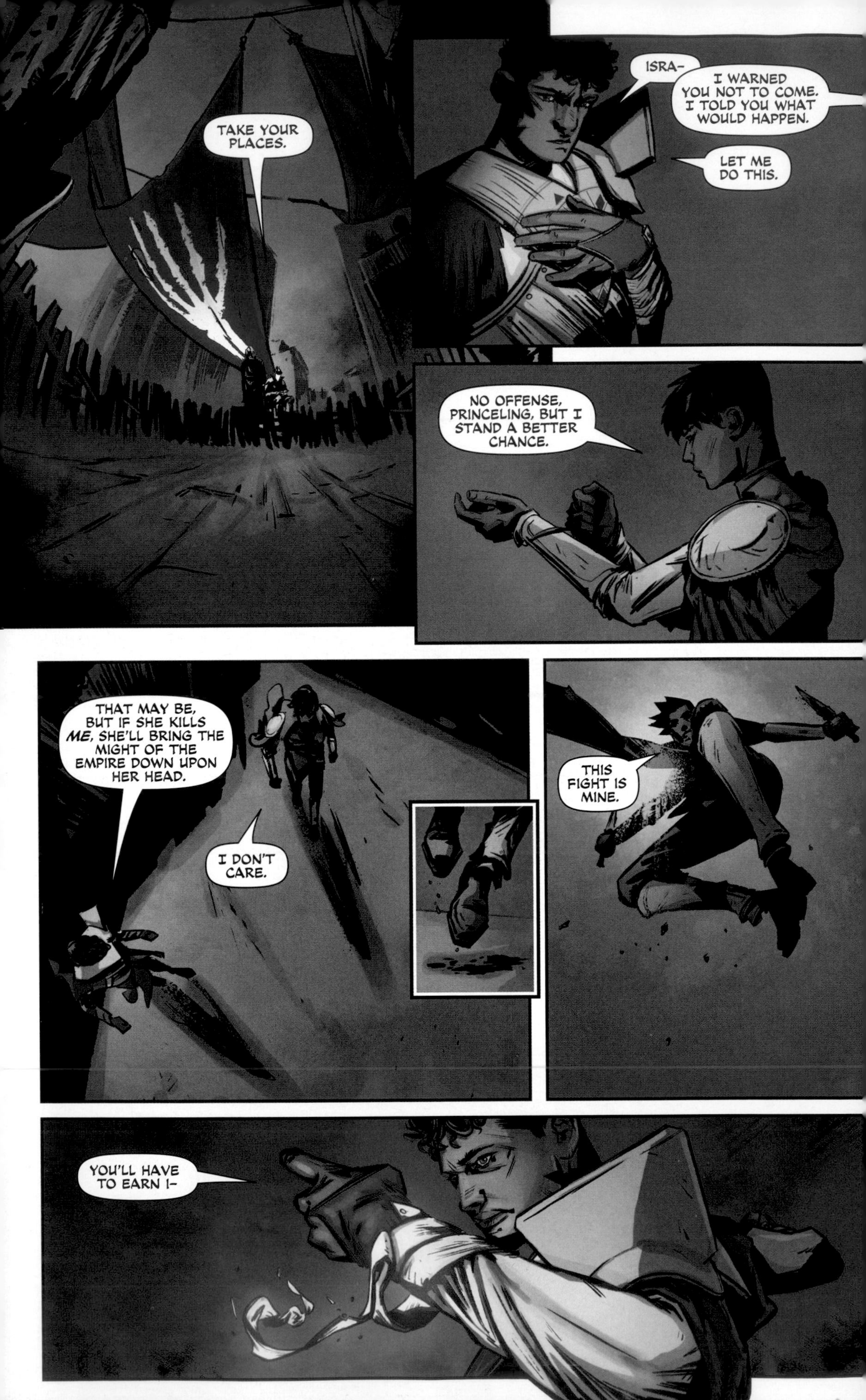
TAKE YOUR PLACES.
ISRA-
I WARNED YOU NOT TO COME. I TOLD YOU WHAT WOULD HAPPEN.
LET ME DO THIS.
NO OFFENSE, PRINCELING, BUT I STAND A BETTER CHANCE.
THAT MAY BE, BUT IF SHE KILLS *ME*, SHE'LL BRING THE MIGHT OF THE EMPIRE DOWN UPON HER HEAD.
I DON'T CARE.
THIS FIGHT IS MINE.
YOU'LL HAVE TO EARN I-

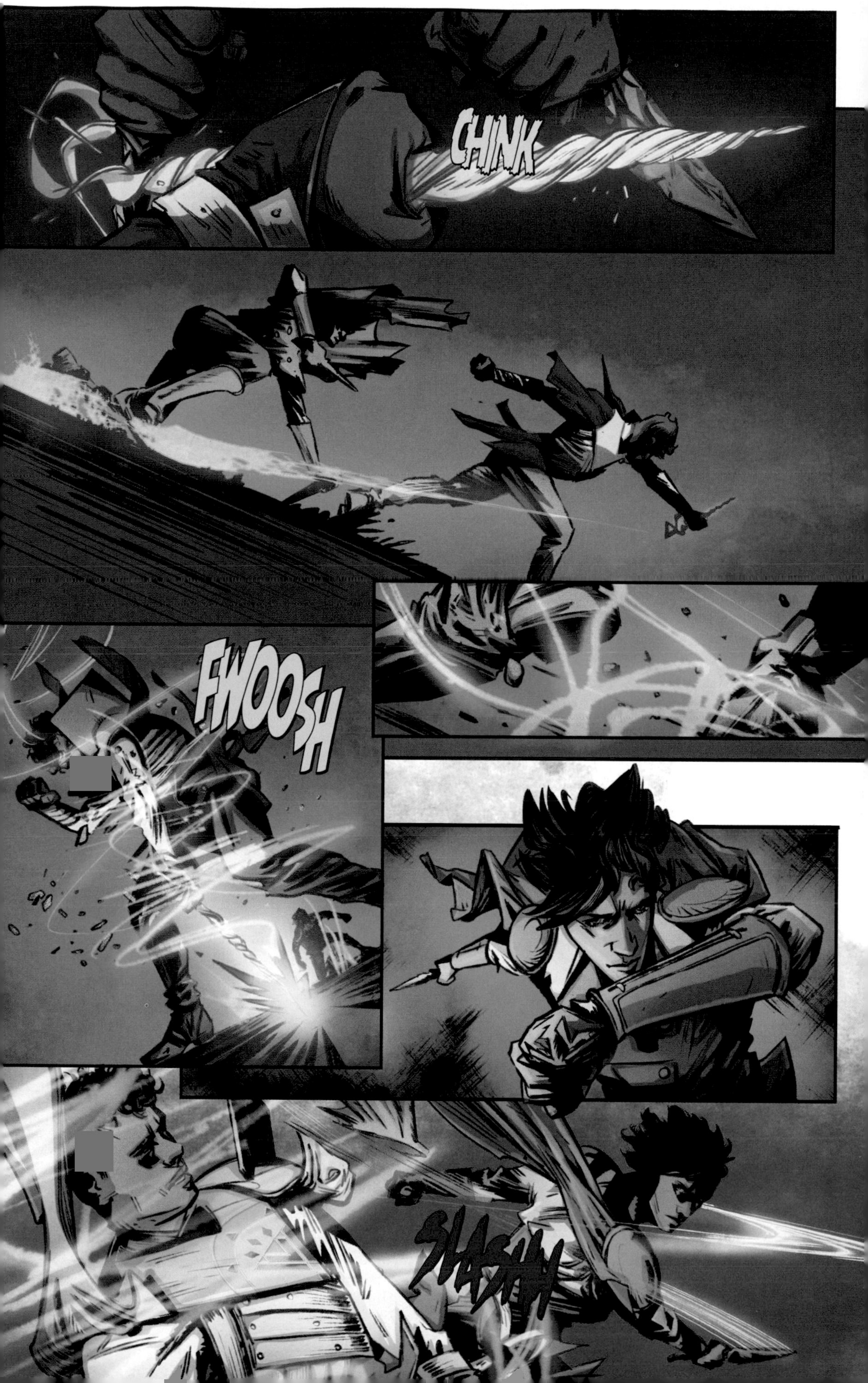
CHINK
FWOOSH
SLASHH

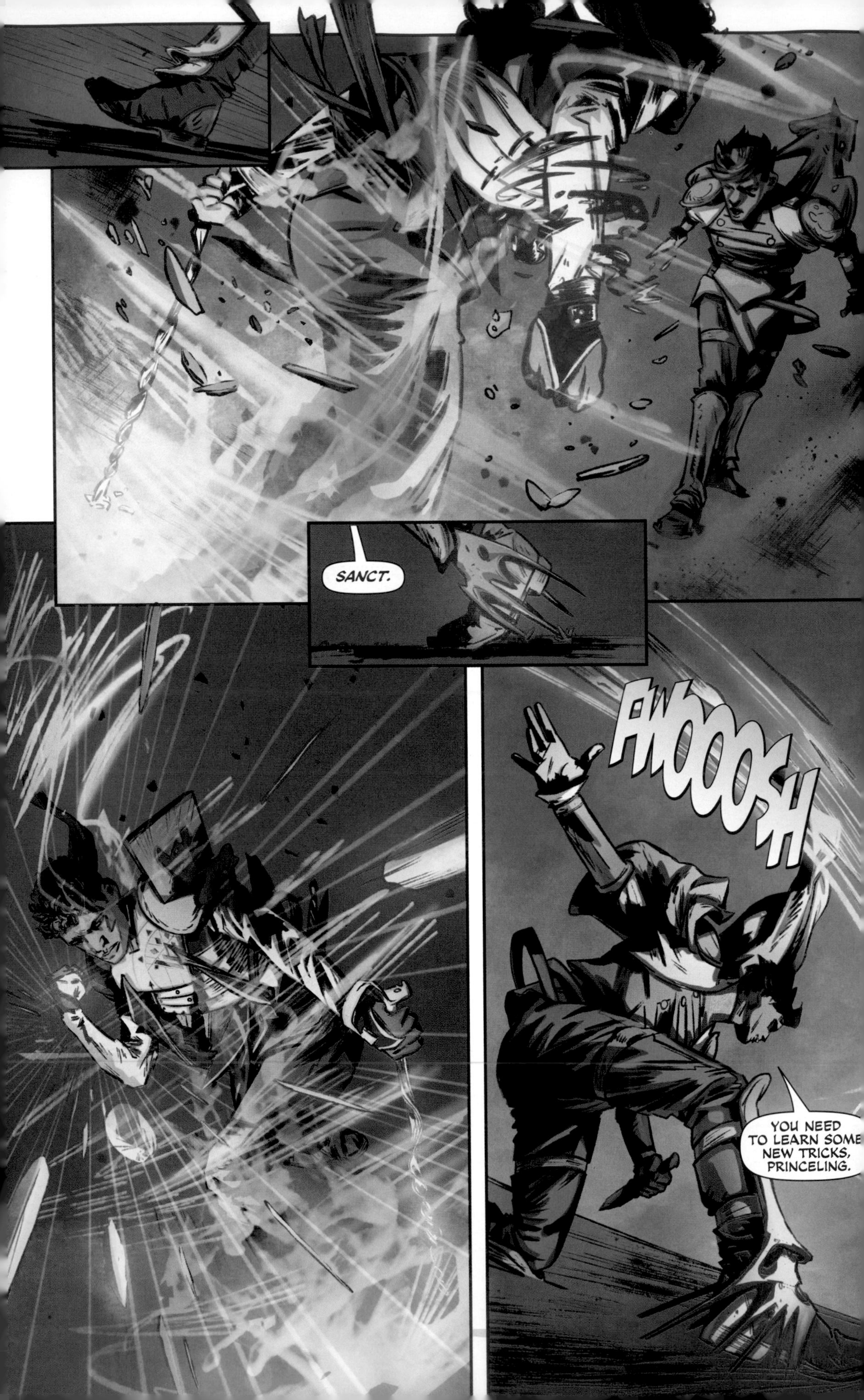
SANCT.
FWOOOSH
YOU NEED TO LEARN SOME NEW TRICKS, PRINCELING.

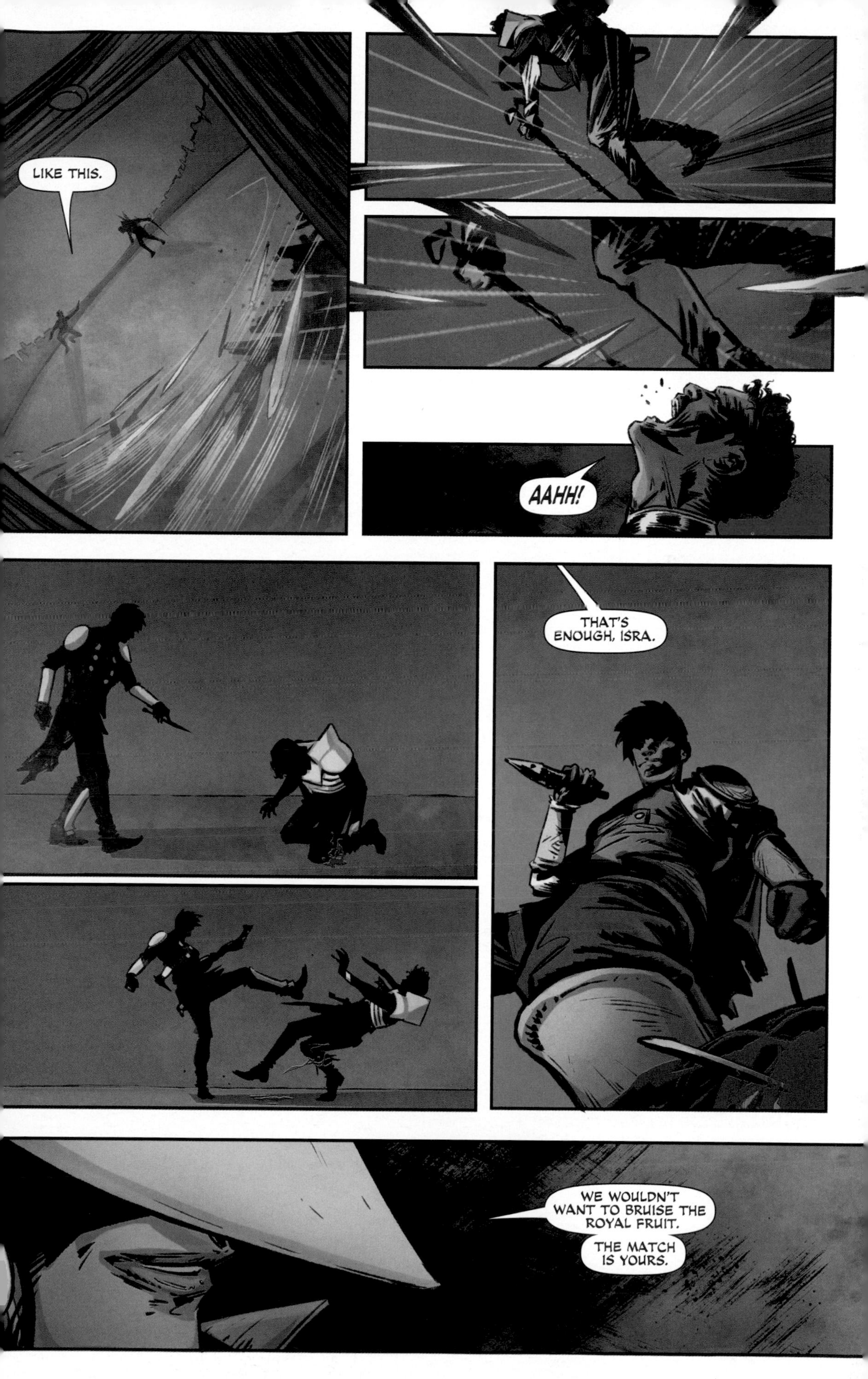
LIKE THIS.
AAHH!
THAT'S ENOUGH, ISRA.
WE WOULDN'T WANT TO BRUISE THE ROYAL FRUIT.
THE MATCH IS YOURS.

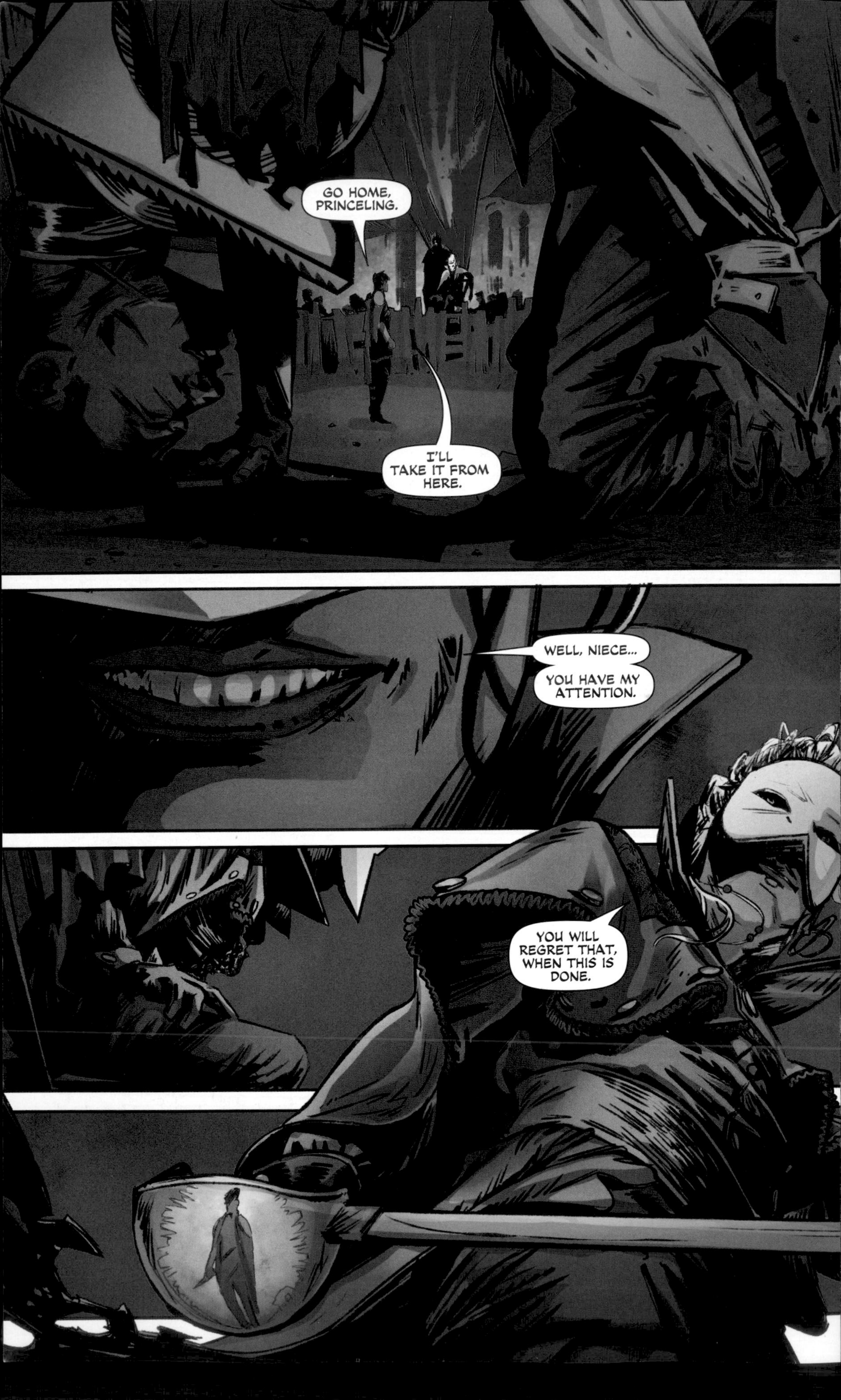
GO HOME, PRINCELING.
I'LL TAKE IT FROM HERE.
WELL, NIECE...
YOU HAVE MY ATTENTION.
YOU WILL REGRET THAT, WHEN THIS IS DONE.

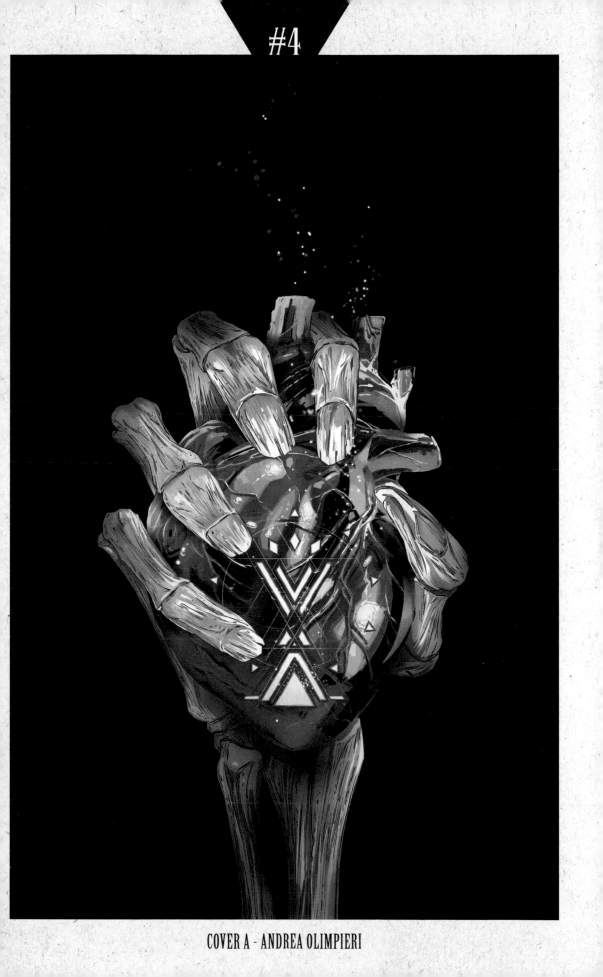

#4

COVER A - ANDREA OLIMPIERI

#4

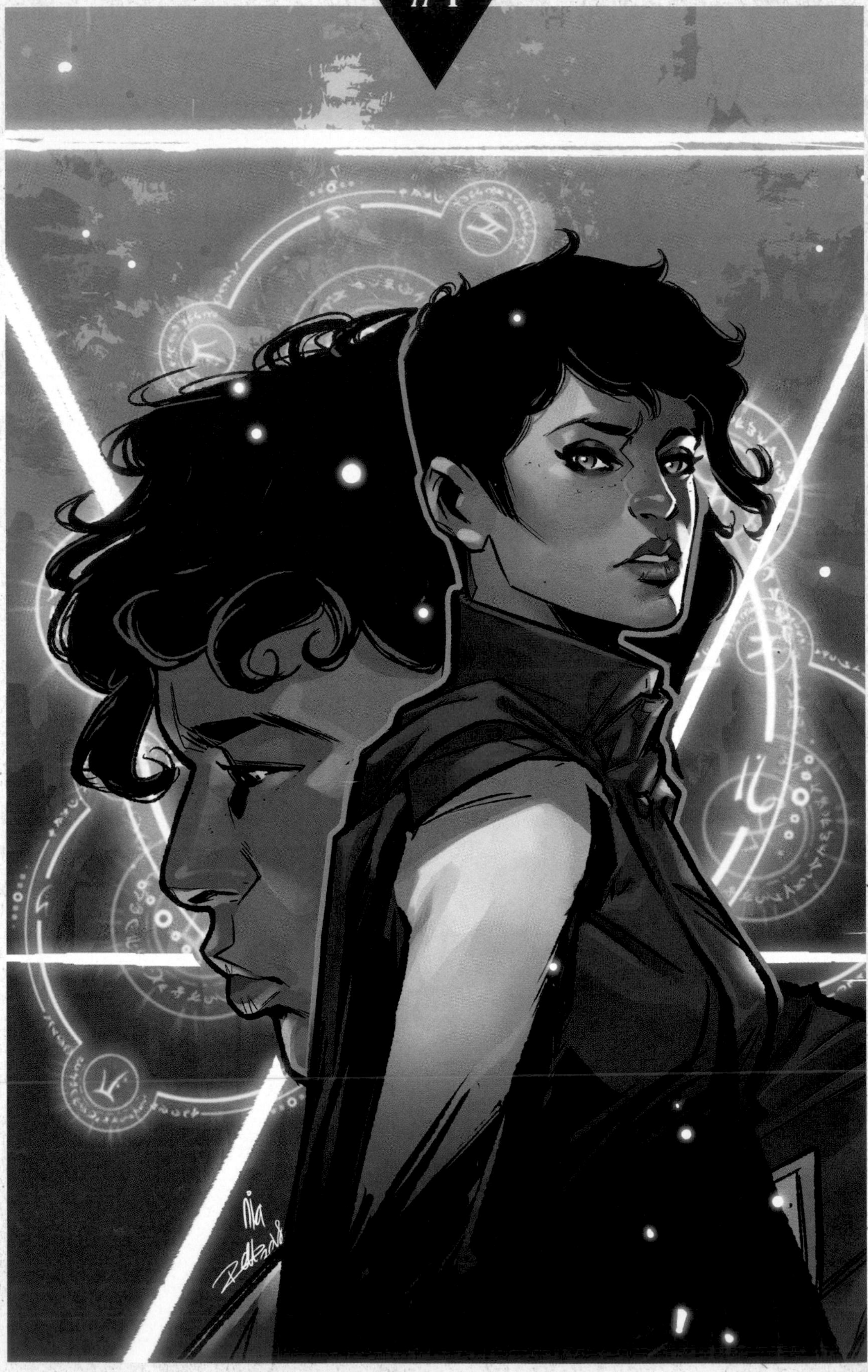

COVER B - ROBERTA INGRANATA & WARNIA SAHADEWA

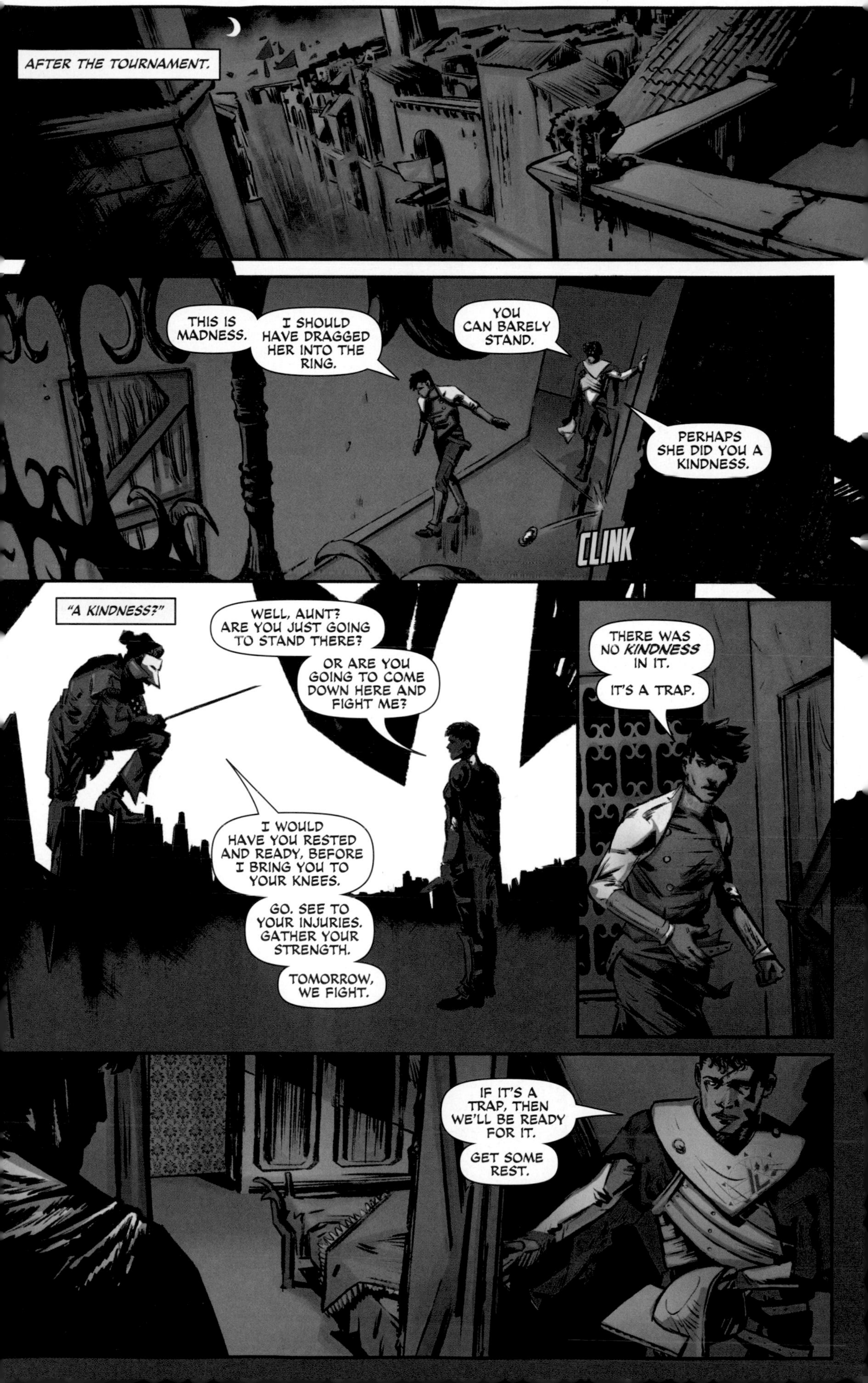
AFTER THE TOURNAMENT.
THIS IS MADNESS.
I SHOULD HAVE DRAGGED HER INTO THE RING.
YOU CAN BARELY STAND.
PERHAPS SHE DID YOU A KINDNESS.
CLINK
"A KINDNESS?"
WELL, AUNT? ARE YOU JUST GOING TO STAND THERE?
OR ARE YOU GOING TO COME DOWN HERE AND FIGHT ME?
I WOULD HAVE YOU RESTED AND READY, BEFORE I BRING YOU TO YOUR KNEES.
GO. SEE TO YOUR INJURIES. GATHER YOUR STRENGTH.
TOMORROW, WE FIGHT.
THERE WAS NO KINDNESS IN IT.
IT'S A TRAP.
IF IT'S A TRAP, THEN WE'LL BE READY FOR IT.
GET SOME REST.

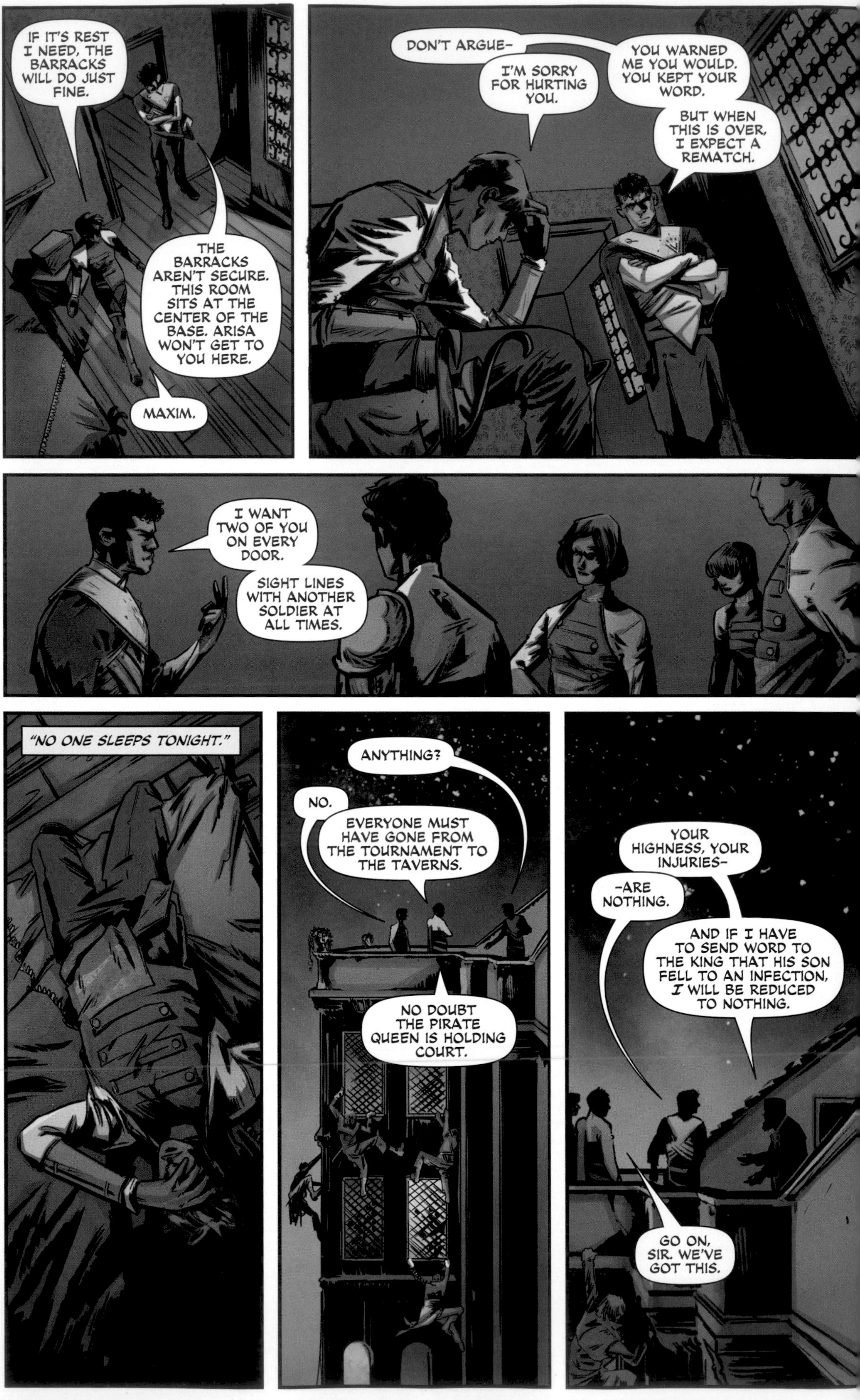
IF IT'S REST I NEED, THE BARRACKS WILL DO JUST FINE.
THE BARRACKS AREN'T SECURE. THIS ROOM SITS AT THE CENTER OF THE BASE. ARISA WON'T GET TO YOU HERE.
MAXIM.
DON'T ARGUE-
I'M SORRY FOR HURTING YOU.
YOU WARNED ME YOU WOULD. YOU KEPT YOUR WORD.
BUT WHEN THIS IS OVER, I EXPECT A REMATCH.
I WANT TWO OF YOU ON EVERY DOOR.
SIGHT LINES WITH ANOTHER SOLDIER AT ALL TIMES.
"NO ONE SLEEPS TONIGHT."
ANYTHING?
NO.
EVERYONE MUST HAVE GONE FROM THE TOURNAMENT TO THE TAVERNS.
NO DOUBT THE PIRATE QUEEN IS HOLDING COURT.
YOUR HIGHNESS, YOUR INJURIES-
-ARE NOTHING.
AND IF I HAVE TO SEND WORD TO THE KING THAT HIS SON FELL TO AN INFECTION, I WILL BE REDUCED TO NOTHING.
GO ON, SIR. WE'VE GOT THIS.

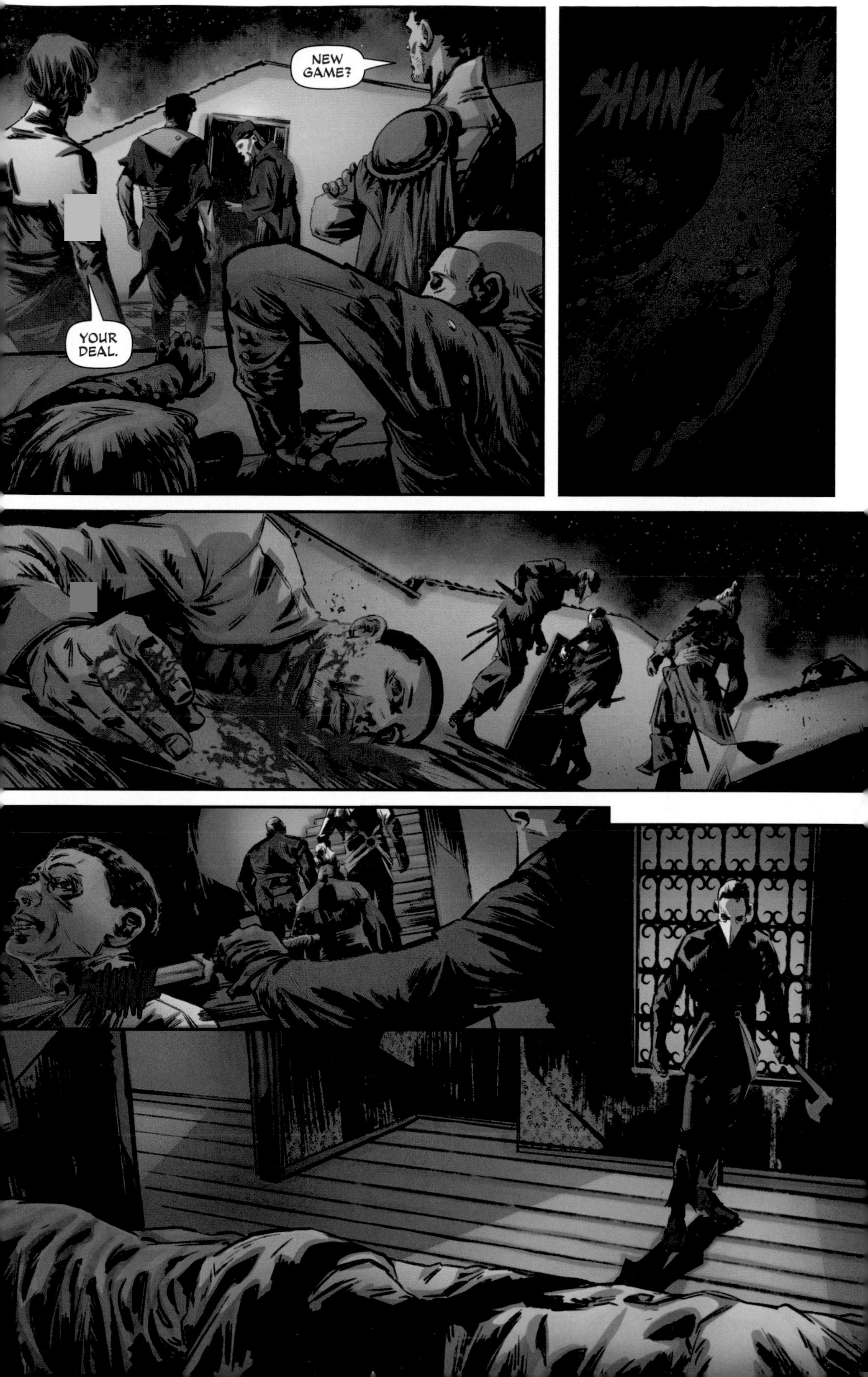
NEW GAME?
YOUR DEAL.
SHUNK

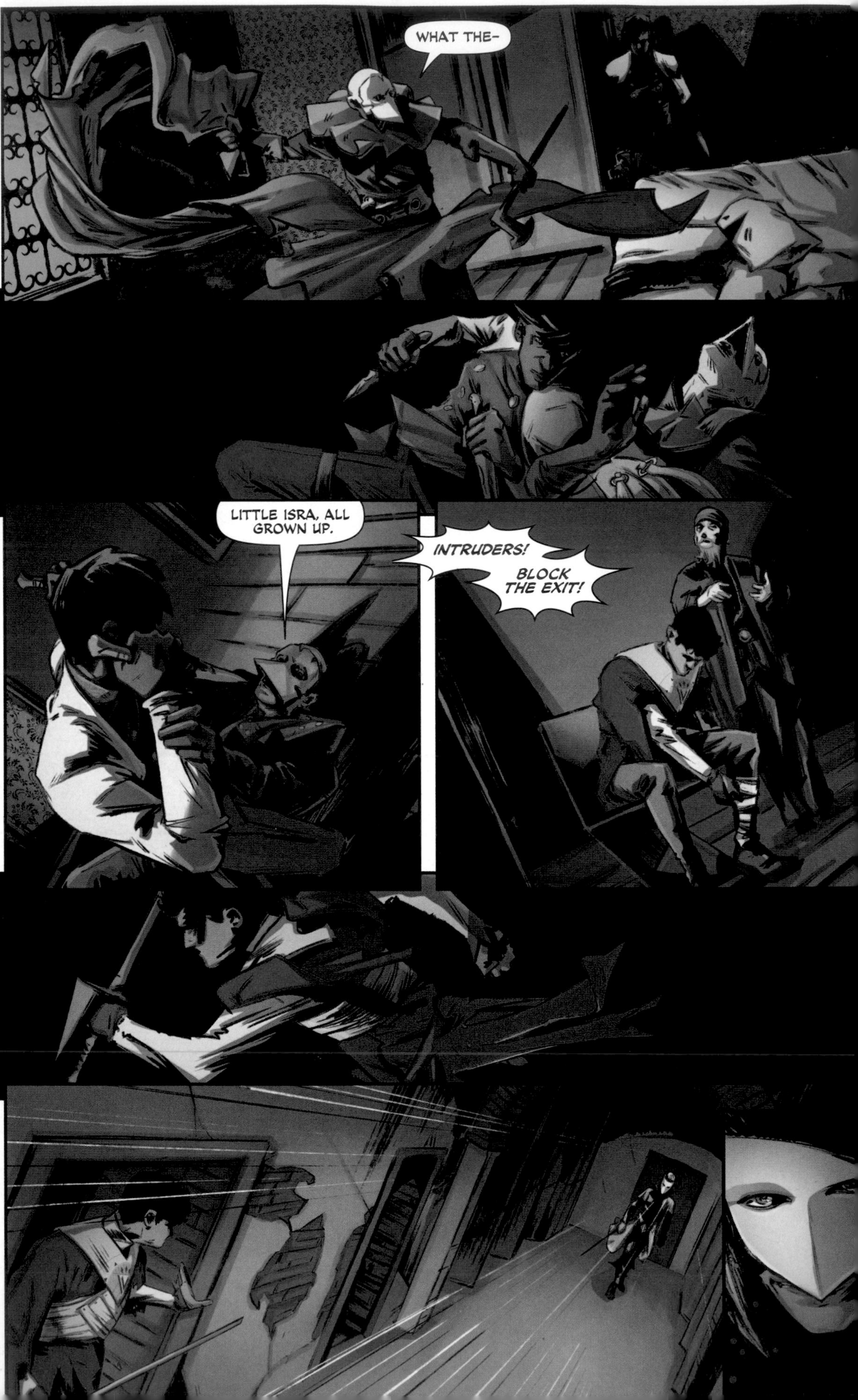
WHAT THE-
LITTLE ISRA, ALL GROWN UP.
INTRUDERS!
BLOCK THE EXIT!

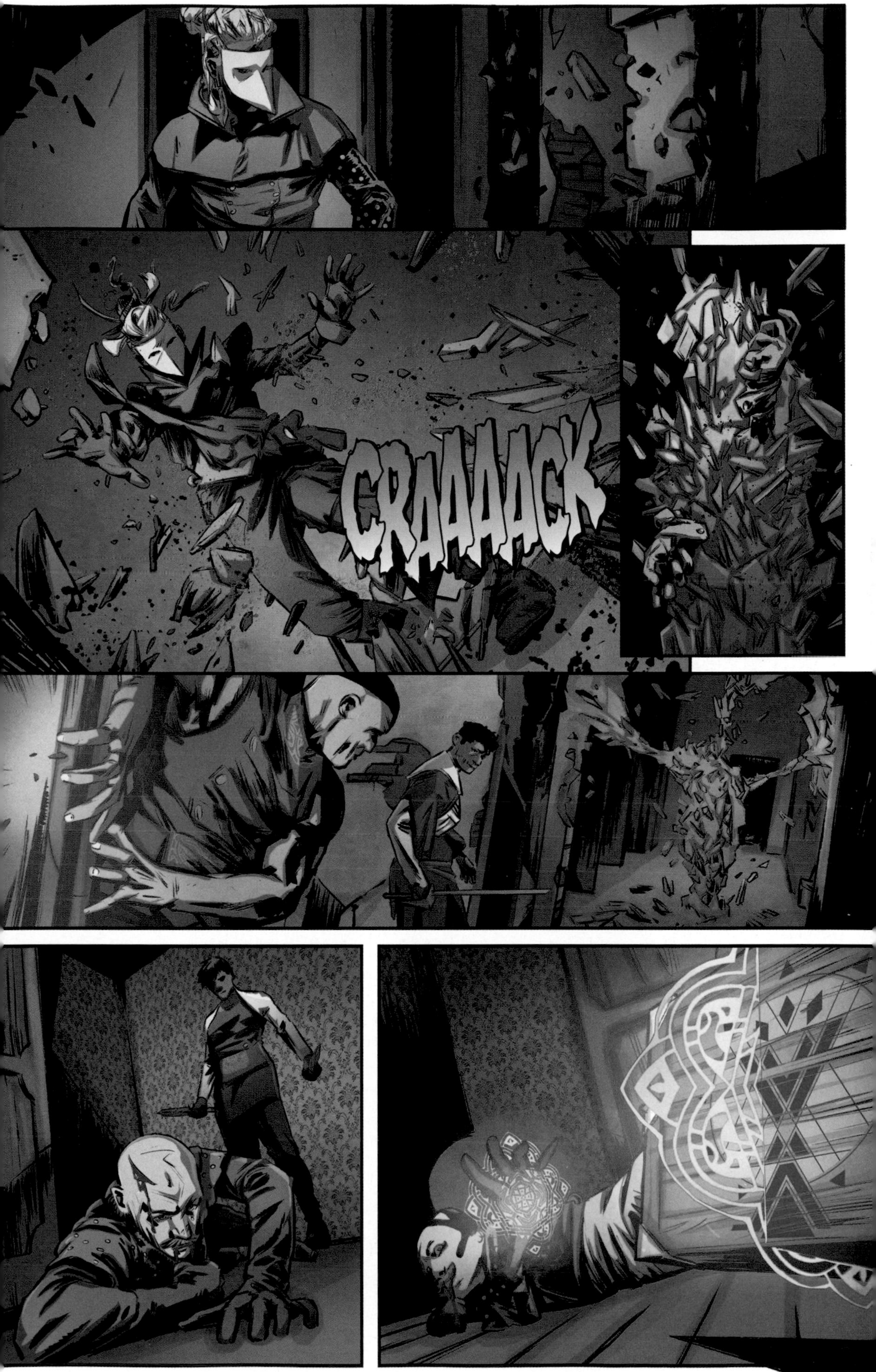
CRAAAACK

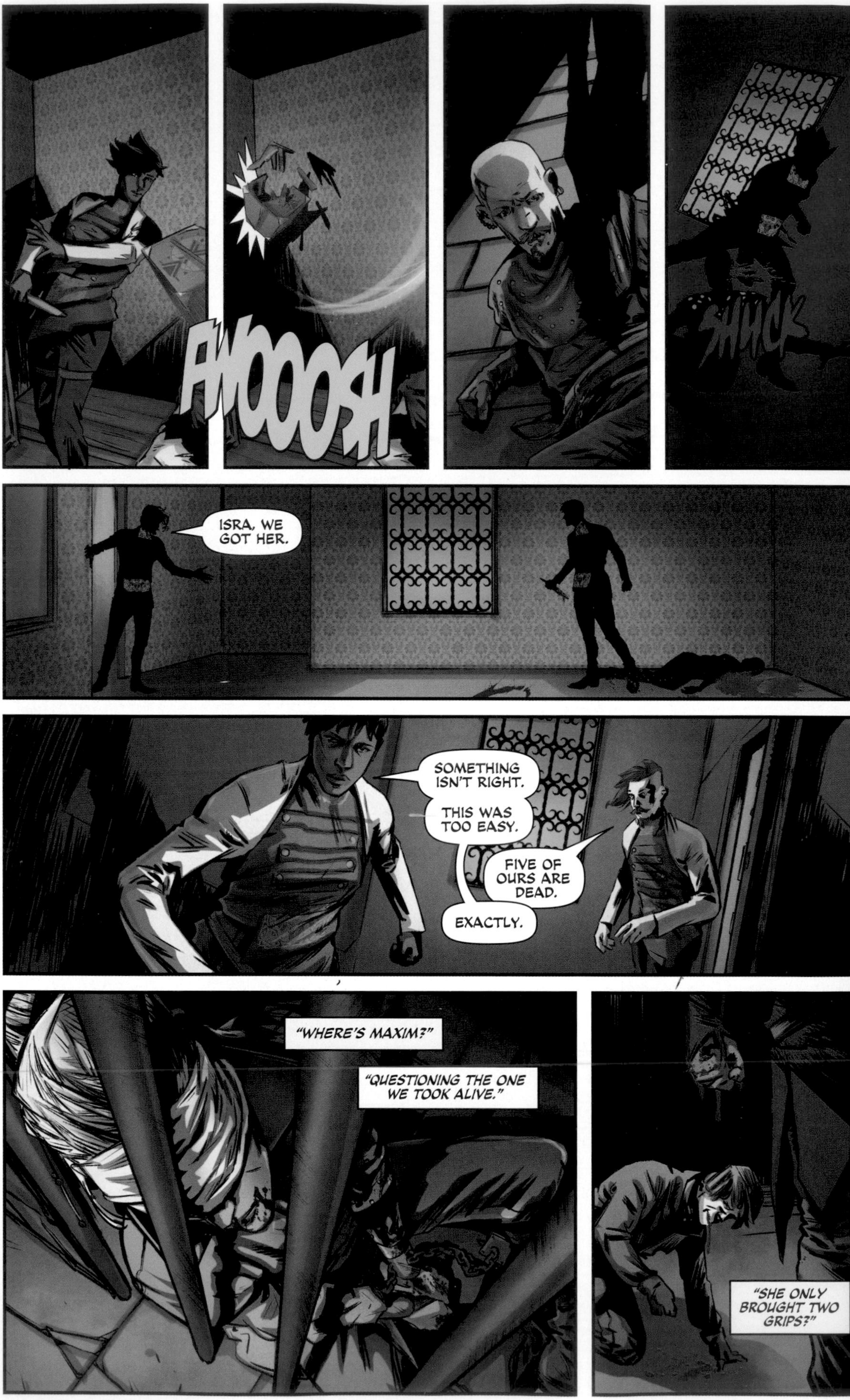
FWOOOSH
SHUCK
ISRA, WE GOT HER.
SOMETHING ISN'T RIGHT.
THIS WAS TOO EASY.
FIVE OF OURS ARE DEAD.
EXACTLY.
"WHERE'S MAXIM?"
"QUESTIONING THE ONE WE TOOK ALIVE."
"SHE ONLY BROUGHT TWO GRIPS?"

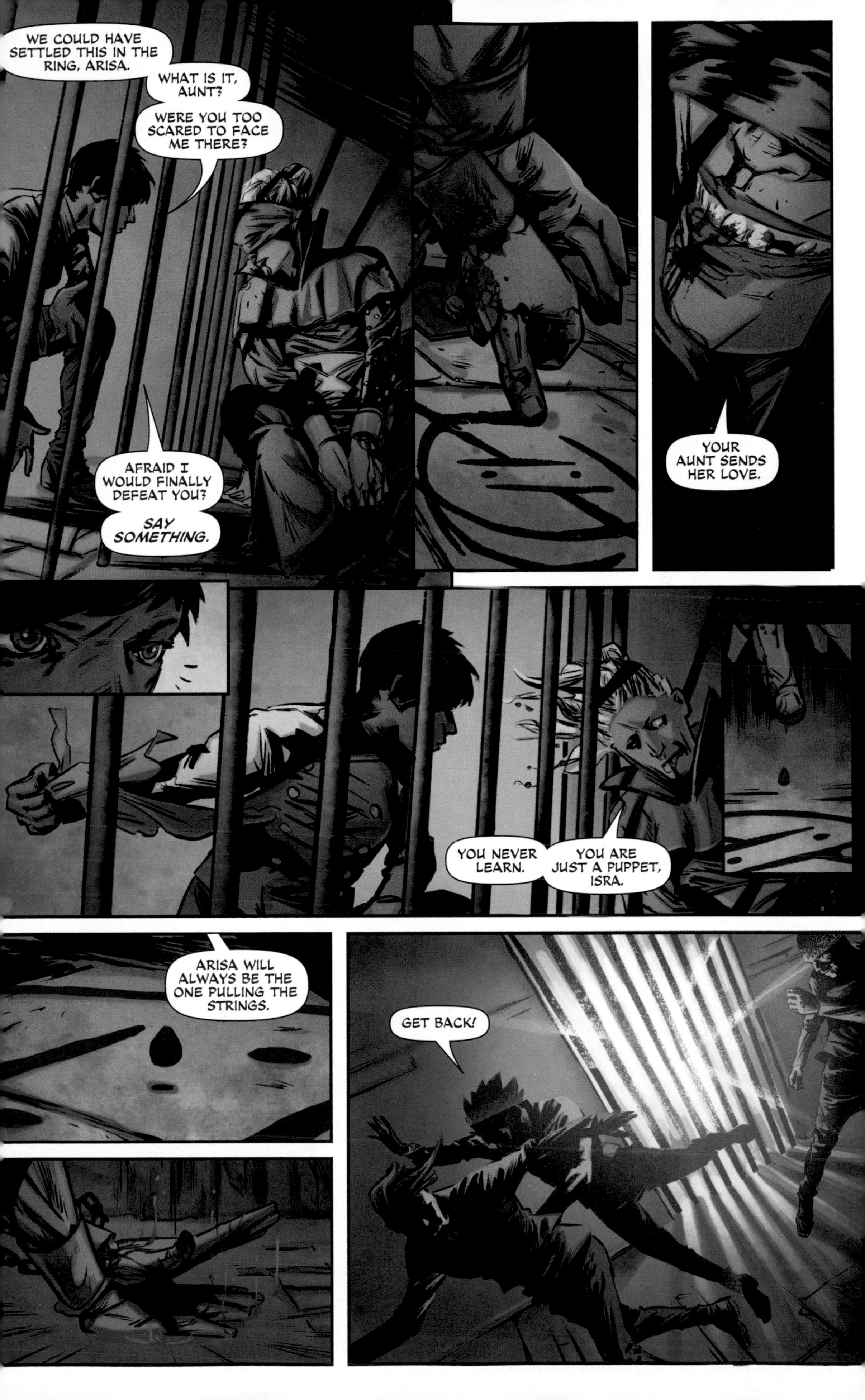
WE COULD HAVE SETTLED THIS IN THE RING, ARISA.
WHAT IS IT, AUNT?
WERE YOU TOO SCARED TO FACE ME THERE?
AFRAID I WOULD FINALLY DEFEAT YOU?
SAY SOMETHING.
YOUR AUNT SENDS HER LOVE.
YOU NEVER LEARN.
YOU ARE JUST A PUPPET, ISRA.
ARISA WILL ALWAYS BE THE ONE PULLING THE STRINGS.
GET BACK!

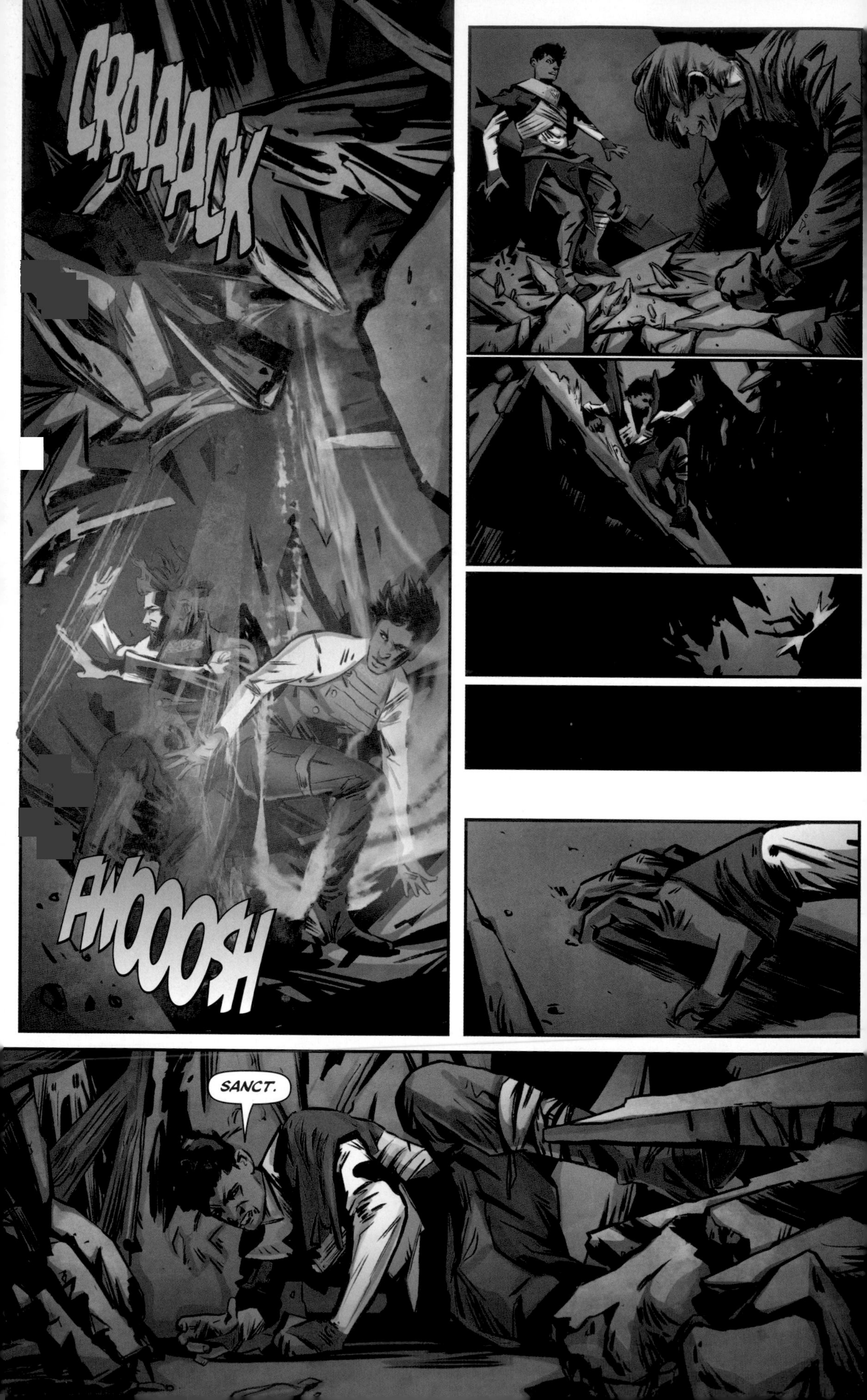
CRAAACK
FWOOOSH
SANCT.

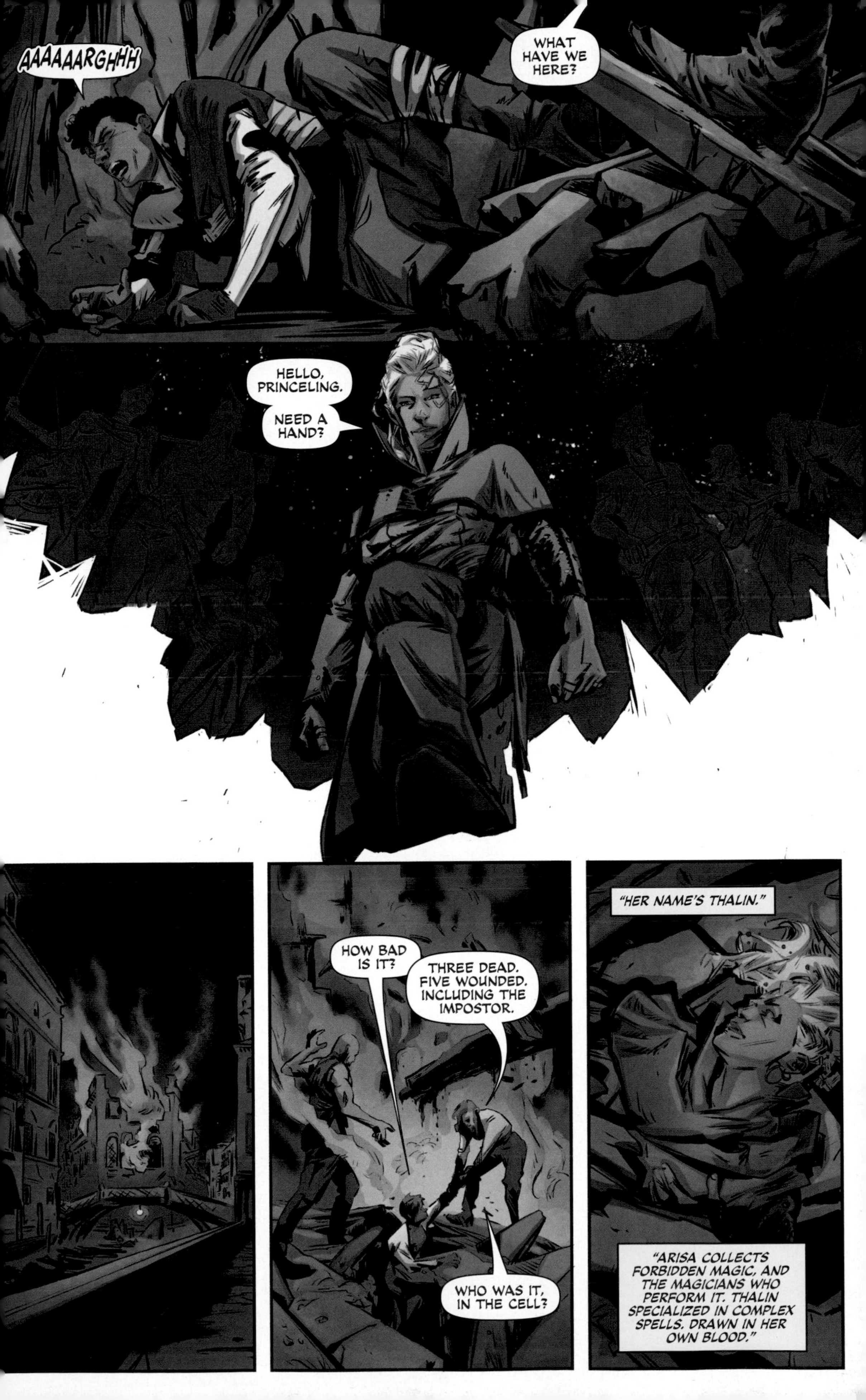
AAAAAARGHHH
WHAT HAVE WE HERE?
HELLO, PRINCELING.
NEED A HAND?
HOW BAD IS IT?
THREE DEAD. FIVE WOUNDED. INCLUDING THE IMPOSTOR.
WHO WAS IT, IN THE CELL?
"HER NAME'S THALIN."
"ARISA COLLECTS FORBIDDEN MAGIC, AND THE MAGICIANS WHO PERFORM IT. THALIN SPECIALIZED IN COMPLEX SPELLS. DRAWN IN HER OWN BLOOD."

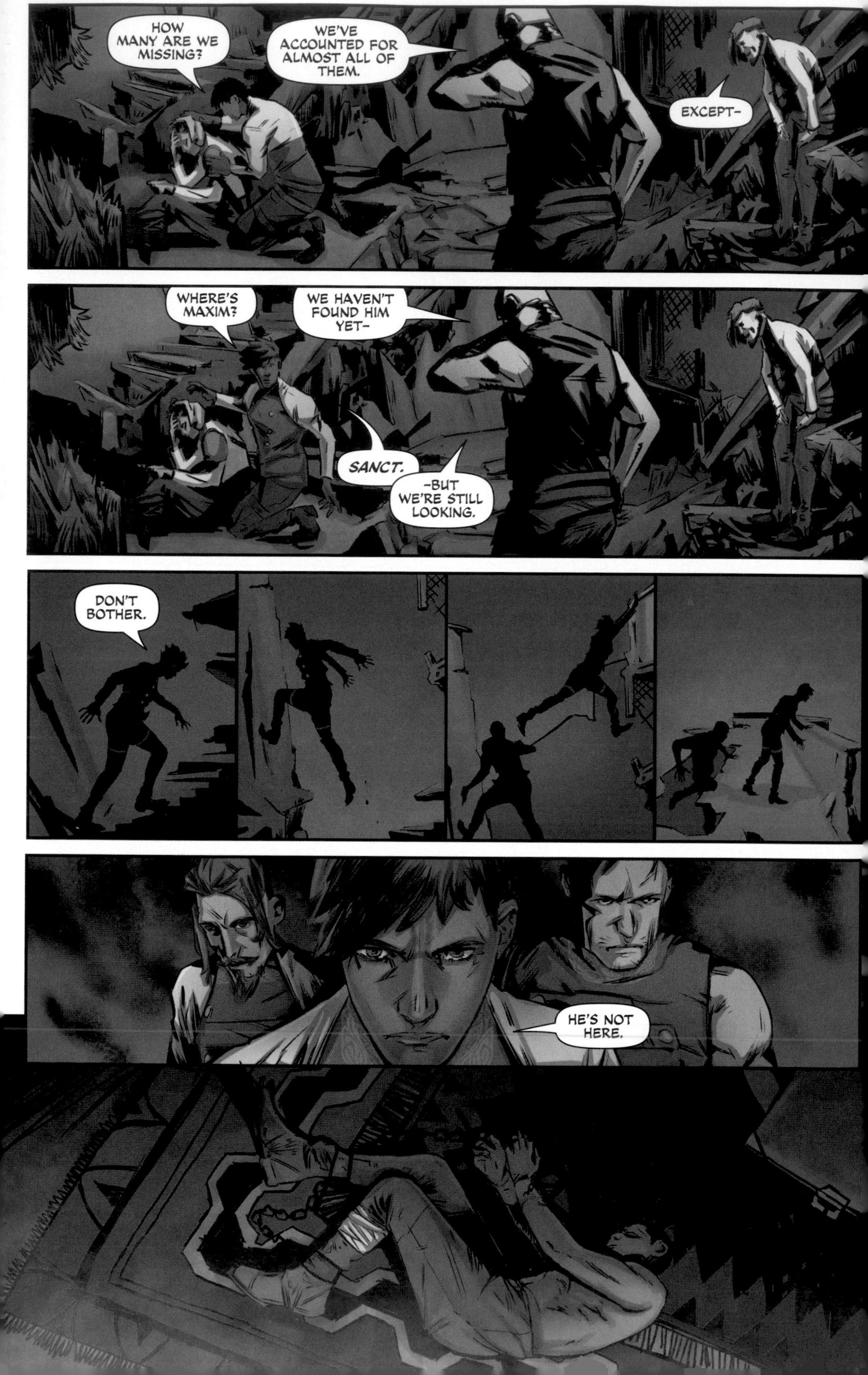
HOW MANY ARE WE MISSING?
WE'VE ACCOUNTED FOR ALMOST ALL OF THEM.
EXCEPT–
WHERE'S MAXIM?
WE HAVEN'T FOUND HIM YET–
SANCT.
–BUT WE'RE STILL LOOKING.
DON'T BOTHER.
HE'S NOT HERE.

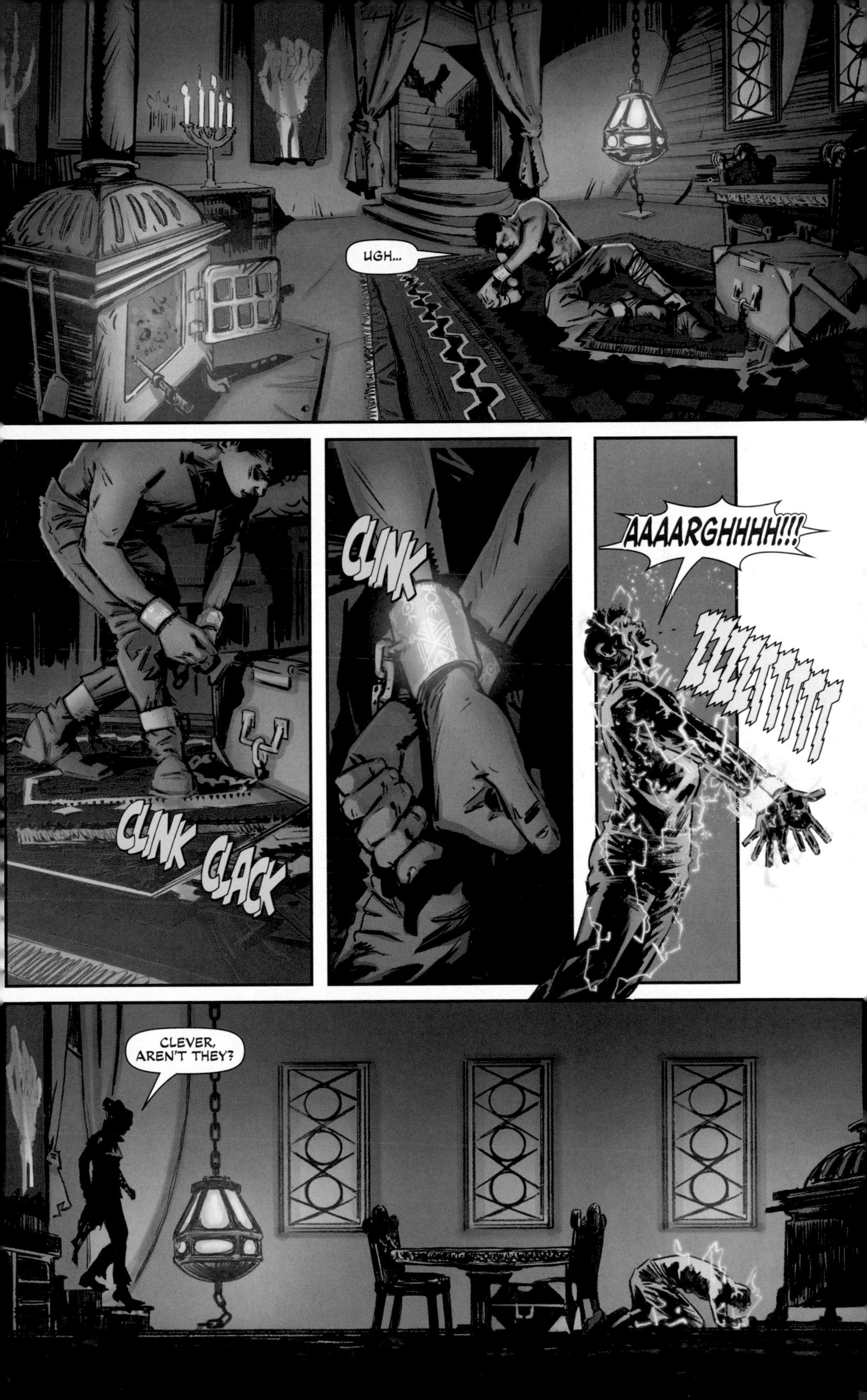
UGH...
CLINK
CLACK
CLINK
AAAARGHHHH!!!
ZZZZTTTTTT
CLEVER, AREN'T THEY?

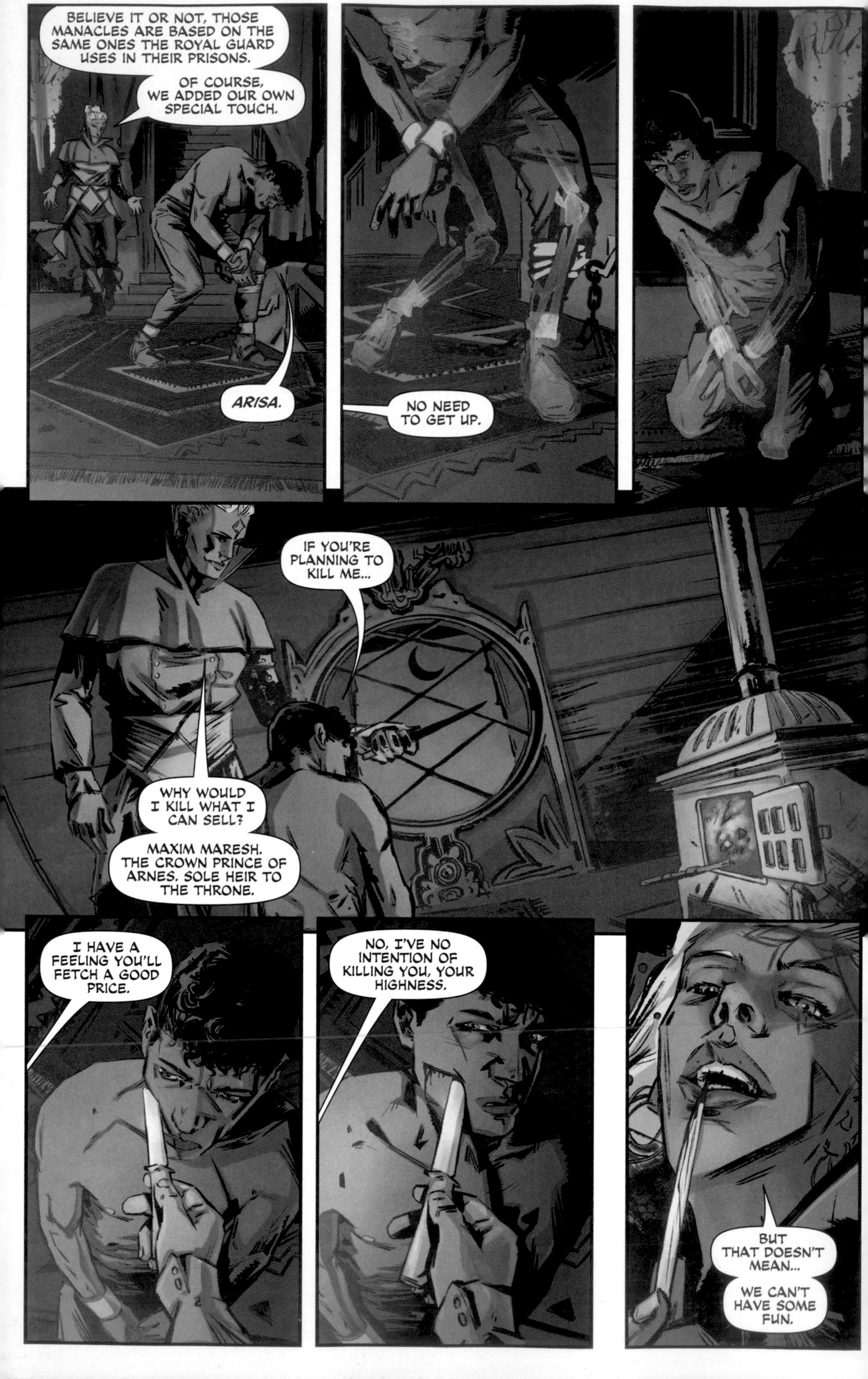
BELIEVE IT OR NOT, THOSE MANACLES ARE BASED ON THE SAME ONES THE ROYAL GUARD USES IN THEIR PRISONS.
OF COURSE, WE ADDED OUR OWN SPECIAL TOUCH.
ARISA.
NO NEED TO GET UP.
IF YOU'RE PLANNING TO KILL ME...
WHY WOULD I KILL WHAT I CAN SELL?
MAXIM MARESH. THE CROWN PRINCE OF ARNES. SOLE HEIR TO THE THRONE.
I HAVE A FEELING YOU'LL FETCH A GOOD PRICE.
NO, I'VE NO INTENTION OF KILLING YOU, YOUR HIGHNESS.
BUT THAT DOESN'T MEAN...
WE CAN'T HAVE SOME FUN.

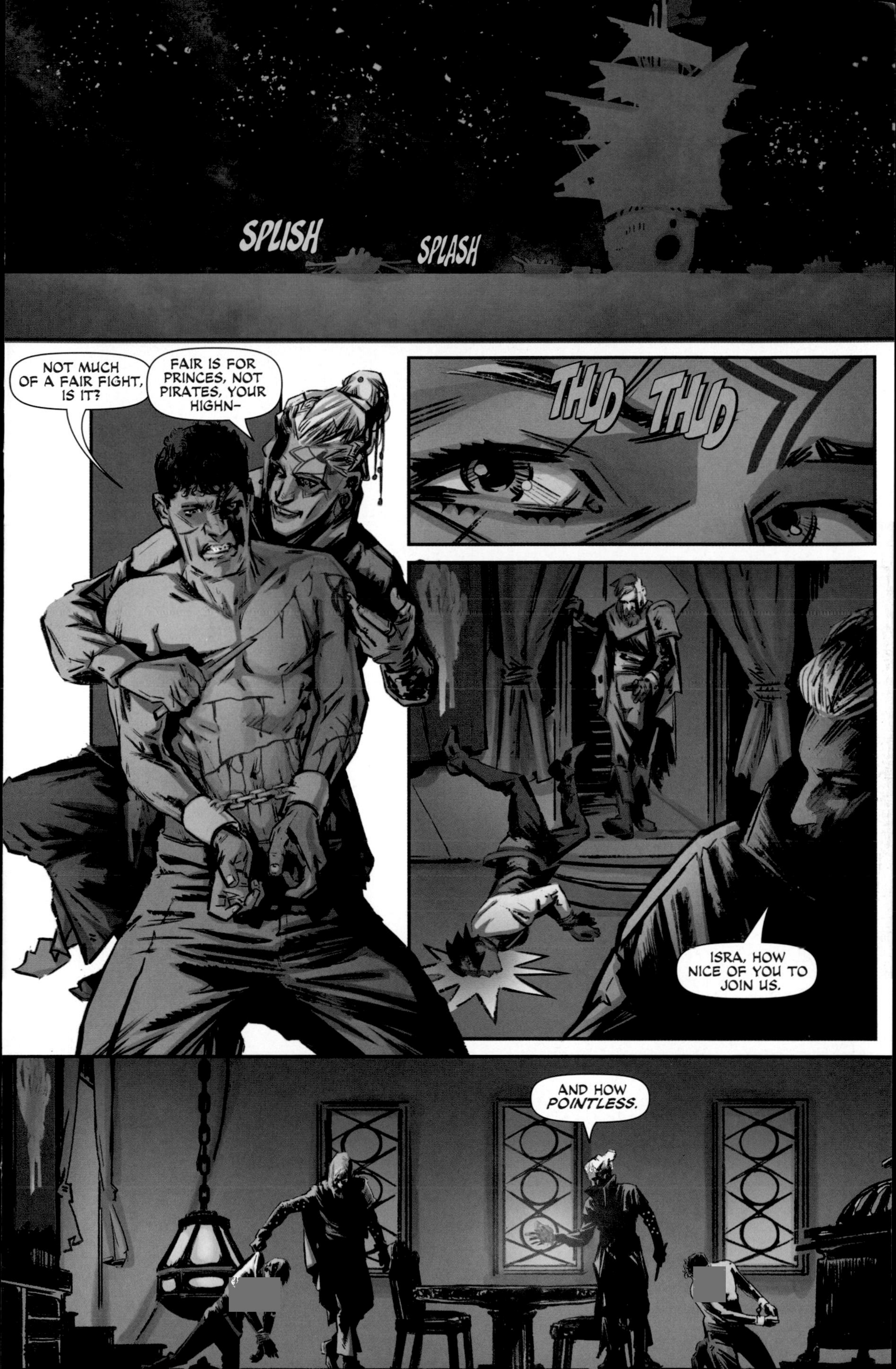
SPLISH
SPLASH
NOT MUCH OF A FAIR FIGHT, IS IT?
FAIR IS FOR PRINCES, NOT PIRATES, YOUR HIGHN-
THUD THUD
ISRA, HOW NICE OF YOU TO JOIN US.
AND HOW *POINTLESS*.

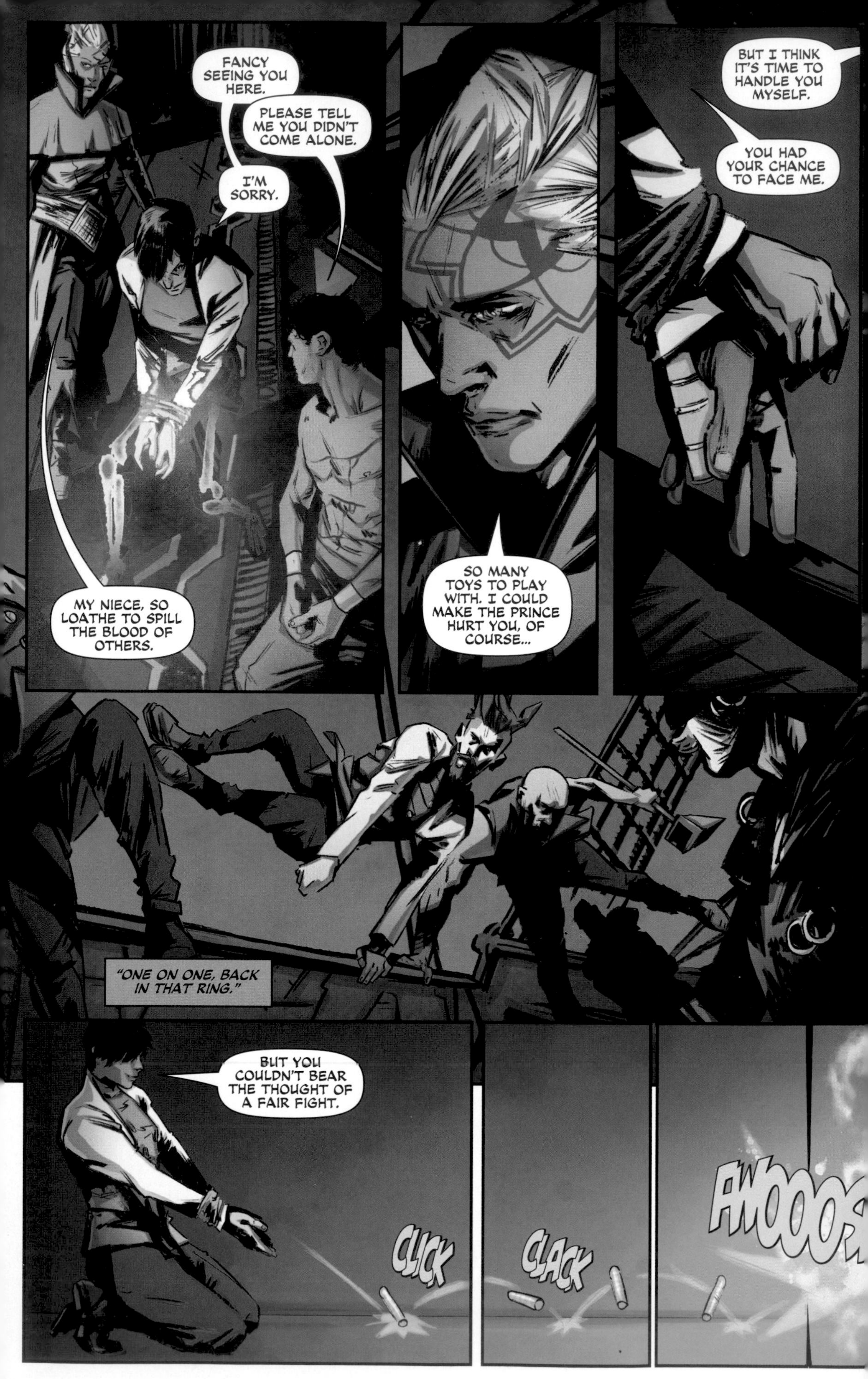
FANCY SEEING YOU HERE.
PLEASE TELL ME YOU DIDN'T COME ALONE.
I'M SORRY.
MY NIECE, SO LOATHE TO SPILL THE BLOOD OF OTHERS.
SO MANY TOYS TO PLAY WITH. I COULD MAKE THE PRINCE HURT YOU, OF COURSE...
BUT I THINK IT'S TIME TO HANDLE YOU MYSELF.
YOU HAD YOUR CHANCE TO FACE ME.
"ONE ON ONE, BACK IN THAT RING."
BUT YOU COULDN'T BEAR THE THOUGHT OF A FAIR FIGHT.
CLICK
CLACK

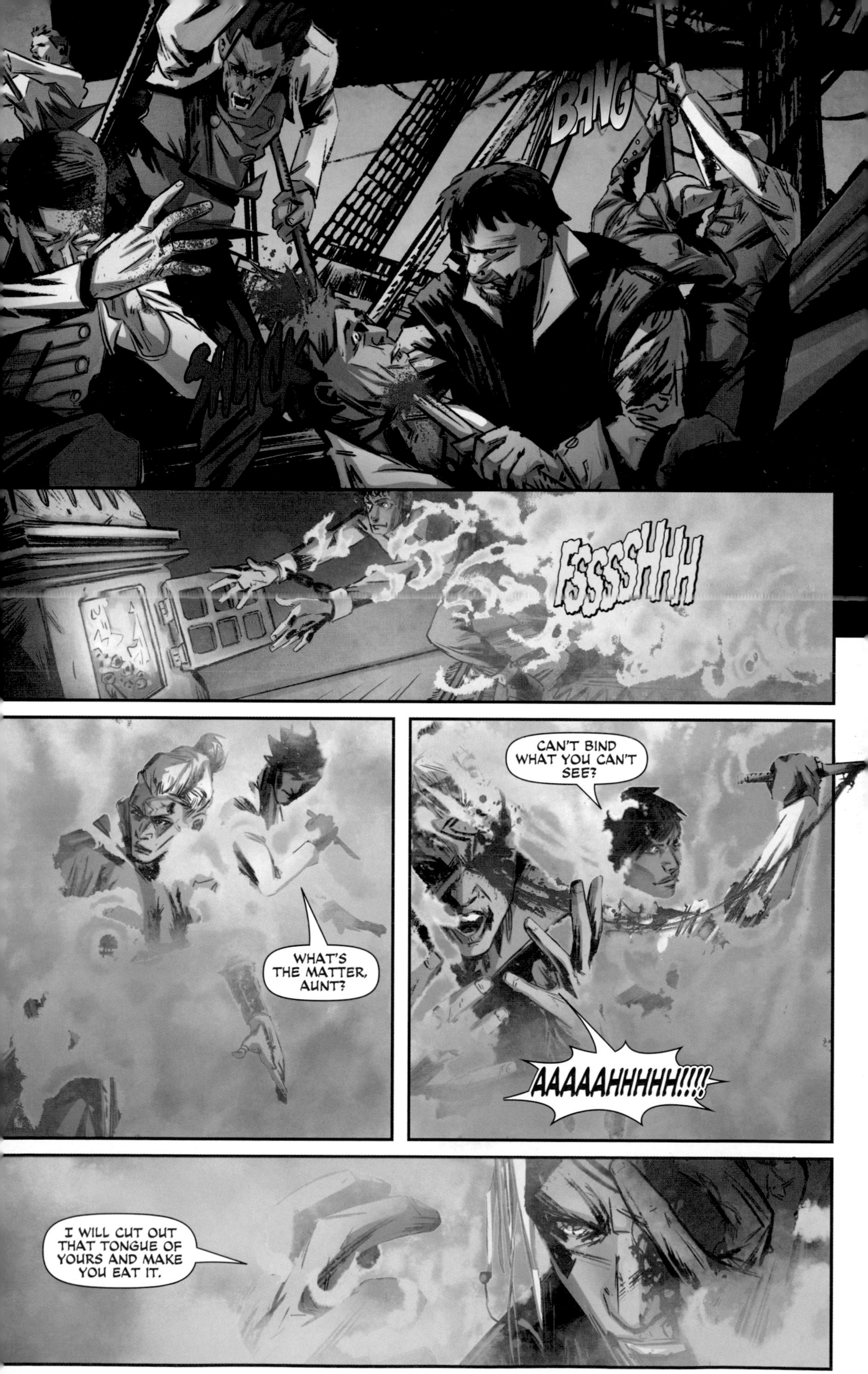
BANG
FSSSSHHH
WHAT'S THE MATTER, AUNT?
CAN'T BIND WHAT YOU CAN'T SEE?
AAAAAHHHHH!!!!
I WILL CUT OUT THAT TONGUE OF YOURS AND MAKE YOU EAT IT.

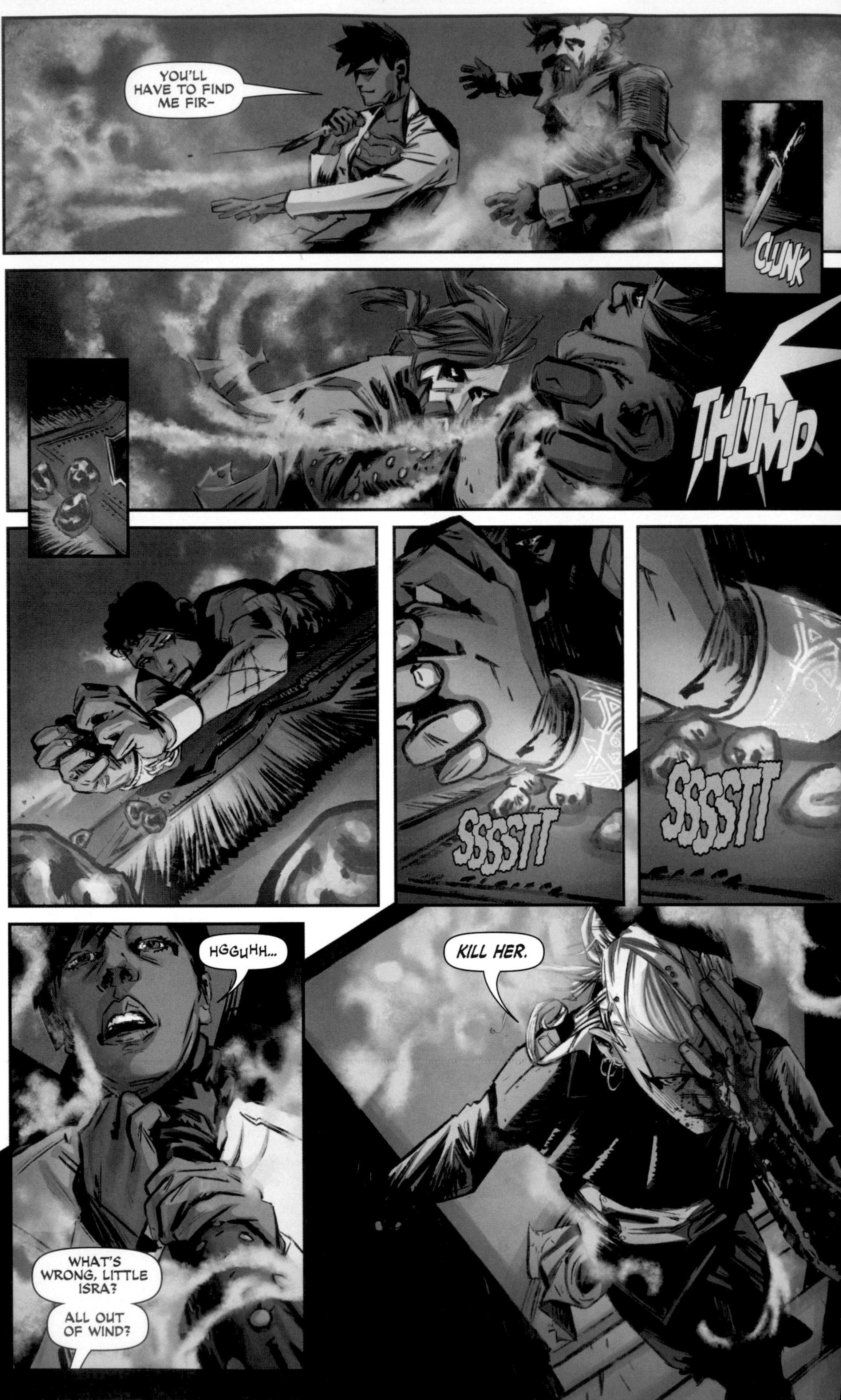
YOU'LL HAVE TO FIND ME FIR-
CLUNK
THUMP
SSSSTT
SSSSTT
HGGUHH...
KILL HER.
WHAT'S WRONG, LITTLE ISRA?
ALL OUT OF WIND?

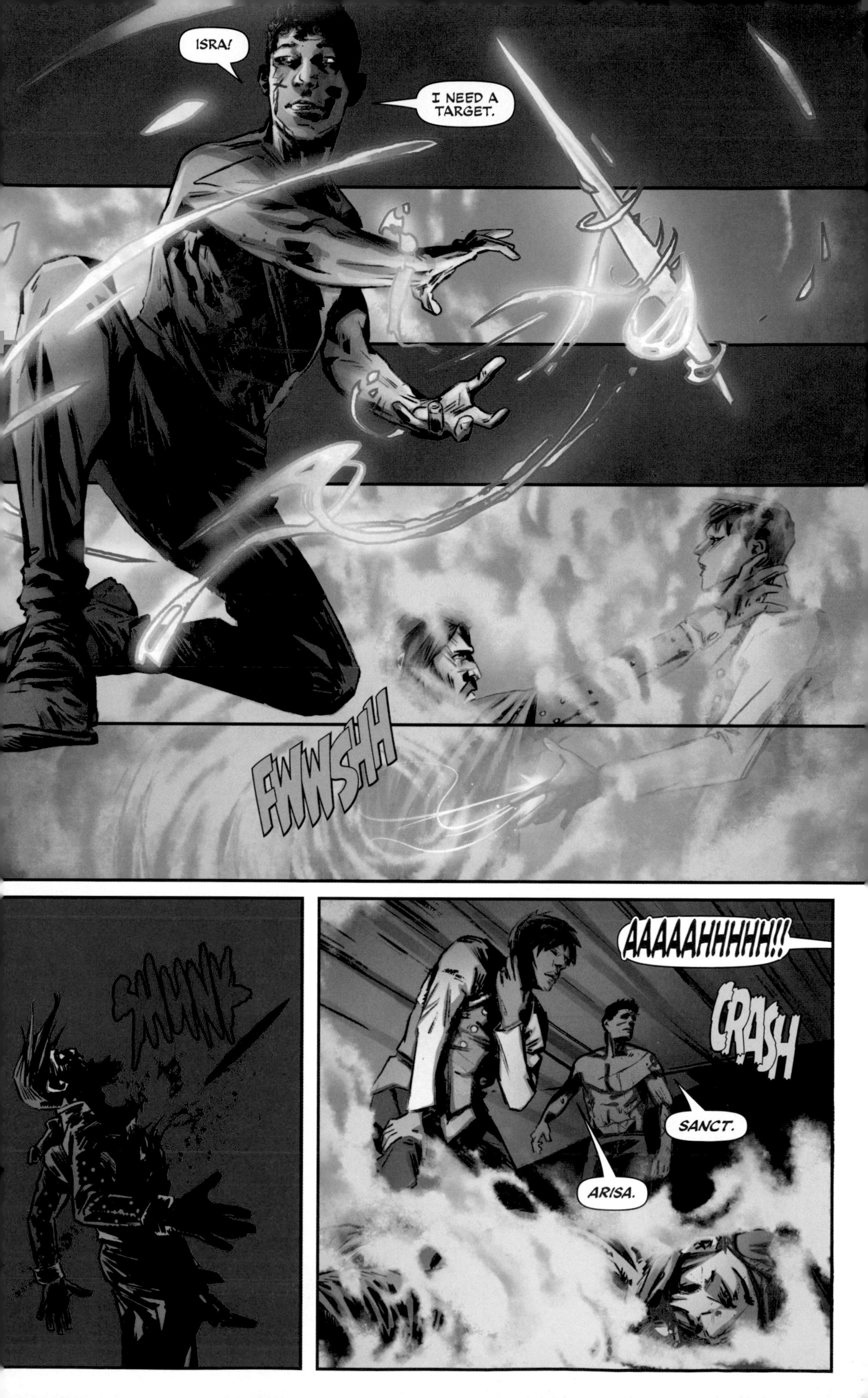
ISRA!
I NEED A TARGET.
FWWSHH
SHUNK
AAAAHHHHH!!
CRASH
SANCT.
ARISA.

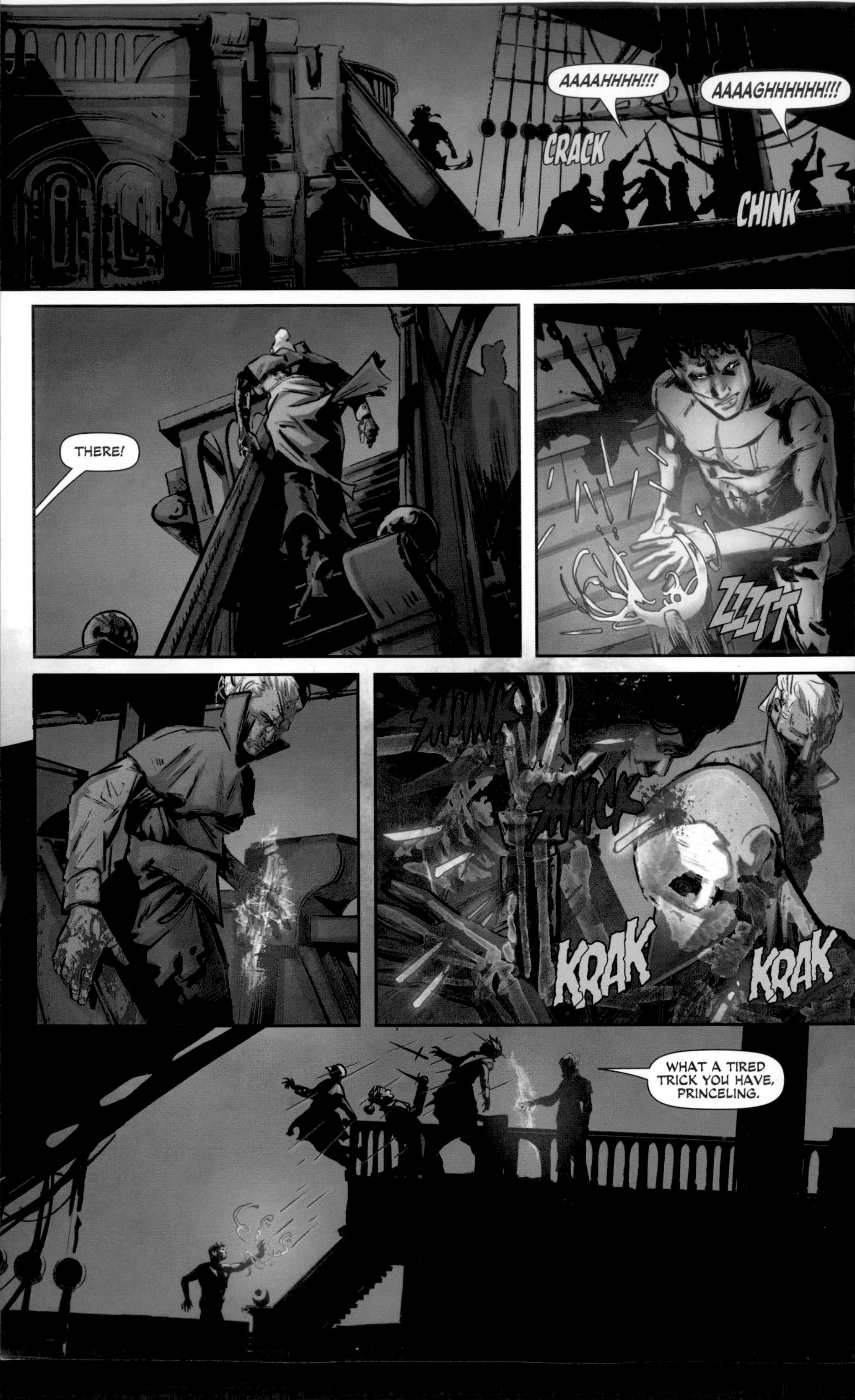

AAAAHHHH!!!
AAAAGHHHHHH!!!
CRACK
CHINK
THERE!
ZZZTT
SHUNK
SHACK
KRAK
KRAK
WHAT A TIRED TRICK YOU HAVE, PRINCELING.

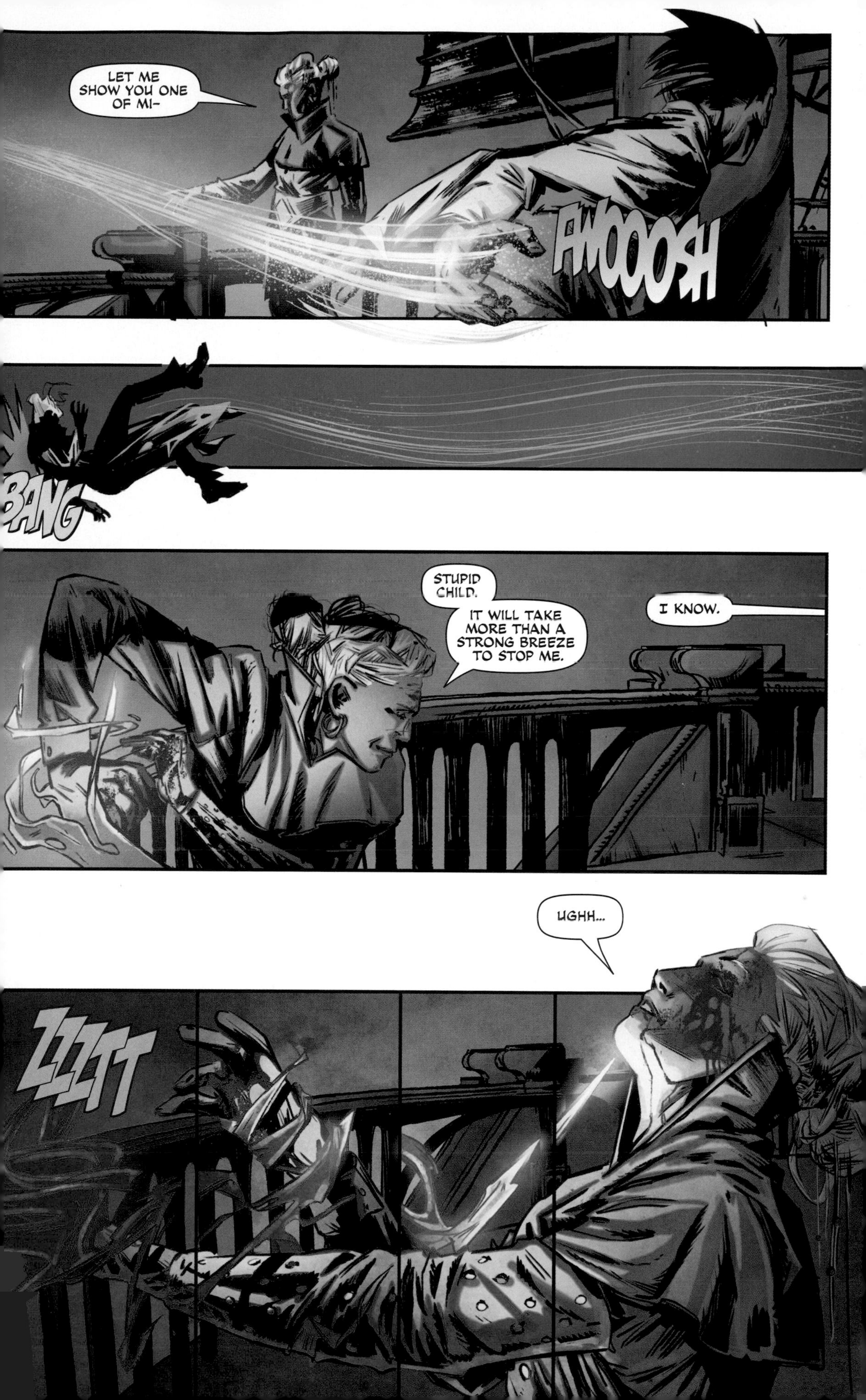
LET ME SHOW YOU ONE OF MI-
FWOOOSH
BANG
STUPID CHILD.
IT WILL TAKE MORE THAN A STRONG BREEZE TO STOP ME.
I KNOW.
UGHH...
ZZZTT

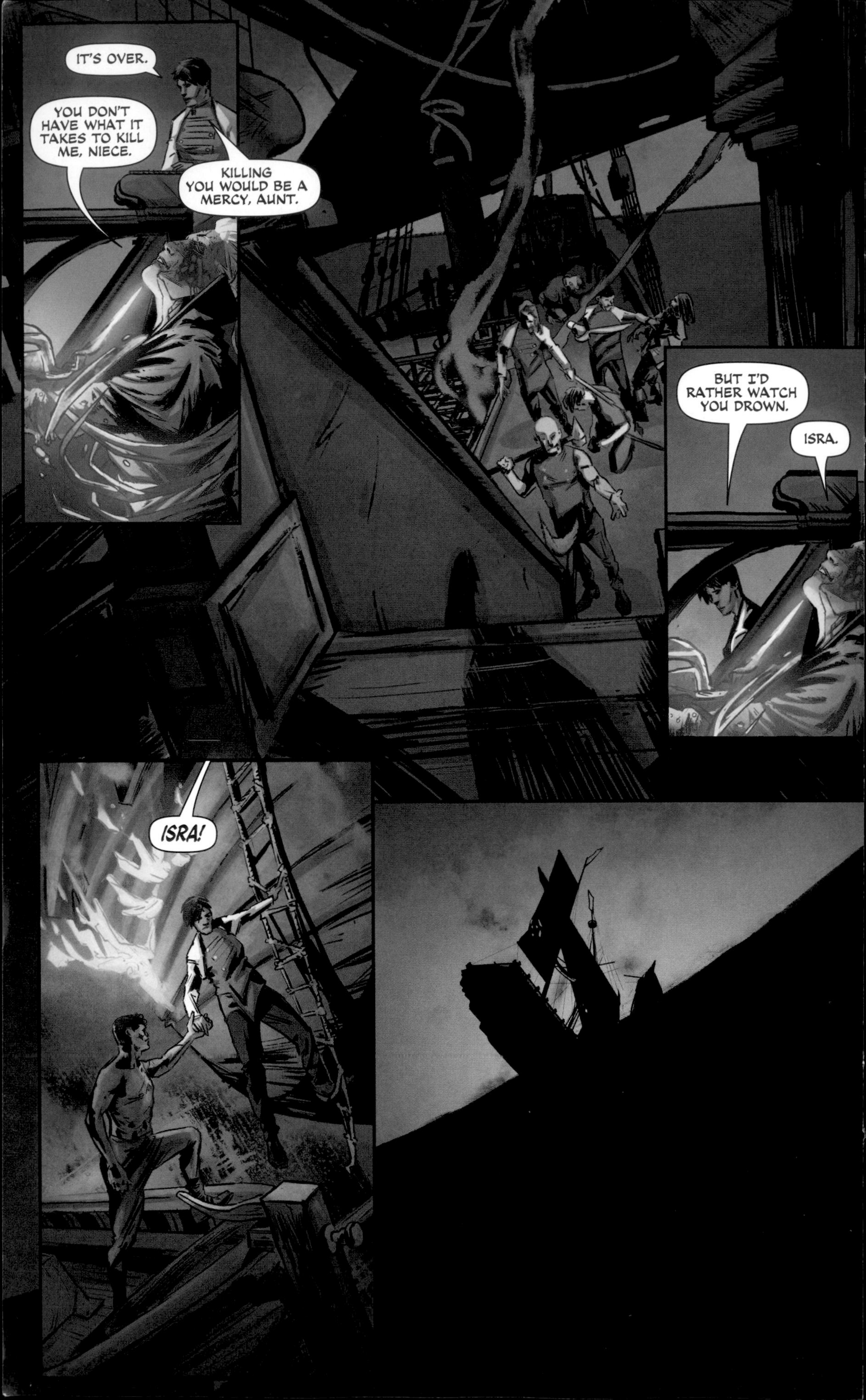
IT'S OVER.
YOU DON'T HAVE WHAT IT TAKES TO KILL ME, NIECE.
KILLING YOU WOULD BE A MERCY, AUNT.
BUT I'D RATHER WATCH YOU DROWN.
ISRA.
ISRA!

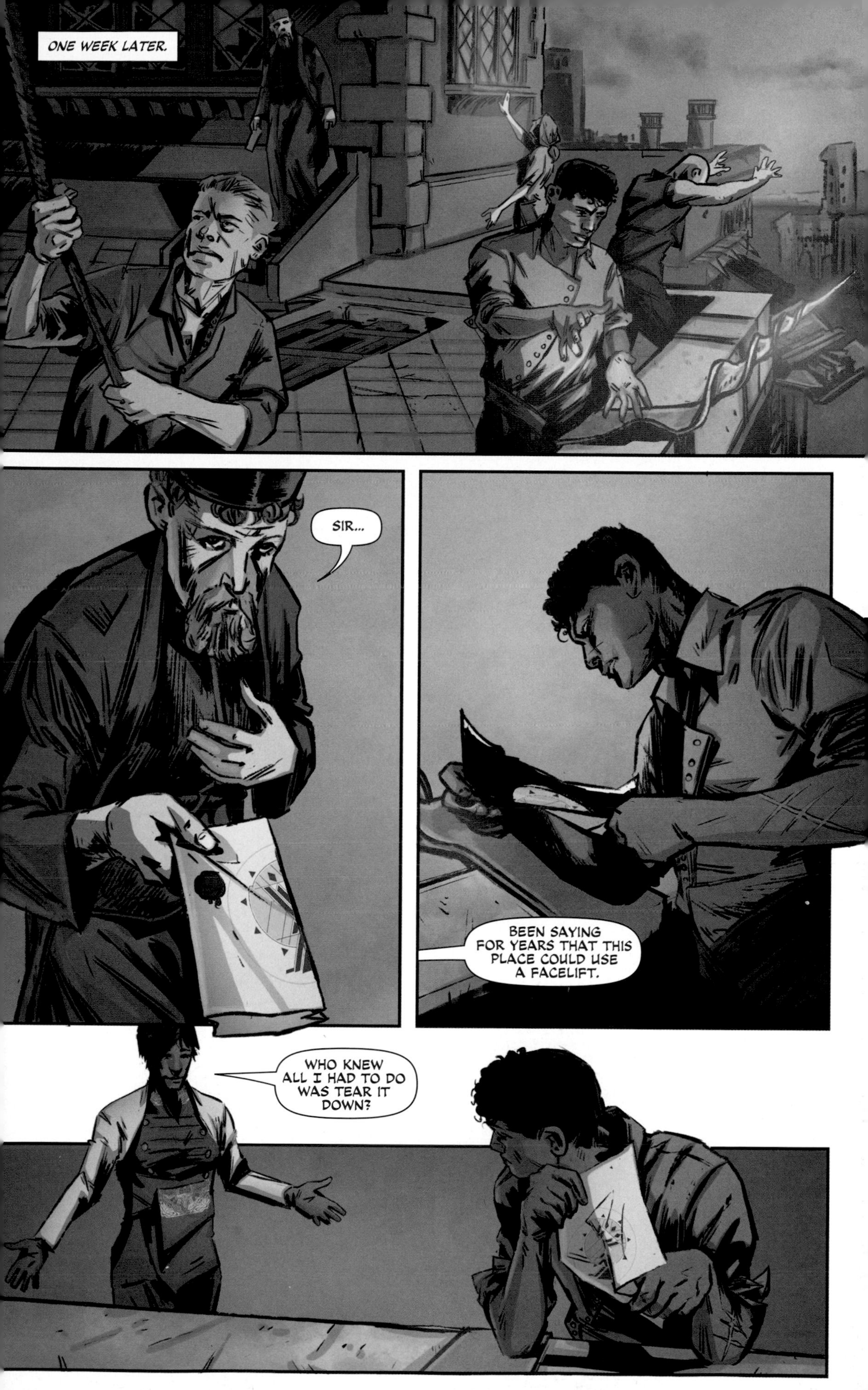
ONE WEEK LATER.
SIR...
BEEN SAYING FOR YEARS THAT THIS PLACE COULD USE A FACELIFT.
WHO KNEW ALL I HAD TO DO WAS TEAR IT DOWN?

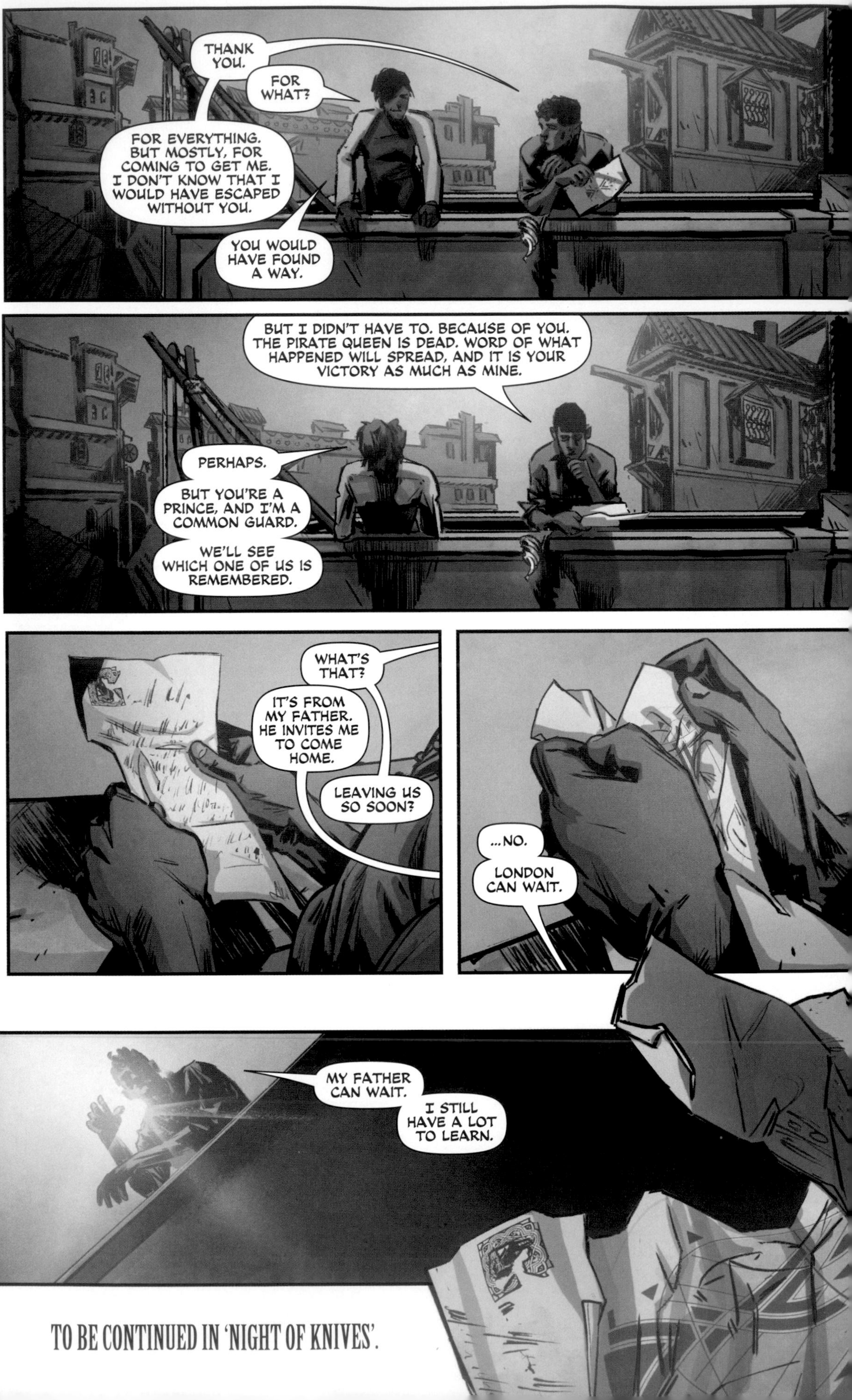
THANK YOU.
FOR WHAT?
FOR EVERYTHING. BUT MOSTLY, FOR COMING TO GET ME. I DON'T KNOW THAT I WOULD HAVE ESCAPED WITHOUT YOU.
YOU WOULD HAVE FOUND A WAY.
BUT I DIDN'T HAVE TO. BECAUSE OF YOU. THE PIRATE QUEEN IS DEAD. WORD OF WHAT HAPPENED WILL SPREAD, AND IT IS YOUR VICTORY AS MUCH AS MINE.
PERHAPS.
BUT YOU'RE A PRINCE, AND I'M A COMMON GUARD.
WE'LL SEE WHICH ONE OF US IS REMEMBERED.
WHAT'S THAT?
IT'S FROM MY FATHER. HE INVITES ME TO COME HOME.
LEAVING US SO SOON?
...NO.
LONDON CAN WAIT.
MY FATHER CAN WAIT.
I STILL HAVE A LOT TO LEARN.

TO BE CONTINUED IN 'NIGHT OF KNIVES'.

CREATOR BIOS

V. E. SCHWAB

Victoria "V.E." Schwab is the #1 NYT, USA, and Indie-bestselling author of more than a dozen books, including *Vicious*, the *Shades of Magic* series, and *This Savage Song*. Her work has received critical acclaim, been featured by EW and the New York Times, been translated into more than a dozen languages, and has been optioned for TV and Film. The Independent calls her the "natural successor to Diana Wynne Jones" and touts her "enviable, almost Gaimanesque ability to switch between styles, genres, and tones."

...

ANDREA OLIMPIERI

Andrea is an up and coming comic book artist based out of Italy. He has been instrumental in creating the visual aesthetic for the *Shades of Magic* comic series. He has also contributed artwork to a number of high-profile titles, including *Monstri*, *True Blood*, and *Dishonored*.

...

ENRICA EREN ANGIOLINI

A skilled colorist and an accomplished fencer, Enrica has colored for books such as *Doctor Who: The Thirteenth Doctor*, *Warhammer 40,000*, *Terminator*, and *The Order of the Forge*. She lives and works in Rome, Italy.

...

ROB STEEN

Rob Steen is an experienced letterer, whose skilled calligraphy has enlivened the works of many publishers, from *Wolverine and the X-Men*, to *Arrowsmith* and *Astro City*, *Harbinger* and *Bloodshot*, *Rivers of London* and *Warhammer 40,000*.

AN INTERVIEW WITH
V. E. SCHWAB

Even though we are just starting, how did you find writing your first comic book? Was there anything you found hard or strange about the process?
VES Honestly, it's been an incredible process. Publishing novels takes a village, but the writing process is often solitary. Getting to be involved in a project like this, where the teamwork and collaboration starts on page one—it's wonderful. Getting to describe a shot, and then see Andrea's interpretation of it, getting to see the transmutation of one art form into another, is such a thrill.

What made you want to write a comic book series, was this something you had planned on doing for a long time?
VES I've been a fan of comics for years—from Marvel and DC staples to *Saga, Monstress, Wicked + the Divine* more recently—and I've wanted to write a comic for quite a while now. The Shades of Magic world was a

perfect fit, thanks to the intensively visual aspects of the magic. But truth be told, I've always been drawn to the visual aspect of storytelling. When I first started writing, I assumed I'd go into screenplays, because I so desperately wanted to see the stories played out in a visual media. It turns out comics is a perfect manifestation of that desire. I get to define the parameters of the story, while also leaving room for the artists interpretations.

What has been your favorite thing so far about the process?
VES Definitely seeing the artwork, watching a couple lines of art direction turn into something so much more powerful.

Any favourite comics or comics writers?
VES I'm a huge fan of Matt Fraction, Marjorie Liu, Al Ewing, Brian K. Vaughan, Kelly Sue DeConnick, Kieron Gillen (and Jamie McKelvie—feel like the two can't be separated for *The Wicked + The Divine*, since half t glory is in the art).

The Steel Prince is a story that's been stewing for a while. Is there a specia reason for this story that you thoug it was best told through comics?
VES I've always wanted to see the Shades of Magic world portrayed through a visual medium, but rather than just translate the existing story,

> "I THOUGHT COMICS WOULD BE A PERFECT WAY TO TELL SOME OF THE STORIES THAT ARE PERHAPS TANGENTIAL TO THE MAIN TRILOGY."

I thought comics would be a perfect way to tell some of the stories that are perhaps tangential to the main trilogy. Stories that center characters and narratives and arcs that I hadn't been able to fully explore in the books, but that lived fully in my brain.

What more can we learn about the world of Shades of Magic through *The Steel Prince*? Or what does it add to the book series canon?
VES In addition to getting to travel beyond Red London—the series' central setting—and explore some as-of-yet unseen forms of magic, *Steel Prince* will delve into the life of the king—and often antagonist—Maxim Maresh, before he ever took the throne. I'm hoping it provides some insight into his character, through the events that made him the man he was in Shades of Magic.

Is there a favorite character you want to introduce (or reintroduce) your readers to – and why?
VES The character I'm most excited to introduce to readers is Maxim's primary ally, Isra. She is given so little page-time in *A Conjuring of Light* (that book had a LOT of ground to cover) where she's introduced only as the head of Maxim's city guard. But I'm over the moon to be able to show this particular soldier in all her glory. Young, fierce, desperate to prove herself, Isra comes with a past that's determined to catch up with her.

Since *The Steel Prince* is a telling of King Maxim's background story, are there any other characters from the original trilogy that you'd also like to give the same treatment if given the opportunity?
VES I'd LOVE to write more about Maris, the ancient female captain at the helm of the Floating Market, a vault ship designed to house and protect some of the world's most dangerous magic ●

CHARACTER BREAKDOWN

DESIGNS: ANDREA OLIMPIERI

SCRIPT EXTRACTS: V.E.SCHWAB

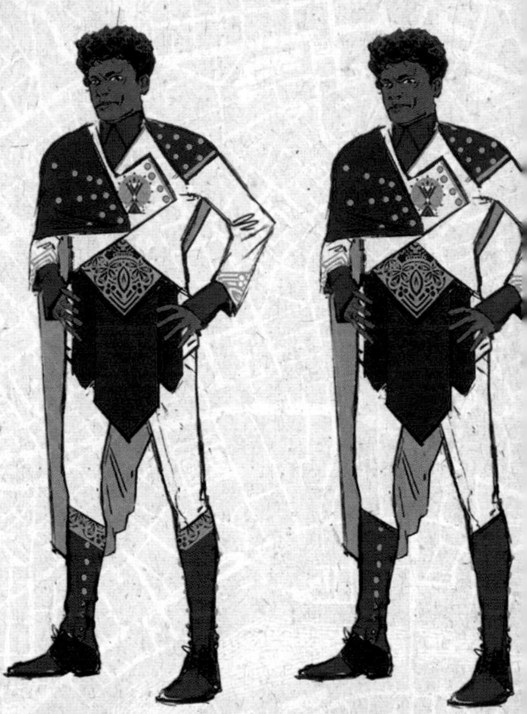

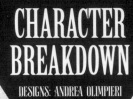

MAXIM MARESH

"Maxim Maresh, early 20s, arrogant, untested. Never without a piece of metal in hand, whether a coin, a ring, or an ornament. A handsome young man with a haughty expression and regal attire."

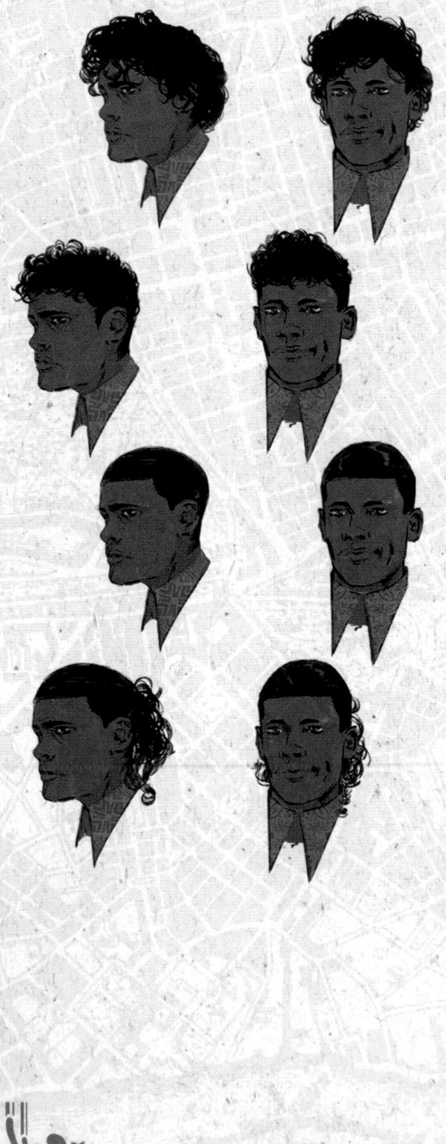

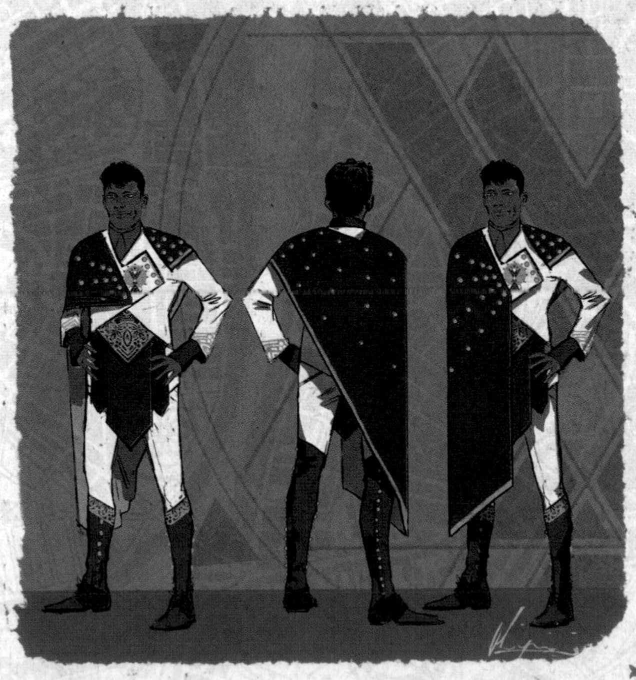

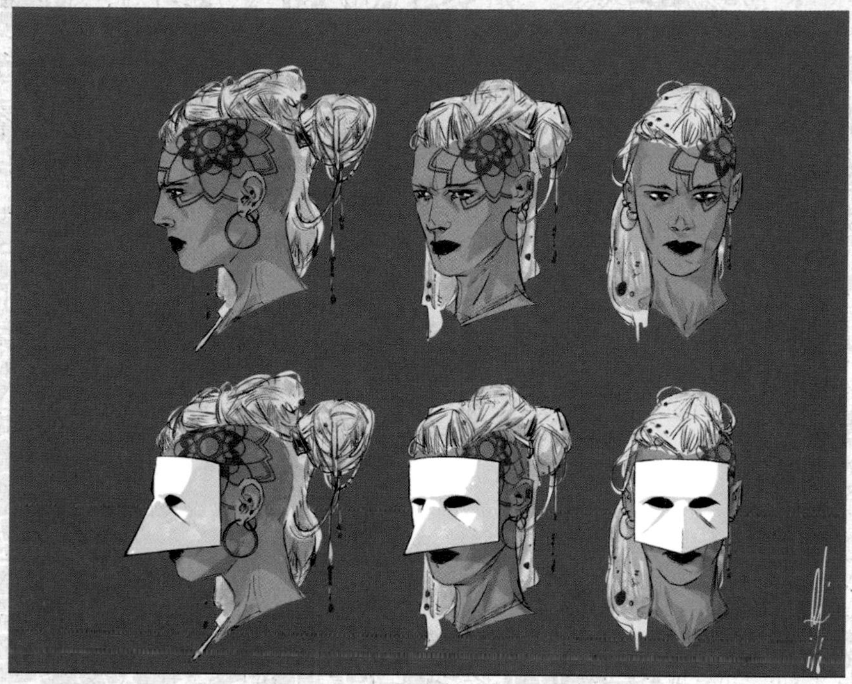

ARISA, THE PIRATE QUEEN

"Our first real glimpse of the Pirate Queen. Arisa stands, hands braced on the ship's rail, her silver hair in a Viking nest of braids, the top half of her face hidden behind a mask."

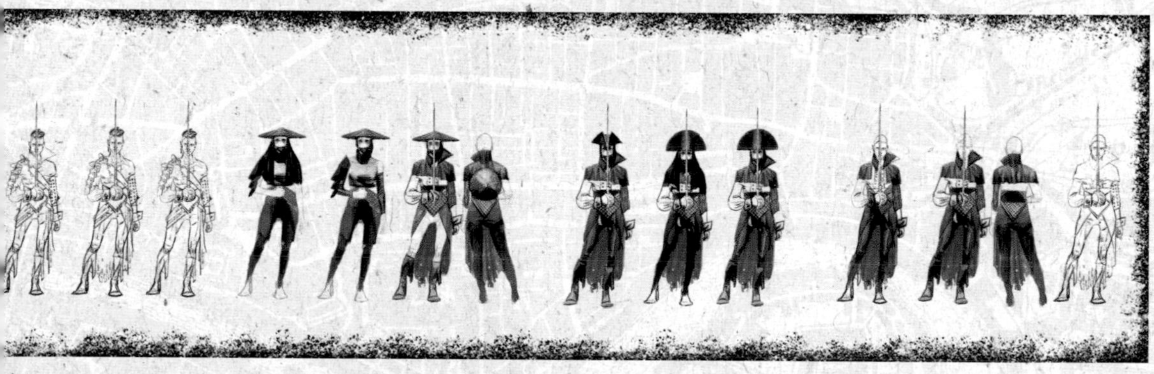

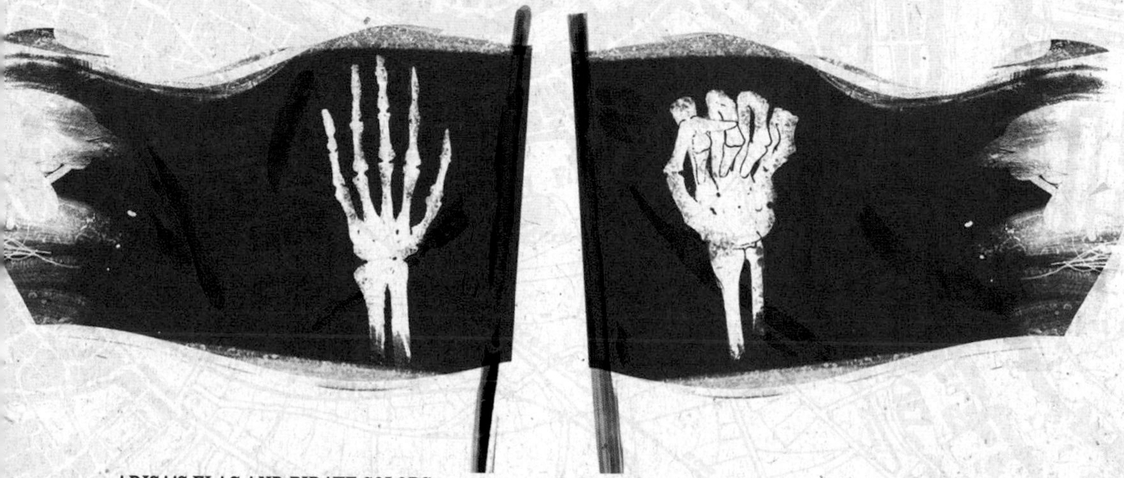

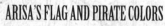

ARISA'S FLAG AND PIRATE COLORS

"A flag whipping in the night breeze. A white skeleton hand against a blood red ground. It changes with the wind. One side an open hand, the other, a closed fist."

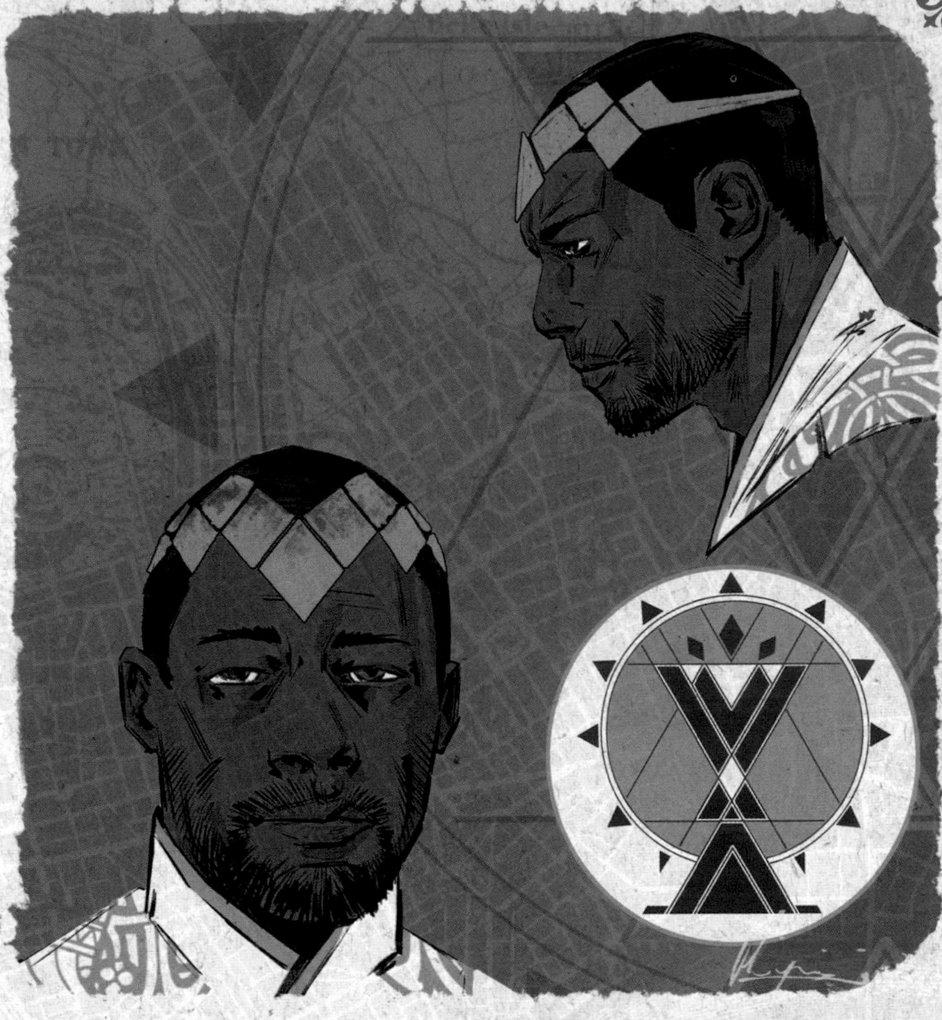

KING NOKIL MARESH

"On a dais at the end of the hall, a gold throne, adorned with silk. On the throne sits King Nokil, crowned and in military-esque regalia, elbow on the arm of the throne, chin resting on his closed fist."

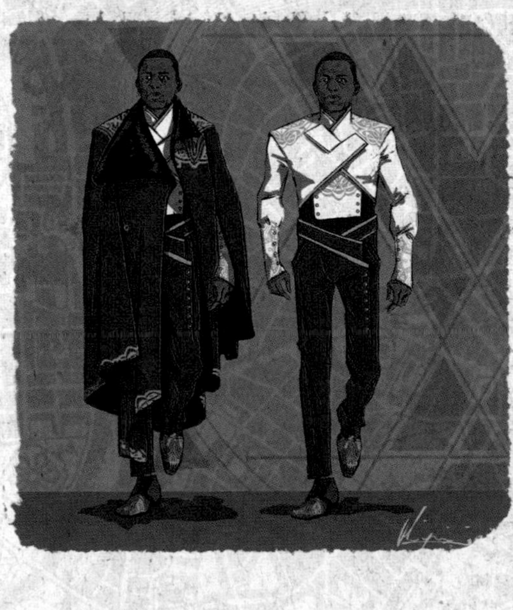

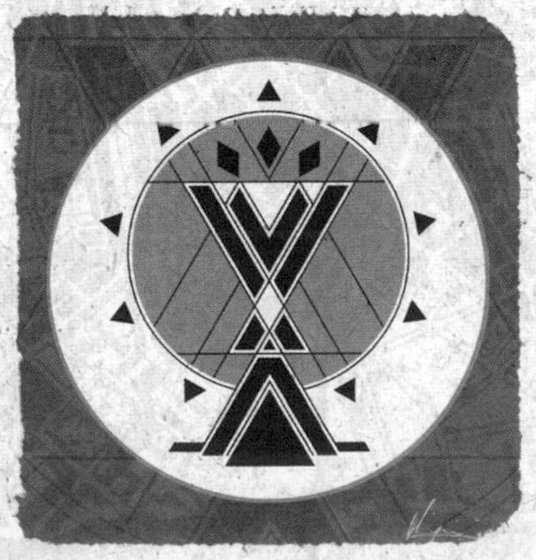

"The brooch features a chalice and rising sun. The symbol of the Maresh royal family."

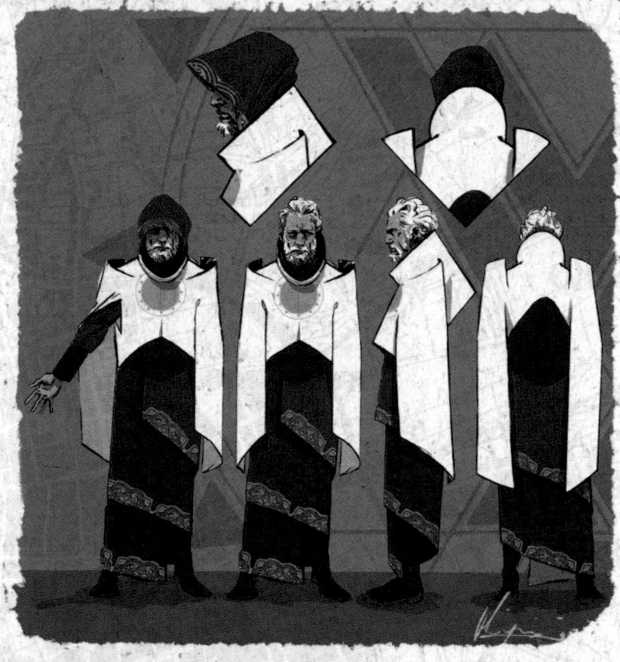

HEAD PRIEST TIEREN SERENSE

"Tieren remains silent, statuesque beyond the King, in crisp white robes trimmed gold.

"Prince Maxim travels with a younger Tieren Serense (who features as Head Priest in the Shades of Magic series). Tieren counsels Maxim on the nature of the sprawling port city."

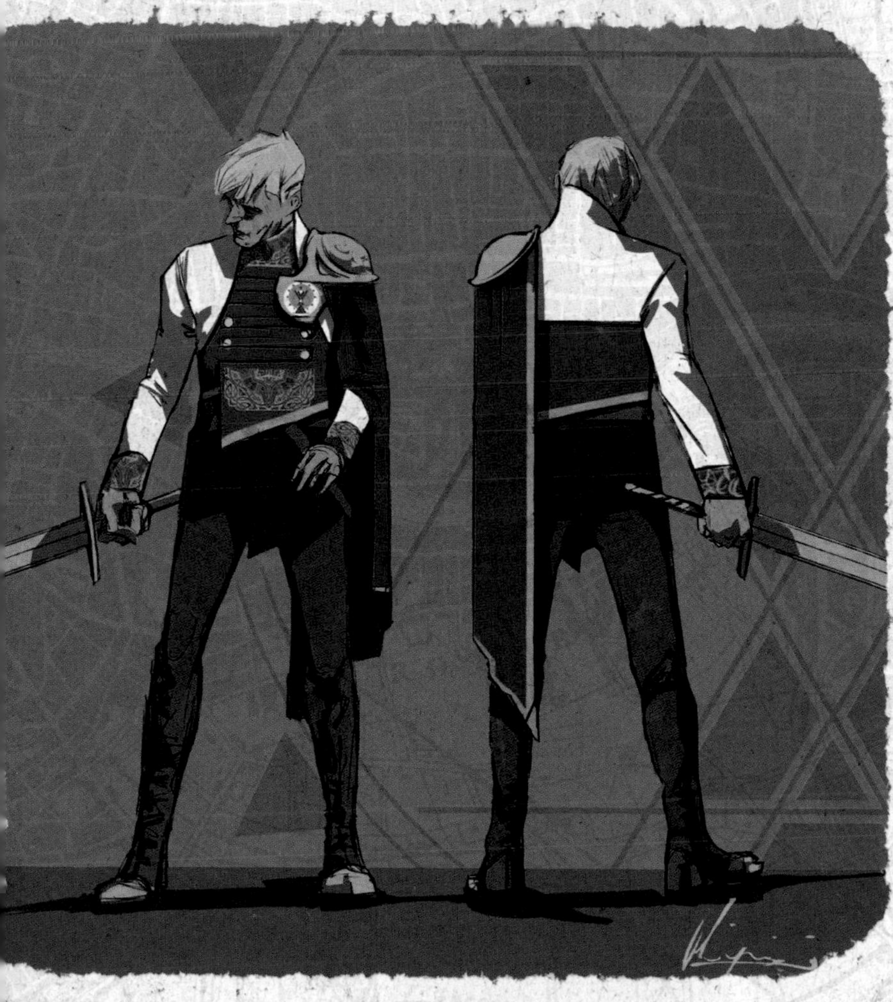

LIVERY OF THE SOLDIERS OF THE KING

"The military look is comprised of high boots, trousers, one short and/or long blade, depending on the soldier's preference, and a jacket.

"The Maresh royal colors are red and gold, so the accents – shoulder loops, buttons, etc. – should reflect that. The uniform is a little gaudy.

"However, the Verose soldiers downplay their attire to blend in, given the dangers of their environment."

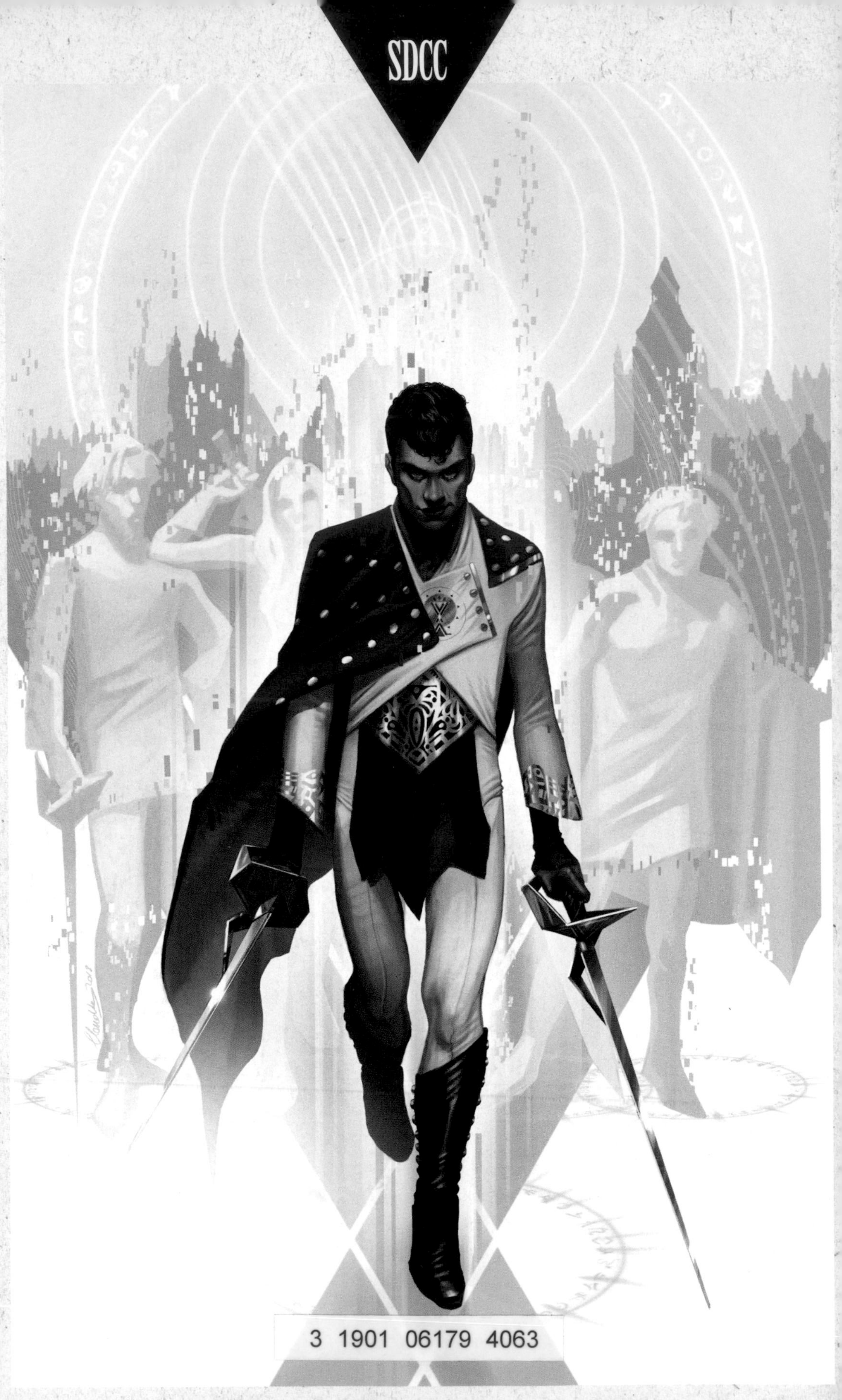
SDCC

SAN DIEGO COMIC COM EXCLUSIVE - CLAUDIA IANNICIELLO